Paul Robeson

Paul Robeson

Film Pioneer

SCOTT ALLEN NOLLEN

McFarland & Company, Inc., Publishers

Jefferson, North Carolina, and London

ALSO BY SCOTT ALLEN NOLLEN
AND FROM MCFARLAND

*Abbott and Costello on the Home Front:
A Critical Study of the Wartime Films* (2009)

*Warners Wiseguys: All 112 Films That Robinson,
Cagney and Bogart Made for the Studio* (2008)

Louis Armstrong: The Life, Music and Screen Career
(2004; paperback 2010)

Jethro Tull: A History of the Band, 1968–2001 (2002)

*Robin Hood: A Cinematic History of the English Outlaw
and His Scottish Counterparts* (1999; paperback 2008)

*Sir Arthur Conan Doyle at the Cinema: A Critical Study
of the Film Adaptations* (1996; paperback 2005)

Robert Louis Stevenson: Life, Literature and the Silver Screen (1994)

*Boris Karloff: A Critical Account of His Screen, Stage, Radio,
Television and Recording Work* (1991; paperback 2008)

The Boys: The Cinematic World of Laurel and Hardy (1989; paperback 2001)

**Frontispiece: Paul Robeson as Luke in his final
feature-film role, in *Tales of Manhattan* (1942).**

LIBRARY OF CONGRESS CATALOGUING-IN-PUBLICATION DATA

Nollen, Scott Allen.
Paul Robeson : film pioneer / Scott Allen Nollen.
p. cm.
Includes bibliographical references and index.

ISBN 978-0-7864-3520-3
softcover : 50# alkaline paper

1. Robeson, Paul, 1898–1976. 2. African Americans—Biography.
3. African American actors—Biography. 4. African American singers—
Biography. 5. Political activists—United States—Biography. I. Title.
E185.97.R63N65 2010 782.0092—dc22 [B] 2010033997

British Library cataloguing data are available

Front cover: Paul Robeson in *Show Boat*, 1932 Broadway
revival (Photofest); background ©2010 Shutterstock

Manufactured in the United States of America

*McFarland & Company, Inc., Publishers
Box 611, Jefferson, North Carolina 28640
www.mcfarlandpub.com*

For the Reverend David J. Polich,
a man of peace

Contents

Preface

Robeson's prominence in film was not marked by the quality of his films so much as the effort he made, as actor and activist, to seize some small portion of integrity for the black world that cinema claimed to depict.... Robeson's fame, both on screen and stage, and the affection in which he was held by two generations of black Americans emerged in part from modern African Americans' penchant for heroes.
— Clement Alexander Price[1]

Go down, Moses,
Way down in Egypt land,
Tell old Pharaoh,
Let my people go.
— African American spiritual

In an era when real heroes are not only in short supply, but also discouraged and considered only mythological beings, a peerless Renaissance Man like Paul Robeson, an African American born to an escaped slave, *should* loom even larger in the cultural landscape of the United States as more time slips away. To me, he has always been a larger-than-life character, the very stuff of legend and myth.

But Robeson wasn't larger than *life*. No one is. He was one of those rare people endowed with extraordinary talent in a myriad of areas who attempted to use his gifts for the benefit of others. He was an outstanding scholar, athlete, public speaker, writer, singer, actor and the first artist-activist in the United States. Perhaps it is the last of these pursuits for which he is most remembered, and the one that inevitably landed him in the most trouble.

African Americans have been proud to echo the title bestowed on Robeson by Mary McLeod Bethune: "The Tallest Tree in Our Forest." Some who were lucky enough to see him perform on stage, in a captivating drama or singing a spiritual with his potent *basso profundo* voice, described him as "mighty as an oak." And there were some, during the Cold War and after, because of ideological differences and deep-seated prejudice, who would have been more than happy to cut him down. But, look out, this man had unbending principles as powerful as John Henry's Hammer.

Even though the process of his removal from the American scene was more gradual and less violent, Robeson (who survived actual assassination threats and attempts) arguably belongs in the same class with other extraordinary citizens who championed human unity and equality at the cost of their own individual well-being: Abraham Lincoln, John F. and Robert F. Kennedy, Medgar Evers, Malcolm X and Dr. Martin Luther King, Jr., are the most obvious who come to mind.

But in the case of Robeson, a man whose beliefs seemed so extreme to so many, his cultural resurrection has taken longer to develop. His most obvious public valediction occurred in 2004 when the U.S. Postal Service honored him on one of its "Black Heritage

Commemorative" postage stamps, 28 years after his departure from the planet he truly believed could be made a better place.

In its own humble way, this book attempts to provide some evidence that Robeson indeed *did just that*. He appeared in just a dozen films, but those performances comprise a unique, powerful and extraordinary body of work that stands as one of the most significant achievements in the history of World Cinema.

When Robeson began acting during the 1920s, there was no such thing as a Civil Rights Movement. He spent many years in England and Europe in an attempt to escape the rigid racist stereotypes rampant in his homeland. Ironically, like Josephine Baker, Louis Armstrong, and other African American artists, he had to retreat to the Old World to elude the prejudice in the New. When Al Jolson, a Lithuanian-born, Jewish immigrant wearing blackface, was making cinematic history in *The Jazz Singer* and a series of popular follow-up films in Hollywood, Robeson was starring in the original British stage version of Oscar Hammerstein II and Jerome Kern's *Show Boat* in London's West End.

Clement Alexander Price, a Rutgers professor, wrote:

> His trailblazing career in film, during the 1920s and 1930s, was only one of the many facets of his extraordinary life, but it was pivotal to the emergence of a black film aesthetic and, by extension, an African American cultural identity. Indeed, it is virtually impossible to understand the intersection of racism, colonialist influences on popular culture, and black artistic concerns without considering what Paul Robeson accomplished as a singer, stage and film star, and activist and, alas, what he left undone because of the tenor of his times.
>
> Over the course of Robeson's life, 1898 to 1976, the far-reaching legacies of both African enslavement and racial mythology in modern America were acknowledged on an unprecedented level and met with increasingly determined resistance by two generations of African Americans. Robeson was at the forefront of that resistance. He was also among those who paid dearly for their own beliefs when civil rights advocacy, labor activism, and kinship with the Soviet Union were hardly popular causes.[2]

In 1942, Robeson, because of racism, decided to retire from the cinema. But, arguably, the cinema couldn't contain Paul Robeson and the aspirations he had for the medium. What he envisioned for the world of film would have been even more impressive than what he actually was *allowed* to achieve, had the proper conditions existed to fulfill that vision.

For a moment, let's set aside Robeson's sociopolitical aspirations for the cinema. When it came to his performance style, it's not that he (like some actors who can't help but *overact*) couldn't scale down his power to suit the camera; the artistic force that was Paul Robeson needed a larger canvas. Perhaps even the theater stage wasn't big enough. This was a performer, and a man, who needed the world stage to convey his artistic intentions. Sometimes he stood upon it, but there were other times when he was literally deprived of that platform by the powers that be. In 1949, he was blacklisted by the U.S. government, an unconstitutional status that dogged him until his death in 1976.

In November 1957, Robeson wrote in the foreword to his book *Here I Stand*:

> I care nothing — less than nothing — about what the lords of the land, the Big White Folks, think of me and my ideas. For more than ten years they have persecuted me in every way they could — by slander and mob violence, by denying me the right to practice my profession as an artist, by withholding my right to travel abroad. To these, the real Un-Americans, I merely say: "All right — I don't like *you* either!"[3]

Robeson's only child, Paul Robeson, Jr., wrote that a biographer of his father should not "attempt to satisfy those who crave a Robeson icon, those who wish to worship at a shrine,

or those who are beguiled by his political persona."[4] His father was a flesh-and-blood artist whose accomplishments (as well as unattainable goals) have cast him in a role that can easily fall prey to the most blatant of hagiographers. Robeson's achievements were real, and there is neither need nor reason for exaggeration. Paul Jr., explained:

> The reason for his banishment from the nation's public life lies in his relentless challenge not only to anti-black stereotypes but also to the cultural challenges to American racism. Touted in the 1940s as the ultimate black role model and the "proof" that the American system worked for blacks, he nevertheless condemned the system for failing to provide the same opportunities for all African Americans.
>
> The media-nurtured myth that his political persecution stemmed from a "love affair" with communism, or that he was "duped" by Russian or American communists, has always been aimed at obfuscating his dedication to the goal of immediate and full freedom for his people. The truth is that my father was never a communist, nor did he ever seriously contemplate joining the Communist Party. His defense of the Soviet Union and his refusal to abandon his communist friends did not stem from a fascination with left-wing ideology or from personal pride. Rather, these decisions were based on his love of Russian culture and his conviction that the Soviet Union and communists in general were the most reliable opponents of Nazism, colonialism, and racism.[5]

This author was born and raised 60 miles east of the Missouri River, and 66 miles straight north of a place called Shenandoah. Though the provenance of the early 19th-century American folksong "Shenandoah" is impossible to determine, I feel a soulful connection to Robeson while listening to him sing these lyrics in his sublime 1958 recording of the song:

> Oh Shenandoah,
> I long to hear you,
> Away you rolling river,
> Oh Shenandoah,
> I long to hear you,
> Away, I'm bound away
> 'Cross the wide Missouri.

The version of the song involving Shenandoah, Iowa, became very popular during the Civil War. My birthplace in Iowa (named after the *Ioway*, a Sioux tribe) lies in the land between the Missouri and the Mississippi, another river with which I am intimately acquainted: "Ol' Man River," in fact.

In more than 30 years of writing about classic motion pictures, rarely have I found a challenge as great as this attempt to shed some light on the extraordinary celluloid images left behind by Paul Robeson. Prior to this book, very little had been written about his pioneering cinematic career. All of his film work tests the historian and critic, but I found a particular adversary in *Show Boat* (1936), a true masterwork by an admirable director: James Whale, who created one of his most beautiful montage scenes for Robeson's performance of "Ol' Man River." (As documented by Whale himself, Paul literally *chilled his spine*, the same effect this filmmaker has had on so many millions of viewers who have seen his four Universal Horror masterpieces: *Frankenstein* [1931], *The Old Dark House* [1932], *The Invisible Man* [1933] and *The Bride of Frankenstein* [1935].) Printed words cannot adequately describe visual images, and this montage scene in *Show Boat* (cinema simultaneously at its most organic and dynamic) is certainly worth more than, and infinitely preferable to, a thousand of them.

The chapter on the underrated, magnificent adventure classic *King Solomon's Mines* (1937) provides a comprehensive retrospective on the film. Remarkably faithful to Sir H. Rider Haggard's (in some ways, progressive) novel, this Robert Stevenson–directed tour de force features a host of fine performances by a who's who of top British actors, not to mention a unique, mesmerizing turn by Robeson. Just as exceptional are Paul's own two favorite films: *Jericho* (1937), a unique project shot primarily on location in Egypt; and the obscure but brilliant and revelatory independent film *The Proud Valley* (1940), here receiving a much-deserved examination.

In order to address sufficiently the cultural and sociopolitical content of the films, as well as Robeson's performances, plot synopses and significant dialogue passages have been integrated with descriptions of the cinematic techniques used by the filmmakers. This is especially important in the case of Robeson, whose films have not always been readily available for viewing.

The FBI, in collaboration with the CIA, State Department and, at times, British Intelligence, consistently carried out surveillance of Robeson from the beginning of U.S. involvement in World War II until his death. Any educational, political, philanthropic or charitable organization with which he was involved was instantly branded a "front" for the Communist Party. Copious reports sent by field agents to FBI Director J. Edgar Hoover were based on second- to fourth-hand "information" relayed by "confidential informants of known reliability." Though Robeson never joined the Communist Party of the United States, the Bureau considered him as not only a member but also as a "prominent" constituent and even a spy engaged in "intelligence activities." Scrutiny of the FBI files on Robeson (along with those on his wife and son) made available by the Freedom of Information Act has provided considerable material on Bureau activities connected to his acting career.

In 1977, one year after Robeson's death, Gil Noble, writer and producer of the documentary *Paul Robeson: The Tallest Tree in Our Forest*, revealed:

> Surely [Robeson's story] represents a major chapter in America's history. The tragedy is that story has hardly been told. Mass media has, in fact, suppressed large amounts of information about this man. Despite exhaustive research, we were able to come up with precious little news film shot of this man here in this country ... and what little motion picture that we did include in [our] documentary came from overseas. Not even the Library of Congress has much to offer in film on this man, Paul Robeson.... Certainly our children should know that story. It is a story of strength and gentleness, commitment and unbending principle.[6]

I would like to extend a personal thank you to Paul Robeson, Jr., for his encouragement and fascinating reminiscences, particularly about his years in the U.S.S.R. and his father's meetings with the great Soviet film director and theorist Sergei Eisenstein. An accomplished historian, archivist, civil rights activist, and author of the excellent two-volume memoir-biography *The Undiscovered Paul Robeson* (John Wiley and Sons, 2001 and 2010, respectively), Mr. Robeson discussed my approach to his father's film career and approved my outline before I began the imposing task of tackling the material in earnest. His well-researched and articulated theory about his father's conspired professional, political and personal devastation (which I have explored through my own independent investigation of primary documents) is both convincing and compelling.

My gratitude also goes to Harriet Akutekha Jenkins, my cultural advisor on Robeson's films incorporating African settings; my good friends, Professors Rudy Pearson and Winsome Jackson, for their comments, enthusiasm and peerless hospitality; the Schomburg

Hollywood Forever Cemetery, Santa Monica Boulevard, July 16, 2005: During the research for this book, the author visited the cenotaph memorial erected for Hattie McDaniel (1895–1952), Robeson's unforgettable costar in *Show Boat* (1936) and the first African American to win an Academy Award. It was McDaniel's last wish to be buried in the Hollywood Cemetery (as it was then called) near her favorite actors, but she was denied this because of the color of her skin. In 1999, the new owner of the property suggested that her remains be moved from the Rosedale Cemetery, the first Los Angeles resting place that had allowed all races and creeds, but her family declined, prompting this granite monument, located on the lawn next to the Douglas Fairbanks tomb and reflecting pond. During the shooting of *Show Boat*, McDaniel was honored to work with Robeson, who called her "one of the best actresses I ever met." [Photograph by Barton H. Aikens.]

Center for Research in Black Culture, a branch of the New York Public Library, in Harlem, for providing access to the records of the Negro Actors Guild; the Paul and Eslanda Robeson Collections at Howard University, Moorland-Spingarn Research Center, in Washington, D.C.; the late Ernest "Sunshine Sammy" Morrison, the first African American actor to sign a long-term Hollywood contract (in 1919), and a wonderful companion while traveling on a Mississippi riverboat (in 1988); the late Anna Lee, a superb actress and true sweetheart, who so graciously discussed her fascinating film career (including the aforementioned *King Solomon's Mines*) with me on a summer day in 1989; and my erudite, eternal comrade, Mr. Barton H. Aikens. A shout-out also goes to my "second family," brothers and sisters Laurah, Lester, David, "Big" Aaron and Najma.

The illustrations in this book were compiled over the course of many years during an effort I can only describe as a treasure hunt of near-archaeological proportions. Original publicity and poster materials from pre–World War II films are often very scarce, and the fact that most of Robeson's best films were produced in Britain makes their discovery even more difficult. During my research and writing, I was very fortunate to acquire country-of-origin pressbooks (perhaps the Robeson-film equivalent of the Dead Sea Scrolls) from the original releases of *The Song of Freedom*, *Jericho* and *The Proud Valley*, three of his best British films. Many images from these rare publicity materials and other sources (which are a strong testament to Robeson's unique status as a major film, stage and concert star in Britain) have been carefully reproduced in the pages that follow.

Though made three-quarters of a century ago, Paul Robeson's cinematic efforts continue to speak to viewers in the era of Barack Obama. There is definitely a need for today's folks to learn about his groundbreaking films, a body of work standing strong, alongside his other landmark achievements in so many areas of artistic, social and political life in the United States and beyond.

Chapter 1

Great Things to Come

> I early became conscious—I don't quite know how—of a special feeling of the Negro community for me. I was no different from the other kids in the neighborhood ... and yet, like my father, the people claimed to see something special about me. Whatever it was, and no one really said, they felt I was fated for great things to come.
>
> — Paul Robeson[1]

Paul Leroy Robeson was born in Princeton, New Jersey, on April 9, 1898, the seventh and last child of the 54-year-old Presbyterian Reverend William Drew Robeson and Maria Louisa Bustill Robeson, a school teacher, aged a mere 44. The dark-skinned William, descended from Nigeria's Igbo tribe, was a former slave who escaped at age 15, with his older brother, Ezekiel, via the Underground Railroad from the Roberson Plantation in North Carolina, where their parents, Benjamin and Sabra, also toiled.

Maria, referred to as a mulatto, hailed from Pennsylvania's Bustill family, whose ancestry blended Igbo African, English Quaker and Lenni-Lenape (Delaware) Native American origins. Her great-grandfather, Cyrus Bustill, an ex-slave, became a baker who provided bread to George Washington's troops during the Revolutionary War, and later helped found the Free African Society, the first black mutual aid association, in 1787.

From birth, Paul heard ragtime, hymns, gospel songs, blues and the soothing sounds of African American spirituals, a transcendent musical form that would prove a staple of his concert repertoire in later years. His father instilled qualities that would inform both his personal values and his artistry, most importantly realizing his individual potential rather than merely coming out the winner, and the concept that all human beings, no matter how diverse, are equal members of a single family.

In 1904, Maria, having suffered an illness that seriously affected her eyesight, tragically burned to death in a household fire after her clothes were ignited by a hot ember from a wood-burning stove. Later Paul could recall few memories of his mother aside from the image of her lying lifeless in her coffin. He wrote:

> [I]t must be that the pain and shock of her death blotted out all other personal recollections. Others have told me of her remarkable intellect, her strength of character and spirit which contributed so much to my father's development and work. She was a companion to him in his studies; she helped compose his sermons; she was his right hand in all his community work.[2]

In 1907, the Reverend moved his family from elite Princeton to the less socially rigid Westfield, New Jersey, where he switched his allegiance to a small African Methodist Episcopal (A.M.E.) Zion congregation of mostly working-class whites who were primarily accepting of blacks. The town, with such a small black population, had an integrated school system. Nine-year-old Paul lived there for the next three years, befriending many white classmates and their family members. He later wrote:

Princeton was Jim Crow ... the grade school that I attended was segregated and Negroes were not permitted in any high school, and I would have had to do the same had we not moved to another town. No Negro students were admitted to the university, although one or two were allowed to attend the divinity school.[3]

When Paul's older brother, William Drew II, was ready for college, he wanted to attend Princeton; but, as Paul wrote, "Reverend Robeson could not push open the doors of that school for his son."[4] Opposed to the attendance of black students was none other than the university's president, Woodrow Wilson, whom Paul later recalled as a "Nobel Peace Prize winner, apostle of the New Liberalism, advocate of democracy for the world and Jim Crow for America!"[5]

The family moved again in 1910, to Somerville, located between Westfield and Princeton, where the Reverend now preached to the black congregation at the St. Thomas A.M.E. Zion Church. Paul attended eighth grade at a small "colored school," where, during his June 1911 graduation oration, he gave what was perhaps the first indication of his career to come. Quoting Patrick Henry, he declared, "Give me liberty or give me death!"

From September 1911 until June 1915, Paul attended Somerville High School, where the student body of 200 included only a dozen blacks. Paul had to endure the racial epithets of the white students, plus the abuse leveled by the "hateful old principal," Dr. Ackerman, who was relentless. One day, when the "watchful hawk" sent him home for punishment, Paul informed his father of what would happen should Ackerman ever "lay a hand" on him: "I swear I'll try my best to break his neck!" "I guess Pop understood," Paul later wrote. "He let it go at that."[6]

The music teacher, Miss Vosseller, however, took extra time in giving Paul voice lessons; and the English instructor, Anna Miller, fostered his debating skills and introduced him to Shakespeare's plays. He later recalled, "Many years were to pass before the American theatre would permit a Negro to play Othello, but the idea seemed eminently right to Miss Miller and she coached me in the part for a high-school dramatic performance."[7]

During his senior year, Paul took a competitive examination to win a four-year scholarship to Rutgers, then a private college in New Brunswick with an enrollment of less than 1,000 students. He wrote:

Well, I won the scholarship — and here was the decisive point in my life.... The important thing was this: *Deep in my heart from that day on was a conviction which none of the Ackermans of America would ever be able to shake.* Equality might be denied, but I *knew* I was not inferior.[8]

Racism was on the rise across the nation when Paul arrived on the Rutgers campus. *The Birth of a Nation* (1915), D. W. Griffith's paean to the Ku Klux Klan, was the most popular film in the land, critically lauded and initially supported by none other than President Woodrow Wilson, who, after screening the film at the White House, reportedly proclaimed it "like writing history with lightning" and "all too terribly true." The NAACP, formed in 1909, condemned this Civil War–era portrayal of blacks (actually whites in blackface) as subhuman beasts who are dealt with by their superior Aryan masters. (One infamous scene features a white girl [Mae Marsh] plunging to her death rather than submit to the advances of Gus, a former slave [a blacked-up Walter Long, later a comic nemesis of Laurel and Hardy], who is subsequently murdered by the heroic Klan.) Paul's father joined other clergymen in preaching sermons condemning the film, which had helped increase national Klan membership to over 100,000.

The third black student ever to attend Rutgers, Paul endured considerable physical abuse when trying out for the football team. Eventually known as "Robeson of Rutgers," he earned 14 varsity letters, was twice named an All-American, and made nationwide news as one of the finest and most intelligent football players in the land, excelling as a pass receiver, offensive blocker and tackle, and defensive linebacker. His academic performance as an English major was no less spectacular, and he was inducted into the Phi Beta Kappa honor society during his junior year. His many triumphs in the college's oratorical competitions pleased his father, who passed away at age 74 on May 17, 1918.

Paul exercised caution around white students and faculty. Though he embraced the progressive views of W. E. B. DuBois (who had forcefully countered D. W. Griffith's "historical interpretation" of the Reconstruction), he only discussed controversial issues with his black peers. When the United States entered World War I in April 1917, he joined the Rutgers Reserve Officers Training Corps (ROTC), in which he served proudly, echoing the patriotic oratory of his companions.

On June 18, 1919, Paul, named class valedictorian, delivered a commencement address titled "The New Idealism." As he walked to the podium to speak, he received a standing ovation from the audience. Across the nation, race violence was heating up, to spark the "Red Summer of 1919" which eventually included hundreds of lynchings and the torching of entire African American communities. Paul mentioned the Americans who had perished during World War I for "a larger and more altruistic form of life" and referred to "the less favored race," whose people "must stand or fall by their own merit." To great applause, he concluded:

> May I not appeal to you who also revere their memory to join us in continuing to fight for the great principles for which they contended, until in all sections of this fair land there will be equal opportunities for us all, and character shall be the standard of excellence; until men by constructive work aim toward Solon's definition of the ideal government — where an injury to the meanest citizen is an insult to the whole Constitution; and until black and white shall clasp friendly hands in the consciousness of the fact that we are brethren and that God is the father of us all.

After graduating from Rutgers, Paul moved to the big city to pursue a scholarship at the New York University Law School. Enamored with the cultural atmosphere of the Harlem Renaissance, he abandoned NYU for the Columbia Law School, where he began attending courses on the Morningside Heights campus during the 1920 spring term. That summer, he was asked by his friend, producer Dora Cole Norman, to play the lead role in *Simon the Cyrenian* with the Amateur Players at the Harlem YMCA. *Simon* had been written by a white playwright, Ridgely Torrence, but was refreshingly free of black stereotypes in its portrayal of an African who shouldered Jesus Christ's cross on the torturous path to Golgotha. (Paul's only true forerunner, Charles Gilpin, who, in 1915, had helped found the Lafayette Players in Harlem, was the first actor to play the role.) Paul agreed to tackle the character as a challenge for himself and as a favor for his friend, but when the curtain fell, he returned to law school with no further plans for a career in the theater.

The 1920 professional football season pulled Paul back into athletics, and he was signed to the Akron Pros, a position that landed him at least $500 per game. The powerhouse team, with Paul on both offense (pass receiver) and defense (left end), went undefeated in 13 games, including the championship contest against the Buffalo All-Americans.

On August 21, 1921, Paul married Eslanda Cardozo Goode, a Columbia graduate and the first African American to become Head Histological Chemist of Surgical Pathology at

New York Presbyterian Hospital. She had met Paul while attending the 1920 summer session at the university.

In March 1922, Dora Cole Norman asked Paul to play the lead in *Taboo*, the debut of playwright Mary Hoyt Wiborg, set on a Louisiana plantation. Although Charles Gilpin had agreed to coach the cast, which included the formidable Margaret Wycherly (who, nearly three decades later, would play the unforgettable "Ma" of the psychotic James Cagney in Raoul Walsh's apocalyptic *White Heat* [1949]), Paul didn't want to return to the theater.

"Essie" saw the role as an opportunity far superior to his working as a postal clerk and attempting to enter the color-conscious legal world. Abandoning her plans to attend medical school, she combined working in the pathology lab with helping him focus on an acting career, which she considered a serious profession. She frequently attended the theater and read the work of leading drama critics, studying acting techniques she thought would be beneficial to her husband. He was reluctant but accepted the role, throwing himself headlong into weeks of rehearsals for *Taboo*, which opened at the Sam H. Harris Theatre on April 4.

The play didn't fare well with critics, though they were generally impressed with Paul, particularly his powerful speaking voice. Both Margaret Wycherly and director Augustin Duncan (brother of Isadora, the innovative and influential dancer) encouraged him to continue accepting major roles, rather than thinking of acting as secondary work. Following the play's brief run, he studied for and passed his second-year law exams, but continued attending the theater with Essie. He later wrote:

> A century ago it was not possible for a Negro actor to appear on the American stage in any role — not even as a buffoon. (Such parts were reserved for "whites only" in the days of the blackface minstrel shows, and only toward the end of that era was "progress" made to the point where a Negro face was permitted to appear in the traditional burnt cork of that happily now-dead form of American theatre.)[9]

In May 1922 Paul was hanging out with friends on the corner of Seventh Avenue and 135th Street in Harlem when he was approached by Harold Browning, the leader of a vocal quartet, the Four Harmony Kings, who were performing in the all-black, hit musical revue *Shuffle Along* at the 63rd Street Music Hall. Browning revealed that the group's bass singer suddenly had left for Chicago, leaving them unable to fulfill their dates in the revue. Paul said he'd fill in, but Browning didn't take him seriously until he agreed to audition. The following evening, after enduring a difficult rehearsal with the quartet, Paul was on stage in *Shuffle Along*, a program of minstrel songs and skits that required the comedians to don blackface. His standout moment was a moving solo performance of Stephen Foster's 1860 plantation song "Ol' Black Joe." Though he deplored the stereotypical content, Paul realized that the show was the first-ever musical revue produced entirely by African Americans, including writers Flournoy Miller and Aubrey Lyles, with music and lyrics by jazz composers Eubie Blake and Noble Sissle. Two of the show's biggest hits were the song "I'm Just Wild About Harry" and cabaret singer Florence Mills, also known as "The Little Blackbird" and "The Queen of Happiness," who had replaced Gertrude Saunders in the role of Ruth Little.

Paul stayed with *Shuffle Along* for a month before accepting a starring role in the British production of *Taboo*, rather than attending law school during the summer. With veteran stage star Mrs. Patrick Campbell as the female lead, the show, re-titled *Voodoo*, was scheduled for a trial run in the provinces before opening in London. In early July, Paul, leaving Essie behind, sailed from New York aboard the S.S. *Homeric*. By July 9, he was in Portsmouth Harbor; the following day, he met Mrs. Campbell. By the time the trial run began the fol-

lowing week, Paul already considered her "a wonderful woman and a marvelous actress. One thousand times better than Miss Wycherly."[10]

The play opened badly in Blackpool on July 17 but, 10 days later, the company scored a major hit in Edinburgh, where Paul received good reviews, then moved on to Glasgow, where Mrs. Campbell encouraged more of his singing, which proved the most popular aspect of the show. In Liverpool on August 7, he decided to remain in England, rather than return to New York for more appearances in *Shuffle Along*. *Voodoo* was booked into Plymouth, so he traveled to London to stay with African American singer John Payne and his guest, arranger-accompanist Lawrence Brown, who would become Paul's most important musical collaborator.

Unfortunately, Mrs. Campbell abandoned the *Voodoo* company, and without her star power the production closed soon thereafter. On August 17, Paul wrote to Essie, claiming that he soon would be sailing home. By this point, *Shuffle Along* was no longer available, so, for a brief time, he worked at the Plantation nightclub in Harlem, singing in the chorus behind Florence Mills in the vaudeville act *The Plantation Revue*. Mills, acclaimed for her performances in *Shuffle Along*, sang the popular J. Russell Robinson–Roy Turk songs "Aggravatin' Papa" and "I've Got What It Takes," but the somewhat crude ragtime material did not impress Paul. (Tragically, after appearing in three more New York shows, Mills developed tuberculosis and died from a post-surgery infection in November 1927. She was only 31 years old.)

In September, Paul enrolled for his final term at Columbia and earned some money during the 1922 professional football season, this time with the Milwaukee Badgers. Although the Badgers won only two of nine games, Paul scored both touchdowns during a 13–0 victory over the Oorang Indians, an all Native American team from LaRue, Ohio, whose coach and star player was the great All-American and Olympic gold medalist Jim Thorpe. Paul's second score incited a brawl with several of the Oorang players, whom he was forced to level in the end zone with some quickly thrown punches.

The fight, which was ended by team managers and police officers, inspired two boxing promoters to visit Paul in the locker room, where they offered him a hefty sum to challenge Jack Dempsey in a heavyweight title bout. Though he turned down the chance to become "The Great Black Hope," *New York Herald Tribune* sportswriter Lawrence Perry reported that he soon would be training as a prize fighter. Paul, possessing no actual boxing skills and worried that such a story would damage his prospects at law school, contacted the Rutgers Alumni Office, who prompted Perry to print a retraction three weeks later.

On February 28, 1923, Paul received his Bachelor of Laws (LL.B.) degree. Through Foster Sanford, his football coach at Rutgers, he landed an interview with Louis W. Stotesbury, head of a major Wall Street law firm. He was hired immediately and assigned to draft a brief for a case involving the will of late financier Stephan Jay Gould. Other than Stotesbury, everyone at the firm was strongly against Paul, and their hostility finally came to a head when a stenographer refused to take dictation "from a nigger." Stotesbury remained helpful but was also frankly practical, telling Paul about the prejudice he would continue to encounter from the white legal profession. His "solution" was to offer Paul the firm's branch office in Harlem.

Rather than be so severely limited by bigotry, Paul focused on his theatrical career. Though Essie suggested seeking work in vaudeville, he valued long-run artistry over a short-run dollar and decided to pursue only legitimate acting roles. He had set his sights on joining the Provincetown Players, specifically meeting one of its top playwrights, Eugene

O'Neill. In March, he approached Otto Kahn, a Rutgers trustee and Players contributor, and Augustin Duncan to provide him with an introduction. Kahn declined, but Duncan wrote to O'Neill, warmly recommending Paul, who soon after sent a letter of his own. O'Neill wrote back in November, agreeing to consider him for a role in a major play.

In December, Paul received word from Kenneth MacGowan, director of the Players, who asked him to read for the lead role in O'Neill's *All God's Chillun Got Wings*, one of the first mainstream American plays to depict the pitfalls of an interracial marriage. His audition was an overwhelming success but, due to publishing obligations, the rehearsals weren't scheduled to begin until April 1924. During the interim, he focused on singing but also accepted the role of an errant preacher in a production of *Roseanne* staged by the all-black Lafayette Players, including Charles Gilpin (the first actor to star in O'Neill's expressionistic *The Emperor Jones* [1920]) and Rose McClendon, in Harlem.

After *All God's Chillun Got Wings* was published in *American Mercury* magazine in February, threats against O'Neill and Paul were made by the Ku Klux Klan, and riots were expected. The play was delayed for another month, and the Players, attempting to draw attention away from the controversy, revived *The Emperor Jones*, with Paul in the lead role of the ambitious Pullman porter who, after killing a guard and escaping from prison, appoints himself ruler of a small island in the Caribbean. O'Neill's use of stereotypical language, including the word "nigger," hadn't appealed to Gilpin, and was initially problematic for Paul, but the revival was wholeheartedly supported by none other than W. E. B. DuBois, who appreciated the playwright's portrayal of true "Negro blood."[11]

The Emperor Jones opened on May 6, when Paul's powerful performance garnered five curtain calls. The next day, he began rehearsing *All God's Chillun Got Wings* during the day and continued to star in *The Emperor Jones* in the evenings. Though a great success, *Jones* closed on May 13 to make way for *Chillun* two days later. Most of the reviews were critical of the new play, but Paul was praised by such journalistic heavyweights as Alexander Woolcott (*New York Times*), Robert Welsh (New York *Evening Telegram*) and Heywood Broun (*New York World*). No protests occurred; but, aside from DuBois, African American leaders (including Marcus Garvey, the Reverend Adam Clayton Powell, Sr., and the Reverend J. W. Brown) strongly disapproved of what they considered negative black stereotypes. Paul, believing that all aspects of African American life should be depicted truthfully, said:

> In *All God's Chillun* we have a play ... emphasizing the humanness, and in Mr. O'Neill's words, "the oneness" of mankind. Any number of people have said to me: "I trust that now you will get a truly heroic and noble role, one portraying the finest type of Negro." I honestly believe that perhaps never will I portray a

Robeson at the dawn of his acting career in the mid–1920s.

nobler type than "Jim Harris" or a more heroically tragic figure than "Brutus Jones, Emperor," not excepting "Othello." ... Negroes ... are too self-conscious, too afraid of showing all phases of our life — especially those phases which are of greatest dramatic value. The great mass of our group discourage any member who has the courage to fight these petty prejudices. I am still being damned all over the place for playing in *All God's Chillun*. It annoys me very little when I realize that those who object most strenuously know mostly nothing of the play and in any event know little of the theater and have no right to judge a playwright of O'Neill's talents.... I am sure that there will come Negro playwrights of great power, and I trust I shall have some part in interpreting that most interesting and much needed addition to the drama of America.[12]

When *All God's Chillun* closed in September, Paul was still playing to a packed house every evening. During the run, he had been visited by the Russian theater critic Alexander Koriansky, an associate of actor-director Konstantin Stanislavski, who offered to teach him acting technique, focusing on a study of the Othello role. Thus began Paul's first formal dramatic lessons.

Paul Robeson, Jr., pointed out the greater depth his father was able to inject into O'Neill's original characterization in *The Emperor Jones*:

Paul's performance, which drew on his own knowledge and experience, added a dimension to the role that O'Neill could not have written. For example, he apparently didn't know that Pullman porters were highly educated. Most, including Paul's brother Bill, had college degrees and possessed a far more sophisticated vision than the character Jones as O'Neill had conceived him. Paul minimized the street-smart aspect of Jones. Playing him as intelligent, rather than merely crafty, Paul brought greater realism, as well as greater dimension, to the role. Furthermore, because of the greater dignity Paul created in the first scene, there was a more shattering dramatic effect when Jones subsequently unraveled.

From Paul's point of view, he achieved his most important contribution to the play by *not* following the playwright's intent exactly. Shrewdly, he avoided public acknowledgment of this digression. Thus, from the beginning of Paul's career, a disparity emerged between his realistic, fully conceived analysis of his stage roles and the critics' overall perception of him as merely an "instinctive" or "natural" actor.... He could not have known that his portrayals of O'Neill's characters were on their way to becoming indelible images of the twentieth century. These images began to redefine the place of black actors in the history of the theater. In Paul's culturally astute interpretations of these roles, he made a breach in the wall holding back both black actors and black playwrights.[13]

Black Preacher's Ambition
Body and Soul (1925)

In the wide acquaintances that I have had over the years, I have never hesitated to associate with people who hold non-conformist or radical views, and this has been true since my earliest days in the American theatre where I first met people who challenged the traditional order of things.

— Paul Robeson[1]

Credits: Director, Producer and Screenplay: Oscar Micheaux; Released by Micheaux Film (U.S.) on November 9, 1925; Running Time: 79 minutes.

Cast: Paul Robeson (Reverend Isaiah T. Jenkins/Sylvester), Mercedes Gilbert (Isabelle), Julia Theresa Russell (Sis' Martha Jane), Lawrence Chenault ("Yellow-Curley" Hinds), Marshall Rogers (Speakeasy Proprietor), Lillian Johnson (Sis' Ca'line), Madame Robinson (Sis' Lucy), Chester A. Alexander (Deacon Simpkins, Church Elder), Walter Cornick (Brother Amos, Church Elder), Tom Fletcher (bit).

In October 1924, Essie Robeson agreed to a contract with groundbreaking African American filmmaker Oscar Micheaux, who was preparing to direct *Body and Soul*, a feature film that would provide Paul with *two* starring roles for his motion-picture debut. Better still, the project guaranteed a salary of $100 per week, plus 3 percent of the gross after clearing the first $40,000 at the box office.

The first African American credited for producing a major motion picture, the Illinois-born Micheaux (1884–1951), the son of former slaves, made his directorial debut with *The Homesteader* (1919), adapted from an autobiographical novel based on his arduous experiences as a farmer in South Dakota. George P. Johnson, brother of noted African American actor Noble Johnson (later to appear in the classic fantasy films *The Mummy* [1932] and *King Kong* [1933]), had read the book and wanted to purchase the rights for his Los Angeles–based Lincoln Motion Picture Company. Micheaux would agree only on condition that he direct the film; when the Johnson brothers refused, he returned to his home in Sioux City, Iowa, where he founded Micheaux's Book and Film Company and sold stock to raise funds for the film. When *The Homesteader* was finished, he traveled from city to city with a print and publicity materials, personally pitching it to exhibitors.

Micheaux's second film, *Within Our Gates* (1919), is his rejoinder to the blatant racism of D. W. Griffith's *Birth of a Nation* and the Chicago Race Riot of 1919, boldly addressing black poverty in the Deep South, interracial relationships and, most courageously, lynching. Authorities in some Northern cities blocked screenings of this "race film," and it took Micheaux two months to obtain approval from the Board of Censors in Chicago, where controversy led to good box office when it finally was released in January 1920.

Body and Soul, Micheaux's 11th film, was shot in the Bronx. Paul's dive into filmmaking body and soul was characteristic of his willingness to take chances in all aspects of his life.

He was presented, not only with the challenge of portraying two major characters with opposing personalities (without being able to use his voice), but also had to work through the entire production without making any mistakes. Micheaux didn't have enough money to shoot retakes. Added to this was the director's penchant for filming the script in sequence, forcing Paul to play both characters during the same session. Trading the wardrobe of Sylvester, a young inventor, for that of his brother, "Reverend" Isaiah T. Jenkins, an escaped convict posing as a preacher, was far easier than juggling their disparate character traits. The "preacher" role seemed a natural fit for Paul, the kinsman of noted men of the cloth. As she had done for his stage roles, Essie rehearsed with him prior to production, and she was often at the studio during the shoot.

The mainstream Hollywood cinema of 1925 was home to the broad histrionics of Rudolph Valentino in *The Eagle*, Lon Chaney in *The Phantom of the Opera*, and Ramon Novarro and Francis X. Bushman in the first feature-film adaptation of General Lew Wallace's *Ben-Hur: A Tale of the Christ*. By contrast, *Body and Soul* opens with a medium close-up of the *back* of Paul's head after the "Rt. Reverend Jenkins" is introduced by the initial title card and a newspaper article noting that he had escaped after being arrested in Tatesville, Georgia. Paul's performance is quite naturalistic as the preacher enters the Autumn Leaf Social Club, a speakeasy run by a "Negro in Business" (Marshall Rogers) to down a shot of "good liquor."

The Reverend speaks proper English, but the proprietor rambles in "Negro dialect," as demonstrated by the title cards:

> Yessuh. Dat's what ah tries tu carry. Uv co'se I gits a li'l money fo' it fum de resta mah customahs; but beins it's you — dat's dif'ent.

The preacher stuffs a pint bottle into his pants pocket and then shakes down the proprietor for a "contribution," threatening to preach about "this house of Hell" if he doesn't pay up.

(Some African Americans criticized Micheaux for depicting their brethren speaking broken English and engaging in unsavory activities on the screen. He responded that some of his previous cinematic efforts had focused on positive, progressive, "uplifting" qualities, only to create an unrealistic atmosphere resulting in audience boredom and disinterest.)

The inebriated Jenkins stumbles down the sidewalk to his dwelling. Meanwhile, a stranger, "Yellow-Curley" Hinds of Atlanta (Lawrence Chenault, a familiar actor in race films), arrives at the Tatesville train station. Across town, Isabelle (Mercedes Gilbert) awakens in her bed, as her mother, Martha Jane (Julia Theresa Russell), clutching money in her hands with the family Bible in her lap, sleeps in a chair. Isabelle walks out of her bedroom to awaken her mother, who reports, "Ah done had a ter'ble dream!" (The significance of this sequence isn't made clear until the end of the film.)

Body and Soul (1925) opens with a newspaper report that the notorious ex-convict "Rt. Reverend Isaiah T. Jenkins" (Robeson) has escaped after being arrested in Tatesville, Georgia [frame enlargement].

"Yellow-Curley" pays a visit to the Autumn Leaf. The scene cross-cuts between Hinds, who questions the proprietor, and the hung-over Jenkins in his bedroom, holding his head and glancing into the mirror.

On Sunday, Hinds attends church. Spying him in the congregation, the Reverend Jenkins experiences a flashback in which Hinds is locked in a prison cell. Embracing the Good Book, the preacher tells a joke aimed at his former acquaintance. A title card reveals that Jenkins now is also speaking vernacular:

"And," said he. "Dem dat am lookin' at me now an' says nuthin', dem will I see latuh."

After the services, the preacher chats with members of the congregation as the scene cross-cuts to a shot of his estranged brother, Sylvester (framed in an iris), walking out of the woods. Resorting to a pinch in the side, Martha Jane "encourages" Isabelle to allow Hinds to walk her home.

Jenkins and Hinds do meet "latuh" over a bottle of hooch. "I tell you that I was not seekin' you out," Hinds claims, "but dropped off here to find girls for 'Cotton Blossom's Shoulder Shakers'—and this little Isabelle—she appeals to muh!"

A title card proclaiming, "Tatesville—other fish in the sea!" prefaces the preacher's brief joyride with a grinning young woman. Sylvester, a timid man of few words, is the opposite of his womanizing, conman brother. Isabelle introduces him to her mother, asking permission to marry. "What's that niggah got tu marry on?" replies Martha Jane.

"Don't say 'niggah,' mother. It's vulgar," Isabelle points out. Disappointed by the harsh response, Sylvester hangs his head and walks out, leaving the two women to argue. The subject turns to the preacher, and the scene cross-cuts to Jenkins downing whiskey and laughing.

"Don't you pass no 'sinuations about my pastuh, that Godly man!" orders Martha Jane, who wants Isabelle to marry him:

An all de money I been savin' is tu buy de home which I'se gwine gib you when you becomes de wife ob my pastuh.

Isabelle accurately calls Jenkins "a drunkard and a sinner" and is therefore accused of being "willful, sinful [and] ungrateful," with a little physical abuse from Martha Jane tossed in for good measure.

Hinds gambles at the Autumn Leaf while Jenkins awakens in his bed from another inebriated slumber. On the street, Isabelle meets Sylvester for a leisurely stroll. Treated like a king, the preacher drops in on Martha Jane, who is entertaining Sis' Ca'line (Lillian Johnson) and Sis' Lucy (Madame Robinson).

Isabelle returns home to discover that Jenkins has arrived to "save her soul," a revelation that sends her crying to Martha Jane. The preacher predictably responds (in proper English):

It is the work of the devil—and that no-account brother of mine! I've warned you, Sister Martha Jane, about letting this child become worldly!

Martha Jane exits the house, and Jenkins grabs Isabelle's right arm (Paul's huge hand engulfs that of Mercedes Gilbert's), twisting it behind her back as the scene fades out. When Martha Jane returns a short time later, the preacher is pleased to report, "It was a great struggle ... but the Lord's will be done. He won."

"Crushed—body and soul," Isabelle tearfully writes a farewell note, picks up her suitcase, and runs from the house toward the train station. Jenkins is accosted on the sidewalk by Hinds, who reports, "That niggah that runs the club cleaned me. I'm broke and you got

to slip me a few dollars." Jenkins is outraged that he dare treat "a minister of the gospel" in such a manner. Blackmail inevitably ensues as Hinds threatens to expose his fakery if he refuses to "come across with some jack."

The preacher squeezes Hinds' money back from the proprietor and the two conmen sit down to inhale some more rotgut hooch. At the house, Martha Jane retrieves her Bible, a "sacred place" where "de wustes sinnuh wouldn't dauh touch" her hidden savings. But the bread has gone missing, only to be replaced by a note from her "heartbroken daughter."

In Atlanta, Isabelle seeks shelter under the viaduct on Decatur Street, where she attempts to scrape by on pennies and rancid food. Months later, she is visited by Martha Jane, who still refuses to believe her comments about Jenkins, who actually absconded with the family savings. Isabelle asks, "Do you recall the Sunday night we were caught in the storm? And didn't come home until morning?"

A flashback depicts the preacher's horse bolting from his two-wheeled cart as a gale interrupts their drive in the country. They wander around in a heavy rain, but manage to find a deserted cabin in the midnight hour. Lightning strikes a tree outside as Jenkins, stepping into another room, tells Isabelle to remove and dry her clothes.

"I was in the act of drying my clothes," she reports as the next flashback scene fades in to a close-up of her sitting naked by the fire, followed by a tight close-up of a door opening and the preacher's feet entering the room. Isabelle's reaction cuts to a medium close-up of the preacher, framed in an iris, slowly advancing toward her (with Paul slightly bowing his head, transforming his smile into a look of subtle depravity). His feet continue to move slowly across the floor, and Isabelle cowers against a wall, attempting to cover herself with a garment as the scene fades out.

A title card stating, "A half hour later" introduces the return of Jenkins' feet, this time moving in the opposite direction, back toward the door. The feet stop and pivot slightly, suggesting that he is turning to taunt the presumably assaulted girl before leaving the room. The rape of Isabelle, told entirely through suggestive visuals and editing, is made more disturbing by what Micheaux *doesn't* show (giving Paul's film debut an extra-sinister and shocking quality).

Isabelle explains that Sylvester, understanding her plight, proposed marriage, only to experience rejection that again left her alone with the lecherous preacher, who forced her into revealing the hiding place of the money. (Paul alternates slightly growling brutality during the arm twisting with a contentedly sinful grin when seeing that the stash box is actually the family Bible.) "Blood money!" the preacher gloats, fondling the cash as a close-up of his hands dissolves to iris-framed shots of clothes being ironed and cotton being picked. ("Reverend Jenkins" is one bad-ass criminal who truly loves his work.)

When Isabelle attempts to grab the money back from his pocket, he lands a right upper cut to her chin, knocking her to the floor, another sadistic act that brings a laughing smile to his face. Before exiting, he advises her "to throw a few things together and beat it on the 4:30 to Atlanta" and then peels off a $10 bill, adding, "That'll pay your fare and keep you for a week. In the meantime, I may decide to run over and marry you." Isabelle finishes her story, collapses exhausted on the bed, and dies.

Back in Tatesville, the congregation gathers at the church as Jenkins prepares "to preach that sermon which is every black preacher's ambition—'Dry Bones—in the Valley.'" An hour passes as generous donations fill his coffers. The sermon increases in intensity and the "Hallelujahs" issue forth. The preacher imbibes hooch from a bottle stashed in the

pulpit and twice knocks Deacon Simpkins (Chester A. Alexander) to the floor. Suddenly, Martha Jane reveals, "I'se just come fum Atlanta wha I bu'ied Isabelle," accuses Jenkins of murder, and recounts "the pitiful story." The worshippers become a mob, driving him from the church with fists and clenched Bibles. (Paul's performance in this scene, informed by his talent as a singer, is carefully developed, like a musical crescendo, as the preacher masterfully builds his delivery of the legendary sermon.)

Later, Jenkins skulks into Martha Jane's home, falls to his knees, and wails, "You pampered me ... ruined me!" before pleading with her to "save" him. She forgives him but, as he attempts to flee through the countryside, he gleefully bludgeons an adversary with a club.

This scene, with Jenkins *attempting* to repent by asking for forgiveness (his "good" side) and then immediately committing a gratuitously violent act (his "bad" side), suggests similar material in Robert Louis Stevenson's seminal 1885 dual-personality classic *The Strange Case of Dr. Jekyll and Mr. Hyde*. In fact, the "good twin/bad twin" dichotomy, a plot often explored in the classic cinema, also suggests the influence of *Jekyll and Hyde*, along with other such oft-filmed duality tales as Alexandre Dumas (père)'s *The Man in the Iron Mask* (1850) and Oscar Wilde's *The Picture of Dorian Gray* (1891).

Asleep in a chair, Martha Jane is awakened by voices outside the door. Isabelle walks in with Sylvester, whose "discovery has been accepted, and he is to be paid three thousand dollars, advance royalty, in sixty days!" "Mammy" retrieves the Bible, hands the happy couple the cash, gives her blessing, and faints. A title card indicates that the previous startling events were merely "All a dream — only the night-mare of a tortured soul!" All is well as a brief epilogue depicts the honeymooners being welcomed into their swank new home by Martha Jane.

Micheaux's basic visual style is primitive (by 1925 standards), consisting of medium two-shots, with the occasional inter-cutting of medium close-ups (and the use of irises to emphasize certain elements within shots). Used only rarely, tight close-ups strongly emphasize key dramatic moments. His camera primarily remains static, and he relies on simple montage strategies, advancing the narrative by cross-cutting between two separate but related incidents. Unbound by the conventions of the Hollywood cinema (and always bound by extremely limited budgets), he told his stories in a direct, unadorned manner and was unconcerned with shooting retakes to cover technical mistakes.

Although the silent format deprives the viewer of hearing Paul's powerful voice, his believable performance carries the film. His style differs very little from his later portrayals in sound films, and his decision to maintain a level of naturalism, rather than embracing the often exaggerated pantomime of the era, indicates that he instinctively understood the possibilities of cinematic acting. His convincing nonverbal technique (which Essie had helped him develop during their rehearsals) includes the masterful use of the full range of his smile, his most charismatic visual trait, one which easily could have been overplayed by a lesser actor. Micheaux's entire cast, in fact, resists histrionics, and their credibility is disrupted only by the skin-lightening facial makeup worn by many of the actors (a convention of the era).

Micheaux's original cut of *Body and Soul* ran nine reels, but the disapproval of the Motion Picture Commission of the State of New York forced him to edit it mercilessly, resulting in a five-reel version that eliminated material the censors considered "immoral" and "sacrilegious." The negative depiction of a minister, in particular, resulted in the major alteration of the ending, which writes off the entire narrative as a dream. This five-reel,

truncated version of the original film premiered in Harlem on November 15, 1925.

The censorial butchering of Micheaux's plot changed the intent of his screenplay. In an effort to depict the black community accurately, he based his novels and films on actual people he had known. The often erratic nature of the narrative (even in the restored, eight-reel version) is partially due to scenes that are either missing or replaced by a few words on a title card.

Director Charles Burnett, a specialist in African American subjects, noted:

Body and Soul (1925). Robeson's decision to portray the bogus preacher "Isaiah T. Jenkins" in a naturalistic style, rather than embracing the often exaggerated pantomime of the silent era, indicates that he instinctively understood the possibilities of cinematic acting [frame enlargement].

For me, that first generation of independent African American filmmakers resonates more than those of the Sixties and later, because they had to be exceptional. They were fighting social issues more extreme than we have today. They were independent in the truest sense of the word.[2]

Burnett agreed about Paul's acting in *Body and Soul*:

Robeson's performance perfectly spotlights his range and talent. While he dives with glee into Jenkins' almost exaggerated evil, it's as the innocent Sylvester that he appears most natural. It's nearly invisible acting, devoid of the histrionics typically found in performances of the period. He seems to fully understand that he's acting for film, which is particularly impressive given his stage background and the fact that the language of film was still being developed at the time.[3]

In late January 1925, Essie negotiated a contract with theatrical impresario Sir Alfred Butt for a British stage production of *The Emperor Jones* to open in London that September. Paul was guaranteed six weeks' work at $300 per, 5 percent of the gross over $1,000, and two round-trip tickets. In the meantime, he teamed with Lawrence Brown, who recently had come to New York for a series of concert performances, and began visiting with Eugene O'Neill at the playwright's country home in Connecticut and during evenings in Harlem. He also turned down an offer to costar with Florence Mills and Charles Gilpin in *Lulu Belle*, a play rife with black stereotypes that went on to great commercial success.

That summer, Paul, having completed his first cinematic project, contributed another aspect of his wide-ranging qualities, his powerful physique, to a different visual art. When Italian sculptor Antonio Salemme, who had seen *The Emperor Jones*, asked him to pose nude for a life-size statue, Paul became the first African American performer to accept such an offer. Over the course of the next two years, he enjoyed posing, full length, with his arms reaching for the sky, at the artist's Greenwich Village studio as they discussed social and political issues. During breaks, Salemme, who titled his 7-foot-tall sculpture "Negro Spir-

itual," introduced Paul to his circle of bohemian-artist friends. Paul returned the favor by initiating Salemme into the black culture of Harlem.

In July 1925, Paul and Lawrence Brown cut their first sides at the Victor Records studio in Camden, New Jersey. During these sessions, Paul learned how to adapt his singing voice for recordings, using less volume and standing at a proper distance from the microphone. Much of his concert and recording repertoire consisted of spirituals, a genre he and Brown rescued from an obscurity deliberately perpetuated by their African American predecessors. Paul believed that embracing this traditional material was a legitimate and *necessary* way of exploring the history of the black struggle. He later said:

> I wanted to be a singer of the folk songs of my people, and I just did not want to become a Wagnerian opera singer, because I wanted my voice to come from *inside me*.... Dear Larry [Brown] was one of the great authorities on our folk music, and one of the great arrangers of our folk songs, just a *master* of the rhythm of our music — and our early programs ... were devoted specifically to the folk songs of our own people.[4]

Paul opened in the London production of *The Emperor Jones* at the Ambassadors' Theatre on September 10, 1925. The house was packed, and the reviews were effusive with praise for his performance, but word-of-mouth among Londoners died out rather quickly, and the play closed after a five-week run. Paul and Essie remained in England during the autumn, enjoying a great intellectual friendship with Emma Goldman, the Russian-born, American anarchist and political activist who had been deported after campaigning against military conscription during World War I. Initially supportive of the Bolshevik Revolution, Goldman became increasingly disillusioned with the Soviets during the ongoing civil war. After leaving Russia in 1921, she lived in Germany before moving to England, where she initially was welcomed by such prominent British socialists as H. G. Wells and Bertrand Russell. In a letter to Paul and Essie written just before the opening of *The Emperor Jones*, Goldman noted, "I know you will be great, dear Paul ... I wish with all my heart that Paul's interpretation of The Emperor should make the cold blooded Englishman realize his greatness."[5]

Paul and Essie also visited France, where Paul sang in the Latin Quarter of Paris to an audience including Ernest Hemingway and James Joyce, visited with the widow and daughter of Henri Matisse at the painter's home near Nevilly, and met Jamaican writer Claude McKay (whose novel *Banjo* later would be adapted for the film *Big Fella*) while vacationing at Villefranche. Informed by Paul's sister, Marian, of the death of his oldest brother, Bill, of tuberculosis at age 44, the couple steamed back to New York in December.

In January and February 1926, Paul and Lawrence Brown traveled by rail from the East Coast as far west as Burlington, Iowa, performing concerts in 13 cities, including Paul's old home town of Somerville, New Jersey; Philadelphia; Pittsburgh; Indianapolis; Chicago; Milwaukee; and Detroit. Some of the dates, due to a lack of advertising and small-town audiences unfamiliar with Paul's work, proved a bust. Following a Boston performance in March, Paul, who had strained his voice during the tour, began to take lessons from Frantz Proshchowsky, who aided him with breathing techniques and better vocal control.

In April, Paul received an offer from Cecil B. DeMille to play the lead role in a loosely defined "Negro film." Having no knowledge of the content but trusting the man he considered one of Hollywood's top directors, Paul negotiated his own contract, including a good salary and travel expenses, which he signed on April 21. Three weeks later, however, the deal fell through when DeMille's proposed New York shooting dates conflicted with Paul's commitment to *Black Boy*, a play produced by Horace Liveright that was loosely

based on the life of former heavyweight champion Jack Johnson, a controversial and often brutal boxer who held the title from 1908 to 1915. Paul was bitterly disappointed that his chance to become a top Hollywood star disappeared. While *Black Boy* provided a good stage part, DeMille's film offered far more money, plus the promise of preserving another major Robeson performance for posterity.

Paul began rehearsals for *Black Boy* on August 23, 1926. His costar, light-skinned African American actress Fredi Washington, was cast as his white mistress to avoid any controversy that would have been created by a Caucasian performer. Though Paul tried to concentrate on the play, he was more than infatuated by the beauty of Washington, with whom he began an affair that stretched over the next 20 years. Essie was devastated by her husband's dalliances and, though her personal life became increasingly painful, she chose to focus on their professional relationship, rather than to seek a separation or divorce.

Paul also made a cameo appearance in *Camille: The Fate of a Coquette* (1926), a short amateur film adapted from Alexandre Dumas (fils)'s novel *La Dame aux camellias* (*The Lady of the Camellias*) by caricaturist Ralph Barton, who received some assistance from Charles Chaplin. This primarily improvised, 33-minute burlesque features a staggering cast, headed by Chaplin, Ethel Barrymore, Richard Barthelmess, Roland Young (who later would costar with Paul in *King Solomon's Mines*), Pauline Starke and Patsy Ruth Miller. It also included a host of famous artists, writers and intellectuals, including Sherwood Anderson, Paul Claudel, Clarence Darrow, Theodore Dreiser, Sinclair Lewis, Anita Loos, W. Somerset Maugham, H. L. Mencken, Ferenc Molnar and Max Reinhardt. (In 1931, the unstable Barton committed suicide, two months before his 40th birthday.)

By early 1927, Paul and Essie were inundated with financial problems, prompting Paul to seek additional singing dates. He also considered accepting a part in Paul Green's all-black musical *In Abraham's Bosom*, but Essie argued that he might become typecast in more "all–Negro" projects. Charles Gilpin was cast in the lead role of a North Carolina farmer hounded by segregation, and the play went on to win the 1927 Pulitzer Prize for Drama.

In May and June, Paul and Lawrence Brown again went on tour, hitting Kansas City (where there was a segregation flare-up), Columbus, Dayton, Rochester, Ithaca, New Brunswick and New York City. At Princeton, where Paul had endured the strongly racist policies of the university, the current president wrote him a congratulatory note, which was augmented the following day by a glowing student review in the *Daily Princetonian*.

Essie, now pregnant, suggested that Paul audition for the role of "Joe" in Oscar Hammerstein II and Jerome Kern's new musical, *Show Boat*, which featured a song, "Ol' Man River," that was dedicated to him. However, the opening lyric, incorporating the word "Niggers," didn't appeal to him.

On October 15, 1927, Paul, accompanied by Lawrence Brown, returned to Europe for a series of concerts, including two successful dates at Paris' Salle Gaveau hall, where jazz singer Alberta Hunter attended the first performance. Following a very difficult delivery on November 2, 1927, Essie gave birth to an 11-pound baby boy they named Paul Robeson, Jr. Though she was very ill with post-delivery complications, she withheld the truth about her condition from Paul, who finally was informed by Essie's mother. In late December, he arrived back in New York.

Even more strapped for cash by March 1928, Paul, having turned down film projects offering him only stereotypical characters, agreed to replace actor Jack Carter as Crown in Dorothy and DuBose Heyward's play *Porgy*, directed by Rouben Mamoulian at the Guild Theatre. However, the $500-per-week salary did not compensate him for the terrific strain

the performances put on his voice as he spent six weeks trying to sing over the excessive volume of the orchestra.

Deliverance came from Florenz Ziegfeld, who asked him to appear in the upcoming London production of *Show Boat*, to be staged at the Theatre Royal in Drury Lane by Sir Alfred Butt, who was concerned that his star might be wasted in a one-song role (played by baritone Jules Bledsoe in the original 1927 Broadway version). Ziegfeld stood his ground, pointing out that Paul would sing the number three times during the show. Slowly recovering from her infections, Essie again acted as Paul's manager, persuading Lawrence Brown to join him for more European concert dates.

The great Ethel Waters, who had sat for a bronze bust by Antonio Salemme, first met Paul at the Greenwich Village studio, when he was posing for the nude statue. She recalled the scene of his trip abroad:

> Paul was a wonderful young man in those days.... Now he was on the eve of sailing for his ... concerts in London. His boy, baby Paul, had just been born.
> I went to see Paul's wife, who was still in the hospital, the day Paul sailed for Europe, and then went down to the pier to see him off. I gave him a picture of me, inscribing it "from one black bottom to another."[6]

On May 3, 1928, Paul opened in *Show Boat*. The performance was a resounding success, and soon he was giving recitals at the Royal Albert Hall and Drury Lane. He also was pleased that Essie, with her health restored, was able to join him. On May 15, he and other members of the cast recorded "Ol' Man River" for British Columbia at the Gramophone Company's studio in London. Unfortunately, contractual red tape prevented this version of the song (for which Paul eliminated the word "nigger" in favor of alternate lyrics) from being released at the time. On June 15, Paul and Lawrence Brown, backed by an orchestra conducted by Carroll Gibbons, recorded excellent arrangements of James Weldon Johnson's "Seem Lak' to Me" and Will Marion Cook's "Down de Lovers' Lane" at Small Queen's Hall in London. Four days later, they cut several spirituals and "Scandalize My Name," a traditional song that Paul would continue to perform throughout his career, at a studio in Hayes, Middlesex.

Now earning $1,200 per week in *Show Boat*, plus an additional $2,000 from concert performances, Paul finally was able to enjoy commercial success. Artistically he was more popular than ever among the intelligentsia, and he could be seen in the company of Aldous Huxley, George Bernard Shaw and H. G. Wells. He also befriended several Labour Party supporters, from whom he learned about working-class politics, and joined a march with Welsh coal miners who had walked over 200 miles from the Rhondda Valley to London to petition the government for aid. As the group reached downtown London, Paul stopped to sing "Ol' Man River" and a selection of ballads and spirituals. Soon after, he raised enough money to pay for the miners' return trip to South Wales aboard a freight train that included a car filled with food and clothing.

Throughout the autumn and winter of 1928, Paul, accompanied either by Brown or the Gibbons orchestra and chorus, recorded a series of spirituals, plantation songs, and popular favorites associated with Al Jolson ("Mammy" and "Sonny Boy") at Small Queen's Hall. Jolson's influence on Paul's singing is apparent at the conclusion of "Sonny Boy," an element that drew the legendary Jewish entertainer's integration of black music into white popular culture full circle. Unlike the minstrel-show performers who preceded him, Jolson's use of blackface was partially a crude and unsubtle physical manifestation of his rudimentary assimilation of the African American jazz he first heard in its infancy in the back alleys of

New Orleans. His "impersonation" of a black man (which he believed was a *positive* element of his often campy, sentimental and bombastic performance style) was considered offensive by some but, while working on Broadway in 1911, he began a career-long fight against discrimination that later would be taken up by his jazz-influenced, innovative successors, Bing Crosby and Frank Sinatra (who helped break down barriers for African Americans in Hollywood and Las Vegas, respectively). Jazz historian Will Friedwald noted that, during the period of his stardom (which stretched into the early 1930s), Jolson

> summed up everything both positive and negative concerning the evolution of modern vocal style during these years. Exciting and boring, charming and repulsive, all-knowingly funny and pretentiously serious, Jolson is a transitional figure on many levels ... taking the mainstream of popular singing from an operetta-derived style to something if not quite black or jazz, at least which deserves credit for suggesting that black music would be an influence on American pop.[7]

When *Show Boat* closed in February 1929, Paul joined a major Celebrity Concert Tour and studied several languages, enabling him to perform in the native tongues of his audiences in Vienna, Prague and Budapest. Back in London, he sang to a packed house at the Royal Albert Hall. In October, he and Essie returned to New York for a two-month tour of the United States. While most blacks viewed him as a conquering hero, white audiences were intrigued by the news they had heard about the great star of the British *Show Boat*. He played Carnegie Hall on November 5 and then began concentrating on his next stage role, Shakespeare's Othello, which he had signed to play in London, with plans for a follow-up on Broadway.

Chapter 3

The Growth of an Idea
Borderline (1930)

> There are many places in the world where, personally, it would be much easier to live, than in the United States, for an American Negro.
>
> — Paul Robeson[1]

Credits: Director, Producer and Screenplay: Kenneth MacPherson; British Board of Film Censors Certificate "A"; Released by POOL Films (U.K.) on October 13, 1930; Running Time: 75 minutes.

Cast: Paul Robeson (Pete Marond, a Negro), Eslanda Robeson (Adah, a Negro Woman), Helga Doorn [a.k.a. Hilda Doolittle] (Astrid), Gavin Arthur (Thorne, Astrid's Husband), Charlotte Arthur (The Barmaid), Blanche Lewin (The Old Lady), Annie Winifred Ellerman [a.k.a. Bryher] (bit).

English composer and arranger Ray Noble (1903–1978) studied at London's Royal Academy of Music before becoming leader of the HMV Records studio band, the New Mayfair Dance Orchestra, in 1929. Following a successful collaboration with legendary African-born, British jazz vocalist Al Bowlly, he became popular in the United States, where he worked with Glenn Miller, wrote such standards as "Cherokee," "The Very Thought of You" and "The Isle of Capri," and played small roles in Hollywood films. During the autumn of 1929, he arranged and conducted several excellent sides for Paul, including Buddy DeSylva, Lew Brown and Ray Henderson's "Little Pal," which Al Jolson recently had sung in the Warner Bros. film *Say It with Songs* (1929), Nathaniel Shilkret and Gene Austin's "The Lonesome Road," and Ethelbert Nevin's "Mighty Lak' a Rose."

Following a brief series of concert dates in Europe during January 1930, Paul settled in at the Riant Chateau, a mountain inn on the Lake Geneva shore at Territet, Switzerland, to play the lead role in the bizarre silent film *Borderline*. A member of the independent avant-garde POOL Group, Scottish painter and filmmaker Kenneth MacPherson envisioned a project that would combine montage theory with psychoanalysis in a story dealing with racial tension. The Harlem Renaissance (especially African American music and dance) had greatly influenced European culture, and MacPherson sought to blend this influence with the tenets of the experimental film movement, which sought to move cinema away from its reliance on literary and theatrical sources.

In July 1927, the POOL Group began publishing the eclectic journal *Close Up*, the first English-language publication devoted to film theory. The inaugural issue included the article "Cinema and the Classics" by poet Hilda Doolittle (known as "H. D."). The group's logo (concentric ripples in a pool of water) symbolized "the growth of an idea." Their 1929 catalog explained, "POOL is seeking to express new trends and new will ... to make a centre for new ideas and modern thought." MacPherson, who was heavily influenced by the Aus-

trian-born, German expressionist director G. W. Pabst and the montage technique of Soviet filmmakers Sergei Eisenstein, Vsevolod Pudovkin and Lev Kuleshov, was generally contemptuous of commercial cinema, referring to the majority of Hollywood and European films as "trash" and "tripe."

In 1929, a special issue of *Close Up* focusing on blacks in the cinema included the article "The Negro Actor and the American Movies" by African American gossip columnist and radio announcer Geraldyn Dismond. Claiming that "it has been conclusively proven that under the proper director the Negro turns out some of the best acting on the American screen,"[2] Dismond points to the film roles played by studio workers-turned-actors Oscar Smith, Stepin Fetchit and Carolyn Snowden, as well as *Our Gang* kids Ernest "Sunshine Sammy" Morrison and Allen "Farina" Hoskins. Interestingly, she praises the advent of talkies for presenting "the Negro at his best," allowing "White America ... to get particular pleasure out of the Negro's dialect, his queer colloquialisms, and his quaint humor," stressing that "the Negro voice," as exemplified by Fetchit, Clarence Muse and Spencer Williams, "can be a thing of beauty, in spite of the mechanics of this new venture in the art of the movies."[3] Concluding the article, Dismond presents a positive, optimistic prediction of how blacks will be portrayed in the American cinema:

> Three by-products have resulted from this slow recognition of the Negro as movie material — Negro film corporations, Negro and white film corporations, and white corporations, all for the production of Negro pictures. They have the same motives, namely, to present Negro films about and for Negroes, showing them not as fools and servants but as human beings with the same emotions, desires and weaknesses as other peoples, and to share in the profits of this great industry.... Because of the Negro movie, many a prejudiced white who would not accept a Negro unless as a servant will be compelled to admit that at least he can be something else; many an indifferent white will be beguiled into a positive attitude of friendliness; many a Negro will have his race consciousness and self-respect stimulated. In short, the Negro movie actor is a means of getting acquainted with Negroes and under proper direction and sympathetic treatment can easily become a potent factor in our great struggle for better race relations.[4]

Having mentioned Universal's first film adaptation of *Show Boat* (1929), Dismond lists Paul as one member of a group of "officers and directors" included in a "rumor of the formation in New York City of the Tono-Film, an all–Negro corporation for exclusive Negro talking pictures."[5]

The POOL publication of Dismond's Hollywood-talkie endorsement notwithstanding, Kenneth MacPherson proceeded to make a diametrically different film with *Borderline*. The sole feature produced by the group, this experimental silent features Paul as Pete Marond, whose girlfriend, Adah, has an affair with a married white man in a Swiss border town. MacPherson's casting of Essie as Adah was ironic, a symbolic turning of the tables on Paul, who had romantic dalliances in real life. MacPherson was bisexual, and he and his wife, Annie Winifred Ellerman (a.k.a. "Bryher"), shared a lover: Hilda Doolittle, who appears in the film under the pseudonym "Helga Doorn." The only professional actor signed for the project, Paul, enjoying his collaboration with other free-thinking intellectuals, refused to accept a fee for his work. Interior shooting was completed at Kenwin, a Bauhaus-style dwelling overlooking Lake Geneva that served as both home and film studio for the POOL members.

The film presents the fallout from an interracial love triangle but doesn't offer any particular moral position. MacPherson's screenplay focuses on the inner psychology of his

characters, rather than narrative coherence. To accompany screenings of the film, MacPherson and Doolittle co-wrote a booklet emphasizing the psychological metaphors. (During the 1930s, Doolittle enjoyed a friendship with Sigmund Freud, who became her analyst when she sought to understand her own bisexual nature.)

Borderline opens with a rapidly edited montage including Adah (Essie), her lover, Thorne (Gavin Arthur), and his wife, Astrid (Hilda Doolittle), who is attempting to reach Adah's partner, Pete Marond (Robeson), by telephone. Paul is first seen after the barmaid (Charlotte Arthur) knocks on the door of Pete's upstairs room and a title card announces, "Astrid on the 'phone!" A medium close-up shows him in profile, standing by a window as the white curtains billow in. A series of tight close-ups show Pete's profile, Thorne and Adah's faces, and the barmaid continuing to summon him. Pete sends her away, triggering a series of images, including a long shot of Paul from behind, and close-ups of his profile and large hands before the barmaid returns to her post, informing Astrid that Pete refuses to answer.

Adah speaks with Astrid, who tells her, "You must go back to Pete and leave Thorne." Various close-ups of Pete, emphasizing Paul's powerful physique, continue to be inter-cut with images of Astrid in her room and a piano player in the barroom. As Pete lies down on his bed, a sequence showing him and Adah outdoors, smiling and waving at each other, is inserted. Unable to rest, Pete puts on his coat and cap, rushes downstairs through the barroom and into the village. He catches up with Adah, and the two walk hand-in-hand along a brick street.

Back in the barroom, Astrid pounds on the table and rages, "They are niggers, my dear!" Thorne arrives and angrily accuses Astrid of bringing Pete to the inn. Her defense is to shout "Nigger Lover!" before exiting the room.

Pete and Adah continue their perambulations in the countryside. In a stunning montage, close-ups of Paul (some with Essie filmed against a painted backdrop) are combined with various shots of the natural wonders of the Alps. The scene shifts to various local patrons in the barroom, where an old woman (Blanche Lewin) shakes her finger and announces, "If I had my way, not one Negro would be allowed in the country!"

"Why blame the Negroes," asks the barmaid, "when...." A montage showing Astrid and Thorne in their room as they party, then argue (and culminating with her walking out on him) follows. Pete and Adah meet upstairs, where they are interrupted by Thorne, who is accompanied by others from the bar who drag him out.

Playing a solitary game of cards, as a stuffed albatross sits

Borderline (1930). **In this bizarre silent feature, Scottish avant-garde filmmaker Kenneth MacPherson uses close-ups of Robeson, shot from every conceivable angle, in an attempt to convey the "inner psychology" of his character, "Pete Marond, a Negro" [frame enlargement].**

on the table beside her, Astrid deals aces and eights: the dead man's hand. Thorne walks in, carrying a bag, and she pleads with him, pounding her fists on his chest. She attempts to embrace him, but he shoves her away, sparking an emotional outburst that leaves Astrid staring at the ceiling as she lies motionless on the floor. Thorne nervously toys with a *sgian dubh* (the Scottish Highlander's traditional boot dagger, no doubt contributed by MacPherson), which he drops onto the table. Astrid grabs the knife, slashes his left hand and right cheek,

Borderline (1930). Pete (Robeson) prepares to doff his cap as he and Adah meet upstairs at the inn [frame enlargement].

and struggles with him as he wrests it away, killing her as the table topples over.

Pete joins the revelers in the bar as the pianist continues to play. The barmaid places a rose behind Pete's ear and dances with a knife between her teeth. Adah arrives and, as Pete leaves with her, the barmaid removes the knife from her mouth. In a brilliant, seamless bit of editing, the scene cuts to the stained *sgian dubh* being placed in a bowl of water. Thorne, his hand and cheek in bandages, attempts to clean the remaining blood from the wooden floor.

Close-ups of Paul's large left hand and face show Pete knocking on the door. Thorne checks the lock as Adah attempts to turn the handle from the other side. The couple is then shown enjoying another walk in the Alps, just before the scene shifts to a montage of accusatory characters, then back to the barroom, where a bespectacled, mustachioed man offends Adah and is punched out by Pete. Adah leaves, the other drinkers cheer and then angrily shake their fists, and the barmaid runs to the downed man.

A note written by Adah, asking forgiveness from Pete, begins the next scene, in which he is informed that

Borderline (1930). Seated on the bed, Pete (Robeson), whose tryst with Adah has been interrupted by Thorne, ponders his next move [frame enlargement].

"Thorne has been acquitted." The innkeeper receives a sealed letter from the mayor, who advises her of his council's decision to evict "the negro [sic] Pete Marond" from both the inn and the town. (Though his character is listed as Pete "Varond" in previous listings, the mayor's letter in the film clearly identifies him as Pete "Marond.") "What do you think?" asks Pete.

She tears up the letter. "Sorry, Pete!" she says. "What makes it worse is they think they're doing the right thing. We're like that!"

"Yes, we're like that," echoes Pete as he walks out. The pianist removes the photo of Pete displayed on his upright, puts it in his wallet, sighs, and begins to play. A compelling scene of Pete and Thorne shaking hands is followed by the outcast leaving town. Thorne is seen on a hillside, staring into the woods. In the bar, the pianist bids farewell and plays a tune, the bigoted old woman is pleased by the events, the barmaid is depressed, and the innkeeper closes the guest's ledger: The End.

University of London professor Ian Christie noted:

> What makes the film "difficult" upon first viewing, but also truly experimental, is the attempt to combine subjective and objective points of view, often without marking any transition.... It also has a strange rhythm, alternating bursts of staccato editing with brooding — and very beautiful — sustained shots of, especially, Robeson, who is seen here as we never see him in any of the exotic roles he would play in other films, dressed as a fashionable, contemporary figure.[6]

The film includes very few title cards, most of which use minimal verbiage to set up montages that effectively tell the story. Like the best silent films (most notably F. W. Murnau's German expressionist masterpiece *Der letzte Mann*, a.k.a. *The Last Laugh* [1924], which tells its powerful tale sans title cards), *Borderline* is truly effective cinema because it primarily relies on *images*. Contrary to those who have criticized the film for being difficult to understand, *Borderline* (though substituting "psychological" imagery for conventional, linear narrative) will make considerable sense to any observant viewer with a solid attention span.

The footage of Paul, shot mainly in close-up from every conceivable angle, is fascinating in its ability to provide an intimate record of the *man*, as well as the actor, at age 32. He is a "fashionable, contemporary figure" and appears perfectly at ease in an unconventional film. The naturalism in his scenes with Essie imparts a unique cinematic document of this married couple.

The title *Borderline* could refer to any of several elements in the film: the fine line the characters walk in their relationships and behavior; the unconventional interracial love affair that incites the tension and, ultimately, mayhem; and the border town itself. With the possible exception of Pete, all the characters pursue a hedonistic lifestyle that is at the heart of the film.

Banned by many censors in 1930, *Borderline* retained its avant-garde status by never receiving an actual theatrical release, although an "A" certificate was awarded by the British Board of Film Censors "for Public Exhibition to Adult Audiences." A reviewer for *The Bioscope* who actually saw the film wrote, "Mr. MacPherson buries his intentions in a conglomerate of weird shots ... around a dissolute set of unsympathetic characters," and expressed his "natural desire to see and hear Paul Robeson in a first-rate British 'talkie' made for the public."[7]

The film literally disappeared for several decades before being rediscovered by historians. A restoration was completed by George Eastman House and, in 2006, the British Film Institute commissioned a new musical score by jazz composer Courtney Pine, whose

excellent bebop increases the tension in key scenes, making the resurrected *Borderline* a very satisfying viewing experience.

After completing his work on *Borderline*, Paul, during March 1930, starred in a one-week run of *The Emperor Jones* in Berlin before returning to London, where rehearsals for his upcoming role in *Othello* were scheduled to begin on April 15. The play was already creating controversy, due to the casting of Peggy Ashcroft as Desdemona, an issue not quite as thorny for the Brits as it was in the United States, where a black man playing Shakespeare's Moor was still considered distasteful by a public majority. (However, producer Jed Harris had announced that, should the London version prove a success, he was ready to cast Lillian Gish as Desdemona in a Broadway production.) When the play opened on May 19, Paul became the first black actor to play Othello opposite a white cast in nearly a century. Most reviews of his performance were very positive, but more than one critic pointed out his lack of the "grand style" and "highly civilized quality" required by the Shakespearean role. Paul Robeson, Jr., explained:

> In 1930, Paul had not yet jettisoned the "don't upset white folks" dictum of his boyhood days, thus interfering with his ability to project the regal and commanding posture that Othello should exude from the outset.... Paul did not yet possess the confidence needed to deliver the lines with the authority he later found.[8]

On June 8, 1930, a historic radio interview with Paul was broadcast by the BBC via the ABC and CBS networks to 25 million listeners in the United States, who heard about his experiences playing Othello and his hopes of bringing the play to New York. Unfortunately, the interference of Maurice Browne, producer of the London version, scotched negotiations for transporting the Bard to Broadway. Controversy already was brewing Stateside, after Salemme's nude, burnished-plaster statue of Paul had been banned from an exhibition by the Philadelphia Art Alliance, fearing that it would incite further racial unrest in a community where "the colored problem seems to be unusually great."[9] Late in life, Salemme said:

> When I did it, there was no such thing as "Black is beautiful." It was a controversial thing, you see, and I didn't realize it was controversial. All I could see is that Robeson had the body of a great athlete.
> He was very beautiful. I did it quite faithfully, quite accurately, so it was a very great statue. It was refused because Paul Robeson was a black man, which was a shame for Philadelphia. It didn't do them any good, but it made me famous.[10]

(Following further unsuccessful attempts to show the statue in the United States, Salemme, using funds from a Guggenheim Fellowship, shipped the piece to a successful exhibit at the Salon des Tuileries in Paris, where he subsequently left it at a foundry to be bronzed. After the statue disappeared without a trace, he produced another plaster cast to exhibit at a gallery in Palm Beach, Florida. This casting also vanished, never to be seen again.)

During the London run of *Othello*, Paul again couldn't resist an affair with a young, attractive leading lady. His off-stage relationship with Peggy Ashcroft (a newlywed) was another in a series of romantic dalliances that hit his wife very hard, particularly since Essie had lobbied for Peggy's casting and then became a close friend. The fact that Paul was simultaneously seeing Yolande Jackson, another young English actress, was too much for Essie to bear, and she eventually suffered a nervous breakdown. Though the Ashcroft affair soon ended, Paul was unwilling to leave Yolande, who continued to pursue him. On September 9, 1930, he rather irresponsibly wrote to Essie, "I am in a period of transition — where I

shall finally finish is of little consequence to me. I would like to get on with my work. To do that I need to be as far as possible absolutely free."[11]

In the meantime, Essie had published, through Victor Gollancz, Ltd., a biography, *Paul Robeson, Negro*, a self-serving and dubious account written in the third person. Paul was not pleased that his wife openly criticized his behavior and work habits, fictionalized dialogue he supposedly said, and literally invented situations that never actually occurred. (Her substitution of the respected maternal family name "Bustill" for his actual middle name, Leroy, led to the subsequent and ongoing listing of his full name as "Paul Leroy Bustill Robeson" in most reference sources.)

On September 11 and 12, 1930, Paul again joined bandleader Ray Noble in Hayes, Middlesex, to record six sides, including Stephen Foster's "Old Folks at Home," "Poor Old Joe" (a.k.a. "Ol' Black Joe") and "My Old Kentucky Home," a lightly swinging, guitar-driven arrangement of Harry Woods' "River Stay Away from My Door," and a new version of "Ol' Man River" that *does* open with the "Niggers" lyric.

For a time, Paul and Essie considered divorcing so he could marry Yolande, although abandoning a black wife for a white lover would have hurt his standing in the African American community, not to mention the harsh reaction he would have received from whites in the United States. Essie had sent young Paul Jr. with her mother to Territet, where they would remain for the next three years, while she prepared a new apartment for her and Paul in central London.

Following a concert tour of the English provinces, Paul, on December 1, rejoined Essie for a few days and spent the holidays with his family before leaving with Lawrence Brown for a tour of the United States. In between concert dates, Paul received word from Essie that she was pregnant and planned to get an abortion, which was performed by a Dr. West in New York in March 1931.

While in New York, Paul befriended Bob Rockmore, an entertainment lawyer and agent whom he had met during the 1924 production of *All God's Chillun Got Wings*. Rockmore signed him to star in a London production of another Eugene O'Neill play, *The Hairy Ape*, to open in May 1931. The story was certainly an unusual one, dealing with a ship's stoker (a role originally written for a white actor) who is abused to a point where he degenerates into a gorilla-like state and cages himself at a zoo. Essie had returned to London a few days before Paul's arrival, and once again she assumed the role of his acting coach, warning him not to overuse his voice during the performances. Though he received fine notices, he eventually developed laryngitis, and the play closed while he was confined to a hospital.

More than a year had passed when Paul and Ray Noble reunited for another recording session, this time at Abbey Road in London, where they cut Hoagy Carmichael's "Rockin' Chair" on September 17, 1931. One week later at Small Queen's Hall, Paul collaborated with Jack Hylton on a medley of spirituals, then got back to work with Noble during two sessions, one of which, at Abbey Road on December 18, yielded a version of Clarence Muse's "When It's Sleepy Time Down South" (which later became the signature song of Louis Armstrong and His All Stars).

For all intents and purposes, Paul and Essie remained separated, due in part to the anger he felt over her abortion (he believed she had been impregnated by a white lover) and also because of a subsequent dilation and curettage procedure required to correct internal damage done during the New York operation. Paul continued to struggle with the dilemma of wanting "to be free," while still needing Essie's guidance in intellectual, artistic

and career matters. In late 1931, Essie wrote a long letter in which she described her feelings regarding his affair with Yolande, as well as their professional reasons for staying together.

In January 1932, Paul was interviewed by British columnist W. R. Titterton, who asked him about the foundations of his religious faith. Though Essie was an agnostic raised by an atheist mother, Paul explained, "I am a black man, and all black men are religious."[12] He also discussed the significance of the African American spirituals he felt compelled to perform in his concerts and on his recordings:

> [H]ow can God be merciful when such terrible things happen? ... He created men — by what process, evolutionary or otherwise, I don't know — and allowed them to work their own will. God can't be blamed if man's works are evil. We had proof that the suffering of the Negro had ennobled his soul in the Spirituals which I am so proud to sing.... How do I know anything about God? I think that most men know ... as an artist I have my moments of ecstasy when the thing is plain. But I do not exalt the artist above the common man. The common man feels; we artists have the power of expression — that is the difference. Nevertheless, when I sing my Spirituals, in which is the whole history of my race, it is then, more than at any other time, that I am liable to be caught away, and feel and know, that God exists, and God is love.[13]

On May 19, 1932, Paul first sang "Ol' Man River" for an American audience during a revival of *Show Boat* at the Casino Theater in New York. His performance literally stopped the show as the crowd gave him a wild standing ovation. Soon he was receiving more offers than he could accept. During the run of the play, he performed on several radio shows, earning $1,500 for each 20-minute appearance. On June 11, he received an honorary Master of Arts degree from Rutgers during the university's annual commencement exercises. The youngest man ever to receive the honor, Paul was praised by Rutgers president Robert Clothier, who said, "Seldom is it given to one man to bring joy to the hearts of his hearers by the arts of singing and acting as it has been given to you, and you have well discharged the trust which that gift implies."

At this point in his career, Paul was outspoken on cultural issues but remained relatively quiet about politics. He seemed uninterested in the upcoming presidential election between Franklin D. Roosevelt and Herbert Hoover, and he said nothing about the railroading of the Scottsboro Boys, five innocent young blacks who had been sentenced to death for "raping a white woman" in northeastern Alabama. However, in October, he wrote to a friend, admitting, "Have had one of the greatest treats of my life in my first reading of Carl [*sic*] Marx. Loving it."[14]

Paul left the *Show Boat* company and returned to London in September 1932. At an October 20 Abbey Road session with Ray Noble, he recorded "My Curly-Headed Baby," a song he would perform in two of his British films. On December 13, he returned to Abbey Road to work with arranger-pianist Ruthland Clapham, who accompanied him on four sides, including James Weldon Johnson's beautiful ballad "Since You Went Away." Two days later, he cut Clapham's own "Hush-a-bye Lullaby" with Noble's orchestra. Focusing ever more on his career, he chose to end his affair with Yolande Jackson and also to pursue the divorce from Essie. However, by the end of December, the couple had decided to continue with their marriage, a reconciliation that proved to be permanent.

Bloomin' Majesty
The Emperor Jones (1933)

Robeson's greatest contribution to black film history — and the aspect of his work that most disturbed American white moviegoers — was his proud, defiant portrait of the black man. In his best known film, *The Emperor Jones* (1933), Robeson portrays O'Neill's black man who refuses to kowtow to anyone ... he is a black man consciously asserting himself, consciously cutting The Man down to size.

— Donald Bogle[1]

Credits: Director: Dudley Murphy; Producers: John Krimsky, Gifford Cochran; Screenplay: DuBose Heyward; Based on the play by Eugene O'Neill; Script Supervisor: William C. DeMille; Director of Photography: Ernest Haller; Editor: Grant Whytock; Art Director: Herman Rosse; Assistant Director: Joseph H. Nadel; Sound Engineer: Joseph Kane; Production Manager: J. Edward Shugrue; Musical Score: Frank Tours; Vocal Arrangements: J. Rosamond Johnson; Sound Synchronization: Max Manne; Premiered (New York) September 19, 1933; Released by United Artists (U.S.) on September 29, 1933; Running Time: 76 minutes.

Cast: Paul Robeson (Brutus Jones), Dudley Digges (Smithers), Frank H. Wilson (Jeff), Fredi Washington (Undine), Ruby Elzy (Dolly), George Haymid Stamper (Lem), Brandon Evans (Carrington), Taylor Gordon (Stick-man), Rex Ingram (Court Crier), Jackie "Moms" Mabley (Marcella), Harold Nicholas (Young Tap Dancer), Blueboy O'Connor (Treasurer), Billie Holiday, Fritz Pollard, Lorenzo Tucker (extras).

In January 1933, the great English stage actress Flora Robson (who was just beginning a distinguished film career that would stretch over the next five decades) asked Paul to costar in a London version of *All God's Chillun Got Wings*, to be directed by the leftist director André Van Gyseghem at the Embassy Theatre. Robson recently had moved in across the hall from Paul and Essie's flat at 19 Buckingham Street and became fast friends with both of them. While preparing for the run of the play, Paul continued his Abbey Road recording sessions, alternately with Ray Noble and Ruthland Clapham.

His acting during the opening performance of *Chillun* on March 13 was described by the critic for *Punch* as having "a passionate intensity which was overwhelming."[2] The majority of reviewers concurred that he was powerful but lacking sufficient subtlety and control, with E. A. Baughan of the *Daily News-Chronicle* noting, "Of Paul Robeson, I am never sure if he is acting, but is just himself. Only ... his voice persuades one that he is an actor of uncommon gifts."[3]

All God's Chillun was successful but closed after a two-month run (at the Embassy and Piccadilly Theatres) to allow Paul to return to the United States on May 10, 1933, for the film version of *The Emperor Jones*. For the screen adaptation, budgeted at $250,000 (with $30,000 allocated for the film rights to the play), Eugene O'Neill, wanting Paul to transform his powerful stage role for the cameras, insisted that he be billed above the title.

Paul agreed, as long as the film was shot in the North, so producers John Krimsky and Gifford Cochran created an independent company unattached to any of the Hollywood studios, with the completed picture to be released through United Artists. The entire shoot, including the jungle scenes, was conducted above the Mason-Dixon Line at Paramount's studio in Astoria, Queens, and in Westchester. *New Yorker* staff writer Hilton Als noted:

> Often an artist finds himself living in a strange home. But America in 1933 was crueler than most: segregation, the Depression, mob violence, Prohibition — a moralistic age that presaged our own. Still, what better moment for Robeson to tackle the role that would make him a star? For he must have known that Brutus Jones — despite O'Neill's limitations in his conception of the role — was a "bad nigger," that all-too-real being who disavowed what America said he should be: subservient, invisible.[4]

O'Neill based his 1920 play on the career of the U.S.-supported Haitian president Jean Vilbrun Guillaume Sam, who was in office from February 25 to July 28, 1915. His repressive regime, which culminated with the execution of 167 political prisoners on July 27, sparked an uprising in Port-au-Prince that led him to seek asylum at the French Embassy. Discovered hiding in a bathroom, he was savagely beaten to death, tossed onto an iron fence, and torn into pieces which were subsequently displayed in various neighborhoods in the capital. Fearing further political turmoil, President Woodrow Wilson ordered U.S. troops into Haiti, which they occupied until 1934.

The film's director, Dudley Murphy, previously had worked with African American performers while shooting two 1929 musical shorts in which two jazz legends made their screen debuts: *Black and Tan*, starring Duke Ellington, and *St. Louis Blues*, featuring Bessie Smith. For *The Emperor Jones,* Murphy hired another jazz innovator, 18-year-old Billie Holiday, who was just beginning her career by singing in Harlem joints, as an extra. Holiday later recalled that her friend, songwriter Shelton Brooks,

> thought I was ready for a crack at the movies. Not Hollywood, just Astoria, Long Island. He got me a part out there playing mob scenes in a picture with Paul Robeson. From that I got a real part in a short featuring Duke Ellington [the 1935 short *Symphony in Black: A Rhapsody of Negro Life*]."[5]

To prepare for Murphy's shooting schedule, Paul ran, boxed and tossed a medicine ball with Fritz Pollard, a close friend and former football teammate on the Akron Pros, who also landed an extra part in the production. Film audiences who hadn't seen Paul on stage but may have heard him on the radio were eager both to see *and* hear him on the silver screen.

O'Neill's play begins with Brutus Jones already serving as emperor on a small island in the West Indies, with his adventures told in a series of flashbacks. The film's opening credits hint at Jones' ultimate destination by featuring natives drumming and dancing in the background, but the narrative begins when these primitive images dissolve to modern African Americans in South Carolina, singing and bopping at the Hezekiah Baptist Church. The preacher prevails upon the congregation to pray for Brutus Jones, their representative who will travel to the North to work as a Pullman porter.

Brutus, wearing his porter's uniform, is first seen admiring himself in a mirror (the film's most prominent visual motif) and unleashing a big smile (a Robeson trademark he uses to convey a variety of emotions) as his gal, Dolly (Ruby Elzy), praises, "Mmm Mmm, Honey, you sho is wonderful in dem clothes." But Brutus has just returned from his Pullman training in New York, where no one notices such attire. When he mentions "them New York gals on Lenox Avenue," Dolly replies, "Them gals is *fast*, I bet."

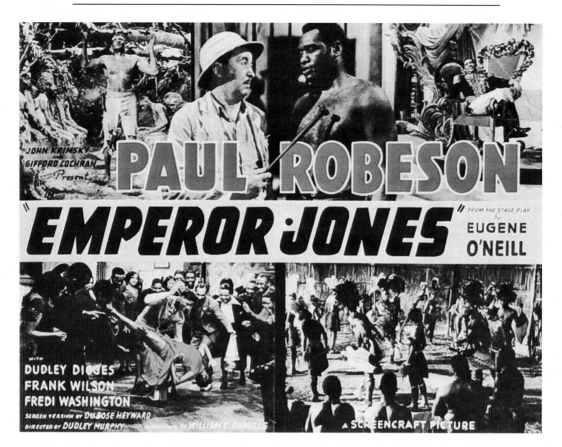

The Emperor Jones (1933). This U.S.–release title lobby card for the film adaptation of Eugene O'Neill's play depicts the similarities between "modern" African Americans partying in a speakeasy and "primitive" blacks dancing in the Caribbean.

"There ain't none of them as pretty in the face, like my gal," he assures her, as the scene cuts back to the preacher, promising his flock that Brutus will *not* go the way of the prodigal son. Back in their room, Brutus describes his experiences in Washington, D.C., instantly conveying to the viewer his true, conman nature when he describes the president of the United States leaving the Capitol building "with a band befo' and a band behind" to congratulate him personally "for landing the job."

Brutus' friend Jeff (Frank H. Wilson) will be on the train scheduled to pick him up at the depot's water tank. Brutus and Dolly enter the church, where she admires his Pullman cap as he embraces the congregants and the preacher before giving voice to "Let Me Fly," a rousing spiritual that is interrupted by the whistle of the approaching train. Brutus introduces Dolly to Jeff and then gives her some money. "But this is too much," she declares. "You is comin' back, ain't ya?"

On board, Jeff schools Brutus in the ways of courting big tippers, of earning "the long green" and, even more importantly, "where to spend it." The scene dissolves to a piano player and a chorus of sisters singing "St. Louis Blues" at a Harlem joint run by Marcella (Jackie "Moms" Mabley, in her film debut). Jeff discovers "his gal," Undine (Fredi Washington), behind a beaded curtain, making time with another man, whom he socks in the kisser. (A light-skinned African American actress, Washington was forced to darken her

The Emperor Jones (1933). The congregation of South Carolina's Hezekiah Baptist Church, including Dolly (Ruby Elzy), places its hopes on Brutus Jones (Robeson), who is about to head north for Pullman porter training in New York City [U.S.–release lobby card].

face to play the role, lest white audiences think miscegenation was afoot.) Marcella gives the bum's rush to the offender, Jeff introduces Undine to "Mr. Jones," and the two new friends happily cavort through the curtain onto the dance floor.

A montage, superimposing a shoe-shining Brutus singing "Little Gal" over a moving train, dissolves back to Marcella's joint, now with the "Big Boy" himself squiring Undine behind the beaded curtain. She fears what Jeff might do, but Brutus assures her, "I can handle that little two-bit porter. You ought to throw him over, anyhow. Then it would just be you and me." He then claims he's been "transferred to the President's private car."

After six weeks of service with Mr. Carrington (Brandon Evans), Brutus, learning of a secret merger, strikes a bargain with the white man. Though he eventually will be sent back to the South, Brutus is soon dressing in a tuxedo, adjusting his black bow tie while again admiring himself in a mirror. This time, Undine can also be seen in the full-length glass, inquiring about the "good fit" of his new attire, acquired from the boss' own tailor. Brutus claims that he's "in partnership" with Carrington, but Undine thinks he won his money "in a crap game." Tossing $40 on the bed, he tells her to go back to Jeff.

Brutus has better things to pursue at the upscale nightclub run by Belle Ledoux, where the floorshow includes a pint-sized version of Cab Calloway (Harold Nicholas, later of the famous Nicholas Brothers duo), who tap dances and conducts a hot swing band. Brutus

and Belle are joined at their table by Jeff and Undine, who stares daggers at the two-timing man as he takes to the floor with his new gal. A catfight erupts with a flurry of choking and hair-pulling, and a bouncer drags Undine out of the joint. "I's travelin' light," Brutus informs the hatcheck girl as he calmly makes his exit.

The train travels south to Washington, Richmond and Savannah, where Brutus crashes Jeff's crap game at Baby Jim's Juke. A would-be singer moans the blues to the accompaniment of a honky-tonk piano as the Big Boy, striding in wearing a straw boater, orders, "Let 'em roll!" much to the dismay of Jeff, who obviously wants nothing more to do with his former friend.

The music stops when "Mr. Jones" raises the stakes. Jeff rolls a natural and starts raking in the loot, but the dealer declares that the dice are crooked. Jeff pulls a knife, and the two erstwhile Pullman brothers wrestle it out. Brutus overpowers Jeff, pinning him to the floor as the knife accidentally slices into Jeff's chest. The scene dissolves to a high-angle shot depicting a macabre tableau: Jeff's lifeless body remains in the middle of the juke-joint floor as the music drones on and the patrons casually continue to drink, smoke and shoot pool. Eventually a Caucasian cop runs in and whistles for backup.

The next sequence fades in on a close-up of chain gang prisoners' shackled ankles as their feet trudge through the dust. Brutus' voice can be heard in the background as he sings

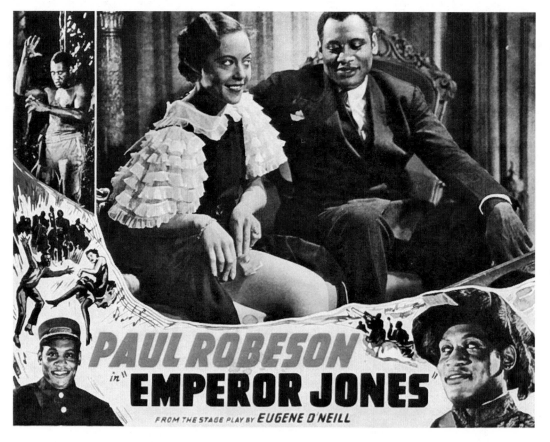

The Emperor Jones (1933). While hanging out in Harlem, Brutus Jones (Robeson) admires the personal banking method preferred by Undine (Fredi Washington) [U.S.–release lobby card].

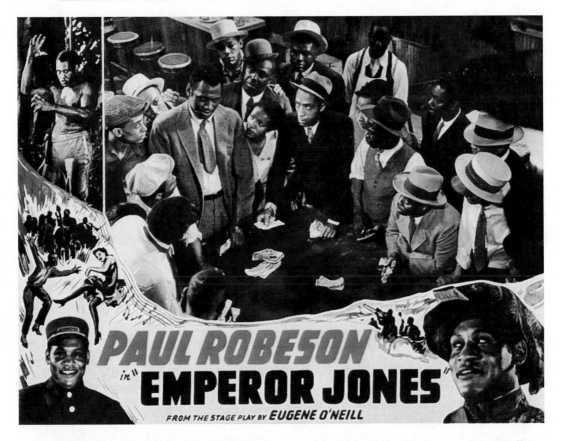

The Emperor Jones (1933). At Baby Jim's Juke in Savannah, Brutus Jones (Robeson) takes on Jeff (Frank H. Wilson), his erstwhile mentor, in a crap game that quickly turns fatal [U.S.–release lobby card].

"John Henry." The close-up dissolves to a long shot of Brutus, stripped to the waist, swinging his sledgehammer into the rock pile as he continues to sing. Paul's powerful physique is seen for the first time in the film; and as the scene cuts to a medium close-up, he segues into another African American work song, "Water Boy."

In a sequence with strong slavery overtones, a white guard orders Brutus to remove a punished prisoner from the sweat box; when he falls out onto the ground, the sadistic man grabs a club, hits Brutus for refusing to wake him, and then unmercifully beats the unconscious man. Framed in a tight close-up, Brutus surveys the area and then grabs a shovel as the scene cuts to a medium shot. Just as he swings the tool at the guard, an abrupt cut leads to a shot of his fellow prisoners sledging rocks near a steam shovel. (The Hays Office ordered this depiction of the killing of a white authority figure by a black man removed, and the footage has never been recovered.) Paul's seemingly invincible physical prowess is demonstrated further as the shackled Brutus scrambles through the rock piles, climbs into a dump truck, and orders another comrade-in-chains to drop a bucket load from the steam shovel directly on top of him. A siren blasts away and armed guards inspect the truck, but the buried Brutus rides away toward the possibility of freedom.

The next scene fades in on one of the most striking images in the film: a medium close-up of Brutus peering into a window, shot from the inside, with Ernest Haller's

chiaroscuro lighting creating an expressionistic mood reminiscent of the great German silent films of F. W. Murnau and Fritz Lang. Brutus taps on the pane. "Dolly, let me in quick!" he orders in a whisper. "Dolly, honey, you hear me?" he asks, frantically rapping again. The great conman has no other choice but to return home, hoping that his abandoned woman still loves him.

"Who dat?" Dolly asks as she sits up in bed. She last saw Brutus in Pullman finery, but now he wears the dirty, striped uniform of the convict. But the Big Boy's bargain pays off: Dolly's love is so blind that she throws her arms around him even before noticing that he's "in trouble." "I gotta leave the country!" he informs her. As soon as the shackles are filed off, he ditches her again.

Stock footage of a steamship at sea dissolves to Brutus, singing "Travelin'," and two black cohorts shoveling coal in the boiler room of a Merchant Marine vessel. Murphy again cuts from a full shot to a close-up of the shirtless Paul as he toils away. Brutus learns that the ship's next port of call is Kingston, Jamaica, but he chooses to take his chances at a "little nigger island" where there is "nothin' but trouble."

"Trouble is my buddy," he tells his pals, who also call him "Big Boy." Robeson of Rutgers, the All-American athlete, demonstrates his athleticism as Brutus announces, "Trouble, here I come!" and dives into the sea, swimming toward the island. (Ironically, Paul wasn't much of a swimmer in real life.) Exhausted, he collapses on the beach, where he is roused by six black "soldiers" wearing sombreros and armed with rifles.

At the post-colonial headquarters of "His Excellency," Smithers (Dudley Digges), a white trader, meets with the island leader (also referred to as "The General"), who appears buffoonish in black top hat and tailcoat. The soldiers burst in with Brutus, who is deemed a "filthy swine" and ordered "locked up" until he can be shipped out.

"I'll take this bloomin' nigger off your hands for you, Your Highness," offers Smithers. Five silver dollars seals the deal, "lock, stock and barrel," and the white master, carrying a riding crop, has a new slave. Noticing the shackle scars on Brutus' ankles, he asks, "So that's what it is, me lad, eh? What they calls in the States a 'bad nigger,' eh? A killer, what? With the law on your trail and the bloomin' gallows waitin' around the next corner, what?"

"Looka here, white man," Brutus fires back. "I comes and I goes, and that's my business."

"Oh, ho! So that's the kind of a nigger you are, eh?" Smithers scoffs. "Not afraid to stand right up to your betters and tell 'em what's what."

Brutus again strikes a bargain with a white man, this time accepting "rum and eats" but not "a stinkin' penny" in return for exacting revenge on the "heathen" who tossed him in jail. "If anybody worries you, you tell 'em you belong to Mr. Smithers," the trader advises.

"I belongs to Mr. Smithers," Brutus repeats, slightly grinning as he bows. But the conman already has a plan: teaching the locals how to shoot dice, which he uses to win supplies they have smuggled down to the beach. At the "Smithers Ltd. Import and Export" shop, the trader wipes the sweat and grumbles, "I wonder what the blazes is keepin' that *black ape*." Brutus arrives with the goods, cart and team of oxen he has filched in the crap game, threatens to open up a rival store next door, and suggests that a "partnership" is a much better idea. Smithers scratches his head as the scene dissolves to a close-up of the altered sign, now reading, "Smithers and Jones Ltd. and Inc."

The new partners ride into the village marketplace on horseback as the locals laze around among chickens pecking the ground. "Why don't you come in and pay your bill?" Smithers asks one of them. (These sombrero-clad natives are a hybrid of black and Latino

The Emperor Jones (1933). Brutus Jones (Robeson, in one of several "beefcake scenes") pretends to bow to one of his "betters," the unscrupulous British trader Smithers (Dudley Digges), who refers to him as a "bloomin', bad nigger" [U.S.–release lobby card].

stereotypes.) Brutus has recruited a new army for the "General," troops he refers to as "fine niggers."

During a contract dispute presided over by the Treasurer (the diminutive Blueboy O'Connor), one of the soldiers fires his gun at Brutus three times. "Don't you know I's got a charm?" he roars at the troops, who all drop to their knees. "It takes a *silver bullet* to kill Brutus Jones!" He grabs the General and shoves him aside. "Take this bush nigger and throw him out of here!" he orders. "*I'm* boss here now!"

Brutus reveals to Smithers how he loaded the inebriated guard's revolver with blanks, and then offers the white man the contract for renovating what stinks like "a chain gang dump" into a real palace. The camera tracks closer as Brutus again admires himself in a full-length looking glass. "I wants mirrors. Plenty of 'em!" he announces. Moving back to the mirror, he considers the titles "President" and "King," but neither is satisfactory. He insists that Smithers light his cigarette (an element nearly cut by the censor) and, as he takes a puff, a tight close-up captures his declaration, "Smithers, you has just had an audience with the *Emperor Jones!*"

The narrative skips ahead to the second year of Jones' reign, when a proclamation orders that the tax on home-made rum and coffee will be doubled to "pay off the National Debt to Mr. Smithers Ltd." A huge crown sits atop an ornate mirror as three footmen dress

Brutus in an 18th-century French military uniform and shine his high riding boots. Smithers arrives to warn him of riots against the tax increase, but he counters, "My army's got them niggers already," and then reveals he has only "six months to go" in his three-year plan to bank his loot "in a foreign land where there ain't no chain gangs and no Jim Crow." Raising his champagne glass, he vows, "In six months, I walks out on this nigger circus."

Framed in a low-angle shot, with the mirror's crown appearing just above his head, he points at Smithers and explains:

> Looka here, white man. There's little stealin' like you does, and there's big stealin' like I does. For little stealin', they get you in jail sooner or later; but for big stealin', they makes you Emperor and puts you in the Hall of Fame when you croaks.

Brutus narcissistically admires himself in a series of mirrors as he struts into the palace to summon his court. In another low-angle shot, as he is about to sit upon his throne, an elaborate symbol featuring an eagle perched on a pair of cannons (bearing a resemblance to the contemporary Nazi icon) hovers over him. When the chained prisoners are brought in, he orders, "Take them niggers into the courtyard and give 'em fifty lashes apiece — and lock 'em up!" When he commands that the village be burned "off the face of the earth!" his repression finally proves too much for his subjects, whose desertion is announced by Smithers, who attempts a little blackmail for good measure: "From what I've been told, it ain't safe for a black to kill a white man in the States!"

"Maybe I does kill one white man back there," Brutus admits. "Maybe I does. And maybe I kills another one right here 'fore long, if he don't look out!" After he loosens his grip on Smithers' throat, the white man reveals that the guards and servants also have abandoned him. Forsaking the remaining six months of his reign, Brutus resigns as emperor and then plans to make his escape through the woods after sundown:

> I has five lead bullets in this gun good enough for common bush niggers, and after that, I's got this *silver* bullet left, to cheat 'em out of gettin' me. I tells 'em, when the time comes, I kills *myself* with it. That's 'cause I'm the only man in the world big enough to get *me*.

A drum begins to beat in the distance. Brutus maintains his verbal bravado, words belied by the fear playing on his face. Smithers attempts to weaken him further with talk of ghosts and heathen spells, but the former Emperor Jones insists his standing in the Baptist Church will protect him in the depths of the forest.

Incorporating a technique from silent and early sound films, the climactic scene is tinted blue as Brutus attempts to flee under cover of the night. Paul begins a soliloquy as the relentless drum of the "bush niggers" steadily increases Brutus' paranoia. The beat increases in volume, and he draws his pistol, firing one of the lead bullets at an imaginary foe. The moon rises, and he stops to rest and sing a few lines, but his paranoia again wins out. A ghostly image of the dead Jeff shaking a pair of dice is superimposed at screen left as Brutus observes, "That sounds like some nigger was shootin' crap." Reaching for the gun, he fires a second lead shot as the specter disappears.

The increasing volume of the drum tells Brutus that his enemies are drawing closer, and he picks up the pace, running through the brush and nearly collapsing from the heat. Finally he throws off his coat to reveal a more exhausted, sweaty and filthy version of his chain-gang self. Unlike the Brutus of the rock pile, this fallen emperor cannot escape, and instead grovels in the dust, pleading with the Lord to spare him from seeing further spirits.

An image of the chain gang is superimposed at screen right as Brutus is overwhelmed by another hallucination. The sadistic white guard also appears, brandishing a whip. "Yes,

sir. Yes, sir, I's comin'," Brutus mutters, grabbing an imaginary sledgehammer and swinging it as the ghostly guard flails his whip in defense. The "white devil" turns his back on Brutus, who loses his hammer after one final flog, and then blasts a third lead bullet from his gun.

An abrupt cut leads to Brutus stumbling through the jungle, stammering about having only the silver bullet left. (A further hallucination, dealing with slavery and culminating with Brutus being placed on the auction block, was cut by the Hays Office, fearing the sequence would prove unacceptable to white audiences. The mirage ended with Brutus blasting the remaining two lead bullets at the auctioneer and the planter intending to buy him. Had the sequence remained in the film, Brutus' egocentric and criminal behavior may have seemed more justified.)

The boots are now missing from his feet as he staggers through a river, left with only the tatters of his trousers. Brutus is now truly terrified, and he confesses his sins to the Almighty. An image of the preacher at Hezekiah Baptist Church is superimposed at screen left as Brutus pleads, "Forgive me, Lord!" and then joins an invisible chorus in singing "Didn't My Lord Deliver Daniel?" The unreal altar fades away and Brutus shouts, "You done saved this sinner, Lord!"

But a fantastical, satanic witch doctor leaps out from the bush to torment the repentant Brutus, who frantically lurches around in the dust, crying out for mercy. "Lord, hear my prayer!" he roars, firing the silver bullet into the mouth of an imaginary crocodile. The image of a hysterical Brutus flailing on the ground dissolves to Smithers, castigating his band of blacks for relying on a "silly drum" and "stinkin' spells." But Brutus' jungle rampage leads him directly into their camp, where he is shot down by Smithers' right-hand man, who has forged a silver bullet by "cooking money."

There is no redemption for the Emperor Jones. Standing over Brutus, the white trader pokes at his lifeless body with the riding crop, pronouncing him "dead as a herring. Where's all your 'igh and mighty airs now, Your Bloomin' Majesty?" In the end, Brutus Jones, a modern African American who adopts repressive colonial ways upon encountering a primitive black culture, is destroyed.

Released in September 1933, *The Emperor Jones* did moderately well at the box office. Most critics lauded Paul but decried the many stereotypes, including the use of the word "nigger," which the black press, of course, denounced. (Censors actually removed the word from prints intended for black audiences.) Nonetheless, Paul's work was considered a step forward for African American performers on the screen.

Paul's image already had received an added boost with the public when his portrait as Jones, shot by ace photographer Edward Steichen, was featured in the August 1933 issue of *Vanity Fair*. Paul Robeson, Jr., noted that his father's "expression of defiance mixed with fear" identified him "with a tragically flawed but heroic character [that] marked the transition in American film from the dehumanized black 'Sambo' caricature to a fully human, though still partly stereotypical, black male image."[6]

Hilton Als wrote:

> As we can see (and hear) in ... *The Emperor Jones*, Robeson stands somewhere to the left of O'Neill's white idea of black speech, not to mention black male life. In a number of scenes, the actor with the legendary basso profundo voice, large chest, and liquid eyes struggles with O'Neill's fantastical, overwrought language as though it were an ill-fitting mask.[7]

Paul's predecessor in the stage role, Charles Gilpin, had refused to use the word "nigger." Paul Robeson, Jr., explained:

There's "nigger" in *Emperor Jones* all over the place. He didn't do anything about that. There's "nigger" in *Show Boat*, [and] he did. How come? What's the difference? Well, all the difference in the world. He recognized the song "Ol' Man River" as a signature song that would be around on records, on film ... for centuries, probably.[8]

Actress Ruby Dee said:

I think Robeson had a dream for universal humanity — and that's why when I see him in some of these films ... how I think it must have hurt him to pretend to be less than he was. To see Robeson try to be this caricature in [*The Emperor Jones*]. I've never liked the film. I can't stand to see this *greatness* deliberately compromise itself.[9]

Ossie Davis commented:

That movie, even with all the degrading language and degrading behavior, and what you have to expose about capitalist power — even so, when that camera is close on his face, man, it is *power*.[10]

Upon his return to London after the *Emperor Jones* shoot, Paul, again giving Essie credit for her coaching (especially her advice not to overplay the negative aspects of Brutus), told an interviewer, "The film has taught me a lot about myself — revealing many little faults. My wife did the rest; she found the remedies, and her advice has been invaluable."[11]

Dudley Murphy's brisk direction benefits immeasurably from Ernest Haller's cinematography (particularly his use of low- and high-angle shots), Herman Rosse's gritty art direction (in both the modern and primitive scenes), and Grant Whytock's editing (including Haller's dramatic close-ups of Paul at strategic points). The acting is uniformly good, with the possible exception of Fredi Washington, who is a bit mannered in her performance. Dudley Digges, a fine character actor who enjoyed a long career in England and Hollywood, is spot-on as the pompous, racist, colonial holdover.

Paul carefully builds his characterization throughout the film, ranging from an ambitious working-class man with somewhat selfish intentions, to a completely self-interested dictator, to a broken man haunted by his past behavior. His most difficult challenge was attempting to affect, with some believability, Brutus Jones' sudden psychic shift from courageous conman to superstitious madman. His charismatic smile, the most distinguishing characteristic of his physical performance style, conveys a full range of emotional states, from optimistic anticipation to personal triumph, from insidious intent to borderline insanity.

Considering that there was no Civil Rights Movement at the time, Paul's achievement, though compromised by offensive language and the primitivism inherent in the depictions of the black characters, was no small one, gaining him the position of top black actor in the United States. His Brutus Jones was the first lead role portrayed by an African American in a mainstream motion picture, an accomplishment that would not be matched by another black actor in the United States for a quarter-century.

Chapter 5

Imperial Palaver
Sanders of the River (1935)

Paul Robeson is the greatest American singer.
— Sergei Mikhailovich Eisenstein[1]

Credits: Director: Zoltan Korda; Producer: Alexander Korda; Screenplay: Lajos Biro, Jeffrey Dell; Additional Dialogue: Arthur Wimperis; Based on the stories by Edgar Wallace; Cinematographers: Osmond Borrodaile, Louis Page, Georges Perinal; Editor: Charles Crichton; Supervising Editor: William Hornbeck; Musical Score: Mischa Spoliansky; Musical Director: Muir Mathieson; Production Manager: G. E. T. Grossmith; Assistant Director: Stanley Irving; Sound: D. Field, L. Fisher, J. Paddon; Recording Director: A. W. Watkins; Visual Effects: W. Percy Day; Camera Operator: Bernard Brown; Technical Advisers: Cecil Grosse, C. O. ("Squash") Lemon, Major C. Wallace; a London Film Production; Released by United Artists (U.K.) on April 8, 1935, and (U.S.) on June 26, 1935; Running Time: 87 minutes.

Cast: Paul Robeson (Bosambo), Leslie Banks (Commissioner R. G. Sanders), Nina Mae McKinney (Lolongo), Martin Walker (J. Ferguson), Robert Cochrane (Lieutenant Tibbets), Richard Grey (Captain Hamilton), Tony Wane (King Mofolaba), Marques De Portago (Farini), Eric Maturin (Smith), Allan Jeayes (Father O'Leary), Charles Carson (Sir John), Luao (Chief of the Wagenia [Congo] Tribe), Kilongalonga (Chief of the Wagenia [Congo] Tribe), Oboja (Chief of the Acholi Tribe), Bertrand Fraser (Makara), Beresford Gale (Topolaka), Jomo Kenyatta (Tribal Chief), Orlando Martins (K'Lova), Anthony Papafio (Bosambo's Son), James Solomon (Kaluba), John Thomas (Obiboo), Deara Williams (Daughter of Bosambo and Lilongo), Robert Adams, Joe Cozier (bits), Members of the Wagenia [Congo], Acholi, Sesi, Tefik, Juruba, Mendi and Kroo tribes (extras).

In 1933, Paul and Essie had both enrolled at London University to study African languages (including Swahili and Tivi) and Chinese. Paul increasingly was becoming more interested in his own identity as an African and carrying this image to his fellow blacks in the Western world in the hope of dispelling the "regrettable and abysmal ignorance of the value of its own heritage in the Negro race itself."[2] Following the release of *The Emperor Jones* in the United States, he and Essie returned to England, seeking a new film project that would fit his new African paradigm.

Paul also continued his collaborations with Ray Noble at Abbey Road, recording a series of spirituals and popular songs, including Harry S. Pepper's "Green Pastures" (which later would provide a motif in *Jericho*), a gently swinging version of Hoagy Carmichael and Johnny Mercer's "Lazybones," new versions of "Ol' Man River" and "Water Boy," and an arrangement of W. C. Handy's superlative "St. Louis Blues."

In April 1934, Essie received a letter from George Gershwin, who was interested in casting Paul in *Porgy and Bess*, the opera he had co-written with his brother, Ira, and DuBose Heyward, author of the original novel *Porgy* and the stage version on which he had collab-

43

orated with his wife, Dorothy. Paul also received a similar offer to sing the part of Amonasro in the Chicago Opera's production of Giuseppe Verdi's *Aida*, but he declined both projects. He believed that, while he might be able to cross the color barrier in the operatic world, he knew that his singing was not up to the challenge of such arduous music and a genre that would limit his audience appeal. Paul enjoyed classical music intended to "please the ear,"[3] such as that of Bach, Mozart and Purcell; and when it came to the sounds of jazz and Tin Pan Alley, he preferred real African rhythms, like those incorporated by "Duke Ellington — with his orchestra, which is really a continuation of the African drum."[4]

Following discussions with producer Alexander Korda, Paul agreed to star in London Films' new African epic *Sanders of the River* (a project originally titled "Wings of the Jungle," in which Alfred Hitchcock was involved only briefly). Korda assured Paul that *Sanders* would present a well-researched, intelligent and positive depiction of African culture based on Edgar Wallace's stories focusing on the tribal leader Chief Bosambo and the British Commissioner Sanders (Leslie Banks).

The prolific, versatile Richard Horatio Edgar Wallace (1875–1932) is well known for his work on the classic fantasy film *King Kong* (1933), for which he wrote the story (from an original concept by producer-director Merian C. Cooper) and a draft of the screenplay (in only five days), but unfortunately he died of pneumonia complicated by diabetes before a final shooting script could be completed. Cooper, who also was stricken with pneumonia, recalled, "I went to the hospital and lived. Edgar refused to go, and he died."[5] (Cooper later claimed that none of Wallace's work survived in the finished film.)

Stationed in South Africa, Wallace had served with the British Infantry and Royal Army Medical Corps before being transferred in 1898 to the Press Corps, working as a correspondent for the *Daily Mail* during the Boer War. Over the course of 17 years, he published his collections of Sanders stories, which originally were serialized, as 12 "African novels," beginning with *Sanders of the River* (1911) and ending with *Sanders Again* (1928). The Ochori chief merited one title all his own, *Bosambo of the River* (1914). Reflecting the tenor of his times, Wallace's stories (like those of his contemporaries) are pro-imperialist depictions of the British master and his (mostly willing) African subjects (living in a nameless colony).

Alexander Korda's brother, Zoltan, who was scheduled to direct Lajos Biro and Jeffrey Dell's screenplay, had compiled 60,000 feet of film (shot by Osmond Borrodaile and Louis Page) and numerous sound recordings during a lengthy trip through central Africa. This footage would then be incorporated with narrative material shot by cinematographer Georges Perinal at Sound City in Shepperton during the summer of 1934. (Some additional exteriors used in the river sequences eventually would be shot on the Thames near Shepperton, as well.)

For Paul, the most important aspect of the production was meeting the 400 blacks, most of them Africans hired from throughout the British Isles (including London's East End, Liverpool and Cardiff), from whom he learned more about his ancestral culture. By the time the shoot ended, he was convinced that he had descended from the Igbo tribe of Nigeria.

Paul particularly enjoyed spending time with Jomo Kenyatta, an anti-colonial activist, who had urged him to play Bosambo. Born Kamau wa Ngengi in 1894 in British East Africa (which became Kenya on December 12, 1963), Kenyatta, a member of the Kikuyu tribe, later became the leader of the nation's independence movement (following a trumped-up seven-year prison sentence for taking part in the Mau Mau rebellion of 1952) and its first prime minister (1963-64) and president (1964–1978). During the shoot, Paul was waylaid

by two British Intelligence agents who "suggested" that he be careful about any "subversive" discussions he might have at the studio. The "technical advisors" on the production were three English army officers, C. O. ("Squash") Lemon, Cecil Grosse and Major C. Wallace.

Paul Robeson, Jr., recalled:

> Several times he took me along to the film set of *Sanders of the River*. There I noticed that he carried his near-regal dominance of his surroundings with a natural ease, making himself accessible to everyone. He was a popular superstar who belonged to the outside world, yet behaved like a regular person.[6]

Traditional tribal music precedes the fade-in on the opening credits of *Sanders of the River*, which bill both Paul and Leslie Banks above the title. The chanting and drumming segue into Paul's voice as the names of screenwriters Lajos Biro and Jeffrey Dell appear on the screen. Credited in the cast listing are members of the Wagenia (Congo), Acholi, Sesi, Tefik, Juruba, Mendi and Kroo tribes. A written prologue unabashedly praises the current colonial administration. Added during post-production, this paternalistic material wasn't exactly what Paul was expecting:

> LONDON FILM PRODUCTIONS wish to record their appreciation of the valuable assistance extended to them in Africa by His Excellency Sir B. Bourdillon K.C.M.G., K.B.E., and all Government Officials during the making of this picture.
>
> Sailors, soldiers and merchant-adventurers were the pioneers who laid the foundation of the British Empire. To-day their work is carried on by the Civil Servants— Keepers of the King's Peace.
>
> AFRICA ... Tens of millions of natives under British rule, each tribe with its own chieftain, governed and protected by a handful of white men whose everyday work is an unsung saga of courage and efficiency.
>
> One of them was Commissioner Sanders.

Part of this prologue was directly inspired by the title of Wallace's "African novel" *The Keepers of the King's Peace* (1917).

A spinning globe halts when Africa comes into view, and a series of dissolves and zooms focuses on Nigeria, then N'gombi, indicated on a colonial map as the "District of Commissioner Sanders." Emerging from his office, Sanders drinks gin and discusses "swamps, jungles and mosquitoes" with his staff. Captain Hamilton (Richard Grey) reveals that he "picked up a queer bird about a mile up the river [who] had a high and important matter to report to ... the Lord Sandi." Sanders is already familiar with the tall black man who enters the office, dressed only in a leopard-skin loincloth, sandals and some jewelry. (This controversial element has been viewed by New York University Africana professor Deborah Willis as "the quintessentially racist image of the underdressed African."[7] However, a colleague, born and raised in Africa and familiar with the region, referred to the costume as "accurate attire for a man of his station."[8])

The black man attempts to use an alias, but Sanders immediately retrieves a file containing a photograph of his guest, captioned, "BOSAMBO: Liberian negro [*sic*], convicted for habitual petty larceny — Escaped from St. Thome prison." Without Sanders' permission, he has made himself chieftain of the Ochori tribe, whose members have been taught to obey the colonial law. "Lord Sandi," he announces, "I lie to anybody if I think it is good for me, but I will never lie to you."

"That will be very wise, Bosambo," Sanders replies with a calm and steady voice as the chieftain tells of the "old king," Mofolaba's, warriors, who are headed toward French-occupied territory. He then refers to himself as the one man in two million along the river who

Sanders of the River (1935). This half-sheet poster produced for the U.S. release depicts some of the stereotypes substituted for what Robeson hoped would be a "well-researched and positive depiction" of African characters in London Films' epic glorification of British colonialism.

will "not run away." Discussing the wise avoidance of war and the prospect of being sent back to prison, Bosambo opines, "Everything is with God." Sanders inquires if he is a "Mohammedan," but he replies, "Oh, no Lord Sandi, I'm a Christian," then rattles off the names of the New Testament authors and "that other John who lost his head over a certain dancing girl."

Sanders offers Bosambo a six-month trial period if he will faithfully serve the British king. He already has been wearing the "chain and medal of chieftainship" (also without permission), but now receives it officially from the commissioner, who orders him to report via carrier pigeon "when the old king's body has come back."

The peaceful people of the French area (depicted with location footage gathered by Zoltan Korda, and including exhilarating scenes of dancing and chanting, bare-breasted young females) are attacked by the spear-wielding, ostrich-feathered warriors of King Mofo-laba, who are on a "slave raid." (Unconvincingly, the "victims" are never shown on-screen in the same shots with the attackers.) Sanders sends a message via pigeon to Bosambo, whose war drums and rousing singing call his enthusiastic troops to battle. More location footage (showing females marching in a circle inside a ring of male warriors) is incorporated, inter-cut with shots of Paul, some of which include him performing in front of a process screen.

Bosambo, now also wearing a leopard-skin headband and armed with a spear and shield, leads his men through the jungle, where he comes face to face with Mofolaba's captain. "I stop you in the name of Lord Sandi," he warns his foe, "who is not pleased when slaves are taken." Bosambo orders the captain to surrender, but he dies as the spears begin to fly (and a hasty dissolve ensures that the battle, in another feeble editing move, "occurs" off-screen).

Successful in the engagement, Bosambo reviews the women, including Lolongo (Nina Mae McKinney), whom he learns is "from the Coast." At this point, only 20 minutes into the film, Paul already has impressively demonstrated several aspects of his character's personality, varying his performance from placating Sanders, to standing tall among his warriors *and* his enemies, and now using warm and soothing tones with a female he admires.

Sanders navigates the river aboard the outdated paddle-steamer *Zaire*. His messenger returns from Mofolaba (Tony Wane) after delivering a summons for both combatants to "palaver" on the field. The two leaders sit down to discuss the question of "buying women" and the fact that the captain of Mofolaba, "the greatest king in these countries," ignored the order of Sanders, representative of "the greatest king on Earth." "If little kings and chiefs disobey his orders," warns Sanders, "I *plough them into the ground!*" Like Robeson, Leslie Banks gives a well-layered performance. Here, he ratchets up his portrayal, breaking from his measured, quiet tones to indicate that Sanders, the colonial commissioner, though he may treat the natives "fairly," does have his job to do, after all. (This scene is faithful to Wallace's literary Sanders, who is not overly oppressive but does resort to force on occasion.)

Mofolaba agrees to retreat "with his spears" to his own country and to accept the return of prisoners as payment for his slain captain. However, he mentions that nine of his war drums bear the skins of "little chiefs who offended him." Glaring eye to eye with Bosambo, he vows, "I know the skin that will be stretched on the tenth."

"If you touch one servant of the government," warns Sanders, "be it so little as a pigeon, then believe me, King Mofolaba, you won't be king any longer." As the king's men leave the field, the pragmatic Sanders tells Lieutenant Tibbets (Robert Cochrane) that circumventing war is essential to avoid an unnecessary burden on the British taxpayer. "Now we have these girls to worry about," he adds.

Sanders questions the giggling women, who wish not to return to their parents but to "marry the chief." "What, all ten of you?" he asks.

"Yes, Lord!" they reply in unison. While the women offer various reasons for their matrimonial wishes, the scene cuts to a medium close-up of the flattered Bosambo (with Paul combining a sheepish movement of his eyes with a subtle version of the trademark Robeson smile).

The chief's gratification is short-lived, however. Sanders warns the would-be brides that Bosambo already has five "old and fierce" wives who would force them to perform oppressive domestic chores. (Leslie Banks relishes the opportunity to inject a bit of slightly overplayed comic delivery into the scene.) Sanders learns that several of the women already have visited the chief's quarters, where the absent Lolongo now is waiting. She tells Sanders that Bosambo has no wives and that she will marry him if the other nine women return to their homes. The following dialogue exchange is particularly clever for a 1935 release, and arguably it would not have survived in a Hollywood film subjected to the puritanical Production Code Administration.

The chief vows, "Lolongo, if you marry me, no other wife will ever come into my house."

"Well, *I'll* take care of that," she advises. Glancing at Sanders, she adds, "I'm a *Mohammedan*."

"Well, *so am I!*" interjects Bosambo.

"*What?*" puzzles Sanders.

"They said you were a *Christian*," adds Lolongo.

"I'm a Christian for *Lord Sandi*," he explains, "but for you, I shall be of the *true faith*."

Bosambo and Lolongo's wedding celebration incorporates more on-location footage (featuring the topless lovelies, children and a furiously shimmying male dancer) and a caption claiming that the scene depicts "the traditional nuptial dance of the Ochori." (Paul was outfitted with a much more elegant loincloth, resembling goat fur, for this sequence.) The cross-cutting between the "documentary" footage and the shots of Robeson, McKinney and Banks filmed on a Shepperton soundstage is followed by the paternalistic caption:

> Five years of harvest, peace and plenty. Under Sanders' just rule the People of the River enjoyed their primitive paradise.

Images of men building thatched dwellings and women happily bearing their loads precede Bosambo's efforts to teach his young son (Anthony Papafio) "the mysteries of chieftainship," namely a song-and-dance initiation in spear-and-shield warfare that ends abruptly when Lolongo enters the room. She objects to the "Killing Dance," claiming that

Sanders of the River (1935). Bosambo, Chief of the Ochori (Robeson), with his wife, Lolongo (Nina Mae McKinney) [U.S.–release lobby card].

the British government's money would allow Bosambo to live elsewhere, out of danger. "I won't stay," she threatens.

Bosambo points out that their boy must be a chief's son to attend the new government school. Furthermore, King Mofolaba will one day be "eaten up" by the British, who could allow their son "to rule all these countries for them." (This scene reflects the title of another Wallace "African novel," *Sandi the Kingmaker* [1922].)

The government, however, temporarily replaces Sanders with a new commissioner, J. Ferguson (Martin Walker), who asks to meet all the current "kings and chiefs" before addressing Mofolaba. Prior to turning over power to Ferguson, Sanders makes the most blatantly paternalistic statement possible: "Now, I want you to obey him as if you were his *own children.*" Ordered to keep the peace, the chiefs appear to bow to their parental authority, with one of them groveling, "We all love one another now, because, if we did not, your Lordship would punish us very cruelly." No matter how benevolent Sanders may appear, this statement proves that the British (like any imperialist power) function as "peacekeepers" only through the omnipresent threat of violence. A subsequent dialogue exchange is rife with further hypocritical political folderol:

SANDERS: Goodbye, Bosambo. You'll be loved by Lord Ferguson just as you've been loved by me.
BOSAMBO: Lord Sandi, you've been Father and Mother to the Peoples of the River.
SANDERS: [laughs] In a year's time, I shall come back, and everything will be just the same as it was before.
BOSAMBO: Remember me, Lord Sandi.
SANDERS: I'll remember you [shakes his hand] always, Bosambo.

Soon after Sanders begins his leave (to marry the sister of Captain Hamilton in London), a pair of unscrupulous white smugglers (one British, one a Mediterranean type) travel down the river to establish an illegal gin still "to make the whole of Africa drunk." "It would give me considerable pleasure," admits Farini (Marques De Portago), the non–British villain, "to teach his black children a thing or two."

"His black children have become pretty civilized," counters Smith (Eric Maturin), the Englishman.

But Farini is the very essence of evil, tapping out a code to the natives, claiming, "Sandi is dead. There is no law anymore," a message hammered throughout the land by native drummers, whose rhythms affect giraffes, birds, crocodiles, elephants, hyenas and even hippopotami before all hell breaks loose. A brief montage of mayhem (replete with dancing warriors, dining buzzards and flaming villages) is followed by the ineffectual Ferguson meeting with Father O'Leary (Allan Jeaves), who arrives to report that his church has also been burned to the ground. This desecration of Christianity angers the interim commissioner, who calls the natives "wild beasts," but the padre points out that their behavior is the result of "two white men ... selling them gin and firearms."

The Africans are not savages, just inferior, infantile beings easily influenced by any member of the superior white race (regardless of intent). "You must be quick and strong now," O'Leary advises, "like a father with his misguided children — like Mr. Sanders would." Ferguson issues orders to his officers and, accompanied by 10 men, prepares to visit King Mofolaba.

On the coast at Government House, well-attired guests dance to "After You've Gone" as word of the troubles arrives from the priest. Sanders is summoned by his commanding officer, who inquires about the activities of Farini. "He's a gun-runner," Sanders explains.

"Ten years ago, I sent him down here in irons. Five years ago, he crossed over my territory, but he slipped over to the Portuguese."

O'Leary's letter requests, "Please send four battalions *or Sanders.*" Choosing his fiancée over King and Country, Sanders declines but is troubled by news of the unknown fates of his comrades.

King Mofolaba's men chant, beat drums, and taunt Ferguson, who is trussed to a pole, while the two smugglers argue in a nearby hut. Ferguson insists that the still-living Sandi will return, kill Mofolaba, and toss his body "to the fishes." The king draws his spear and murders the commissioner with repeated stabs to the chest.

Mofolaba's warriors whip themselves into a frenzy with the "fearsome Lion Dance," while Sanders pilots a biplane back to the district. (Wildlife footage again is inter-cut, making the flight sequence seem interminable.) Back on the paddle-steamer, Sanders asks Bosambo about Ferguson's death. The Ochori chief has passed word to the drummers that "Sandi is not dead. The law is back on the river."

Farini maintains that Sanders is dead, but the drums do not lie. Three of Mofolaba's men drag Farini away to his demise, while Smith tries to escape in a canoe, gunning down a few men as he goes. Using some of the rifles bought from the smugglers, the warriors blast away, but the archers send Smith into the drink with a few deadly arrows. Mofolaba tells his people he can make peace with the English but, to save their honor, still wants the blood of the Ochori chief, whom they will bait "like a leopard."

In a fanciful sequence that bears similarities to the abduction scene in *King Kong* (1933), Lolongo sings a (very European-sounding) lullaby to her son and infant daughter (Deara Williams), as the humming accompaniment of the tribe sends their spear-toting guard off to slumber land. A gang of Mofolaba's ostrich-plumed killers sneaks into the village, bludgeons the sleeping sentry, stabs another servant, and kidnaps Lolongo. (Prior to costarring in *Sanders,* Leslie Banks gave a virtuoso performance as the mad Count Zaroff in *The Most Dangerous Game* [1932], a spectacular jungle thriller made by the *King Kong* producer-director team of Merian C. Cooper and Ernest B. Schoedsack.)

Several chiefs, including Kuluba (James Solomon), meet on the steamer with Sanders, who informs them that he has been greatly shamed before his king, whose law must again be obeyed. Banks gives a sincere, understated performance as Sandi pronounces, "Bosambo, you're a very brave man. You have made the Ochoris the bravest people in the River, and helped me punish the others. You have been my friend," then promises to return "in the spring ... with four battalions and punish King Mofolaba."

During a sequence in which Bosambo returns home with his warriors, Paul appears completely out of focus, framed in a medium shot as he sings in front of a process screen showing a boatload of men rowing as they chant along with him. This inferior image is inter-cut with impressive location footage of large canoes full of men, rushing down the river as Paul's voice booms on the soundtrack.

Bedridden with malaria, Sanders tosses in his delirium as Bosambo reaches the village to chastise Topolaka (Beresford Gale) for not bringing the Ochori women out to welcome the warriors. He orders that his children and a letter be delivered to the commissioner before he sets out alone to deal with King Mofolaba. During a tender farewell, Bosambo tells his son, "I'm sending you to Lord Sandi. He will teach you the things I was going to teach you, and he will make you a great, great chief." He briefly caresses the hair of his infant daughter, turns back to the boy, and adds, "Goodbye, my son" before heading out with spear and shield.

On board the *Zaire*, Sanders receives the children and news of the abduction, then orders the boat to steam up river to the Old King's Country, where no ship has gone before. Bosambo tramps through the jungle, as drummers along the path take up their mallets to announce his impending showdown with Mofolaba, who has used Lolongo to bait his trap. "Lord, I come in peace," announces Bosambo. "This woman is life to me, and I would rather die by her side than live with my people. But if you allow her to go, she will send you two-thousand gold pieces."

Mofolaba wants not gold but Bosambo's skin for his

Sanders of the River (1935). Before leaving to fight King Mofolaba, Bosambo (Robeson) tells his young son (Anthony Papafio), "I'm sending you to Lord Sandi. He will teach you the things I was going to teach you, and he will make you a great, great chief" [frame enlargement].

drum. Subdued by four men, the Ochori chief is lashed to a pole beside his wife. In the nick of time, the knife-wielding warrior intending to execute Lolongo is shot down by a rifleman aboard the *Zaire*, which has made amazing time in its journey upriver. Another fez-wearing black soldier opens fire with a machine gun, the prisoners are freed, and the rejuvenated Sanders reminds Mofolaba about his previous threat: "I said that if you touched

a servant of the government, be it so little as a pigeon, you wouldn't be king any longer."

Mofolaba's men claim that "Farini and Smith chopped Ferguson," but Sanders counters, "That's a lie!" Ordered not to move, Mofolaba raises his spear but is impaled by the deftly thrown lance of Bosambo. With the triumphant Ochori chief at his side, the commissioner proclaims, "I am Sandi Who Gives You the Law!" then demands the truth about Ferguson's murder and insists that he be obeyed without question. Bosambo calls all the chiefs together, and Sanders appoints a new king for the People of the

Sanders of the River (1935). Bosambo (Robeson) spurs on his warriors to go into battle against the forces of King Mofolaba [frame enlargement].

River, a "wise and cunning" leader who will make them "a rich and great nation ... keep the peace and treat all men equally." (Here is Wallace's *Sandi the Kingmaker* indeed.)

The Ochori rejoice as Sanders briefs the new king of the river before again "leaving for twelve moons." "Lord Sandi," says Bosambo, "I've learned the secret of government from Your Lordship. It is this: A king ought not to be feared but loved by his people."

"Go now, my friend," Sanders replies, shaking Bosambo's hand. "Keep the peace of my king."

"Lord, I promise," Bosambo agrees. As the pipe-smoking commissioner steams back down the river, the Ochori accompany the steamer in their canoes and their new king sings a song of high praise for Sandi the "strong" and "wise."

Following the *Sanders* shoot, Paul made arrangements to visit the Soviet Union, ostensibly to meet with Sergei Eisenstein, whom he had contacted through his friend, the English writer Marie Seton. Eisenstein planned to direct a film about Toussaint L'Ouverture, the guerrilla leader on the island of Hispaniola who had driven the British from Santo Domingo in 1798 and the French from Haiti in 1804, making that nation the first in the Western Hemisphere to end slavery.

Unfortunately Eisenstein had fallen from the graces of Joseph Stalin. Following the shooting of his revolutionary film *¡Que Viva Mexico!* (1932), he was tragically unable to complete the project, due to his disregard for a contract in which both the Mexican government and his American investors (including Upton Sinclair) had clearly specified a *short* film with *apolitical* content. After the Mexican Film Trust shut down production, Eisenstein was unable to return to the United States; and, without General Secretary Stalin's blessing, the director had little or no chance of receiving support from the Soviet film authorities.

Before the trip, Paul and Essie sent her mother and Paul Jr. back to the United States. Paul also began to make his first public statements about his political beliefs, especially his positive views of the U.S.S.R. He told one reporter, "There is absolutely no color prejudice there. One reason is they have so many colored races in the Soviet Union."[9] Paul Robeson, Jr., revealed:

> As a result of his African studies, his contacts with Africans in the anti-colonial movement, and his five-year association with British socialists, he had already raised his voice on behalf of the struggle to free Africa from colonialism. Now the trip to the Soviet Union, a country viewed as a reliable ally by the anti-colonial movement, was a striking symbolic gesture.[10]

On December 23, 1934, Paul and Essie, joined by Marie Seton, arrived at the Berlin train station on their journey to Moscow. As Essie went for their bags, leaving Paul and Marie on the platform, two groups of brown-shirted Nazi storm troopers formed a semicircle around them. Segregated from all the other passengers, Paul and Marie tensed up as he recognized the racial epithets being shouted at them. Paul told her that the brown-shirts thought she was German, advising her not to move or show any sign of fear, which, he assured her, was a prime way to incite a lynching. When Essie returned, all three boarded the Moscow train unmolested. Safe in his seat, Paul explained, "I never understood what fascism was before. I'll fight it wherever I find it from now on."[11]

At the station in Moscow, Eisenstein headed a group (including Essie's brother, John Goode) who had gathered to meet them. Eisenstein accompanied them to their hotel, where he and Paul had a lengthy discussion in Russian, during which the director explained that, although currently forbidden from making films, he was allowed to teach at the Film Uni-

versity. Two interviews for Paul had been scheduled: one with Tass, the Soviet news agency, and another (in English) with a correspondent from the *Chicago Defender*. Due to the recent murder of Leningrad Party leader Sergei Kirov (rumored to have been ordered by Stalin), the political climate was becoming increasingly more hard line, and Eisenstein counseled Paul to focus on cultural topics and avoid any political or religious statements. He followed this advice during the Tass interview but made certain to mention his intention to collaborate with Eisenstein on the L'Ouverture film.

Witnessing racial tolerance firsthand (bolstered by discussions with Essie's brothers, John and Frank, who both were living in Moscow), Paul told Eisenstein, "Here, for the first time in my life, I walk in full human dignity. You cannot imagine what that means to me as a Negro."[12]

Paul delivered a brief speech in Russian to a group of Soviet cinematographers at the House of Cinema, where he also performed the aria "Prayer and Death" from Modest Mussorgsky's opera *Boris Godunov*, "Ol' Man River" and other songs. Eisenstein and other Soviet directors attended several films with the couple, who appreciated their explanations of the political and cultural content. During a dinner party on Christmas Eve, Paul discussed the possibility of a war between the U.S.S.R. and Nazi Germany with Marshal Mikhail Nikolaevich Tukhachevsky, who had been chief of the Red Army from 1925 to 1928 (and would later be executed during Stalin's Great Purge of 1937).

Though he was encouraged to become more outwardly political by William Paterson, a representative of the U.S. Communists, Paul remained noncommittal but did express his support of the Party's campaign to help the Scottsboro Boys. Following a visit to Leningrad in January 1935, during which they heard African American contralto Marian Anderson perform at Philharmonic Hall, Paul and Essie returned to London via Copenhagen and Stockholm, where reporters mentioned his roles in *Show Boat*, *The Emperor Jones* and the forthcoming *Sanders of the River*.

Following Paul's concert at the Royal Albert Hall and another tour of the English provinces, during which he performed spirituals as well as folk songs from Russia, Scotland and Finland, *Sanders of the River* premiered at London's Leicester Square Theatre on April 2, 1935. When Paul and Essie arrived at the venue, a large crowd cheered and gathered around their car. Paul Robeson, Jr., later recalled, "Whenever my father attended a public event, he was mobbed. He was like the rock star of his time."[13]

Among the audience were British aristocrats, financiers, captains of industry, cinema stars, and U.S. Ambassador Robert Worth Bingham and his wife, Eleanor. From the outset, Paul realized that the script was rife with stereotypes and positive depictions of colonialism, but again he saw the value in playing an African character as a "good guy."[14] In the end, embarrassed, he skulked out of the premiere early, then attempted to disown the film, which had become an unabashed celebration of the British in Africa. Essie followed but, wanting Paul to wait for the African reaction, convinced him to return to the theater, where he then appeared on stage with Leslie Banks. Paul Jr. elaborated:

> Mom ... realized, "Uh oh, he's out of there." Sure enough, he went back to the apartment ... so she went back and said, "You can't do this. You gotta go back." So they had this big argument, and she said, "Look, Paul, Jomo Kenyatta is sitting up there, and he's got a bit part in there, and all the Africans are staying there. You can't be more African than the Africans. Get over it.[15]

An enormous box-office hit in England, *Sanders of the River* went on to earn the gold medal for Best British Film of 1935 from the Institute of Amateur Cinematographers. It

Sanders of the River (1935). The colonial presence of "Lord Sandi" (Leslie Banks) looms large over Bosambo (Robeson) and Lolongo (Nina Mae McKinney) on this one-sheet poster produced for the film's Australian release.

was also a huge success in Austria, Italy (where Mischa Spoliansky won the Best Music Award at the Venice Film Festival), India (where it was held over in Bombay for a second week), and New York, where the critics, however, faulted the film for its "romantic portrait of the benevolent white father."[16] Paul later informed African American journalist Ted Poston that *Sanders* "was not originally planned as an empire-building epic ... the imperialist angle was placed in the plot during the last five days of shooting."[17]

The success of the film led to another offer from Alexander Korda, who wanted to cast Paul as King Christophe of Haiti in a new epic film. Referring to this offer, Paul also asked Ted Poston, "Could you imagine a Black King being treated seriously in Hollywood?"[18]

During two Abbey Road sessions (April 15 and May 14, 1935), Paul continued his association with *Sanders* by recording four of Spoliansky's songs with an orchestra conducted by Muir Matheson. Spoliansky, a Russian musical prodigy who, in 1933, had immigrated to England to begin a second career as a film composer, would again write material for Paul during the making of *King Solomon's Mines* in 1937.

Sanders of the River provides a prime example of the 1930s film plot (especially prevalent in Hollywood gangster and prison pictures) depicting "bad" *individuals* who create corruption and conflict within a *system* that is essentially "good." The establishment is not responsible for the problems dogging certain factions of folks (often minority groups such as the unemployed, World War I veterans, or convicts); it's those self-interested bad apples who try to spoil the bunch. And here the establishment is one of the biggest in history: the British Empire.

In spite of the film's obvious stereotypes and exotic padding, *Sanders of the River* includes some good writing, fine acting, and admirable production elements. Though toeing the colonial line in noble-savage mode, Paul's characterization of the educated and wily Bosambo contains positive, non-stereotypical elements not present in the typical Uncle Tom roles being offered on the other side of the Atlantic in 1935. His obvious care in crafting a multi-layered performance is proof that he took the role seriously. The fact that he could be simultaneously powerful and understated flies in the faces of those who have questioned his greatness as a film actor. Seven decades later, James Earl Jones pointed out the political complexities of Paul's portrayal:

> When he walked on the screen, the movie had to make way for another kind of creature—not the one who smoked a pipe and talked with a British accent, but this thing that *sang*, sometimes. It certainly *moved*. He was big. It was *strong*, but it does more than carry water and cut wood.
>
> What does it do? They didn't know what it did. They didn't know what the Negro creature did. They were afraid to find out—still are—Hollywood is still afraid to find out.
>
> I suspect they probably shot a lot of stuff that they cut, because they felt, "Oh, that won't work for our public, for our audience, because we're still a colonial power. How do we keep control of these darkies if we admit that Paul Robeson is a human being?[19]

Regardless of the problems with *Sanders of the River*, Paul later wrote of his British experiences:

> It was in Britain—among the English, Scottish, Welsh and Irish people of that land—that I learned that the essential character of a nation is determined not by the upper classes, but by the common people, and that the common people of all nations are truly brothers in the great family of mankind. If in Britain there were those who lived by plundering the colonial peoples, there were also the many millions who earned their bread by honest toil. And even as I grew to feel more Negro in spirit, or African as I put it then, I also came to feel a sense of oneness with the white working people whom I came to know and love.[20]

Whale on the Mississippi
Show Boat (1936)

[T]he spine-chilling effect of that one song I shall never forget.
— James Whale, on "Ol' Man River"[1]

Credits: Director: James Whale; Producer: Carl Laemmle, Jr.; Screenplay: Oscar Hammerstein II (based on his play); Based on the novel by Edna Ferber; Songs: Jerome Kern, Oscar Hammerstein II; Director of Photography: John J. Mescall; Editors: Bernard Burton, Ted Kent; Art Director: Charles D. Hall; Costume Designer: Doris Zinkeisen; Assistant Director: Joseph A. McDonough; Sound Supervisor: Gilbert Kurland; Special Effects: John P. Fulton; Assistant Cameraman: James V. King; Costumes: Vera West; Original Music: Robert Russell Bennett; Musical Director: Victor Baravalle; Vocal and Choral Arranger: Will Vodery; Technical Director: Leighton Brill; Choreographer: LeRoy Prinz; Title Designer: John W. Harkrider; Released by Universal Pictures (U.S.) on May 14, 1936; Running Time: 113 minutes.

Cast: Irene Dunne (Magnolia Hawks), Allan Jones (Gaylord Ravenal), Charles Winninger (Cap'n Andy Hawks), Paul Robeson (Joe), Helen Morgan (Julie LaVerne), Helen Westley (Parthenia "Parthy" Hawks), Queenie Smith (Ellie May Chipley), Sammy White (Frank Schultz), Donald Cook (Steve Baker), Hattie McDaniel (Queenie), Francis X. Mahoney (Rubber Face Smith), Marilyn Knowlden (Kim as a Child), Sunnie O'Dea (Kim at 16), Arthur Hohl (Pete), Charles Middleton (Sheriff Ike Vallon), J. Farrell MacDonald (Windy McClain), Charles C. Wilson (Jim Green, Trocadero Manager), Clarence Muse (Sam, Doorman at Trocadero), Maude Allen (Fat Woman), Eddie "Rochester" Anderson (Young Black Man), Harry Barris (Jake, Piano Player at Trocadero), Patricia Barry (Kim as a Baby), May Beatty (Mrs. O'Brien), Brooks Benedict (Race Fan), Barbara Bletcher (Fat Girl), Donald Briggs (Press Agent), Betty Brown (First Girl), Daisy Bufford (Maid in Chicago), Eddie Chandler (Gambler), E. E. Clive (London Producer), Edmund Cobb (Gambler), Maxine Cook (Thin Girl), Grace Cunard (Mother), J. Gunnis Davis (Doctor at Kim's Birth), Elspeth Dudgeon (Mother Superior), Helen Jerome Eddy (Reporter), Kathleen Ellis (Girl #2), Al Ferguson (Gambler), Stanley Fields (Backwoodsman with Gun), Flora Finch (Woman [footage deleted]), Artye Folz (Fat Girl), June Glory (Girl #3), Dorothy Granger (New Year's Eve Cutie), George Hackathorne (YMCA Worker), Marilyn Harris (Little Girl), Helen Hayward (Mrs. Brecenbridge), Ernest Hilliard (Race Fan), Arthur Housman (Drunk), Jimmy Jackson (Young Man), Selmer Jackson (Hotel Clerk), Matthew Jones (Bartender at Trocadero), Jane Keckley (Mrs. Ewing), Jack Latham (Juvenile), Theodore Lorch (Simon Legree), Frank Mayo (Gambler), Monte Montague (Old Man), Jack Mulhall (Race Fan), Georgia O'Dell (School Teacher), Patti Patterson (Banjo Player), Edward Peil, Sr. (Gambler), Barbara Pepper (New Year's Eve Cutie), Lee Phelps (Gambler), LeRoy Prinz (Dance Director at Rehearsal), George Reed (Old Black Man), Tom Ricketts (Minister), Donna Mae Roberts (New Year's Eve Party Extra), Tiny Sandford (Zebe), Forrest Stanley (New York Theatre Manager), Mary Stewart (Singer/Dancer), Lois Verner (Small Girl), Max Wagner (Soldier), Harold Waldridge (Office Boy), Bobs Watson (Lost Child), Lloyd Whitlock (Gambler Speaking to Sheriff), Renee Whitney (New Year's Eve Cutie), Frank Whitson (Dealer), Mary Bovard (bit).

In London during the spring of 1935, Paul was involved with stage work, including the title role of an African chief in *Basalik* by Norma Munro, an American who wrote under the nom de plume of Peter Garland. In mid–April, the play had a trial run at the Arts Theater but closed after only three days, spurring Paul to re-team with André Van Gyseghem for *Stevedore*, an American play by Paul Peters and George Sklar about black laborers whose attempt to unionize against white management nearly results in a lynching. Opening at the Embassy Theatre on May 6, the production, featuring a supporting cast of amateur actors, fared a bit better than *Basalik*, playing for two weeks to mixed reviews.

While Paul was busy treading the boards, Essie conducted contract negotiations with Universal Pictures, who wanted him to repeat the role of Joe for James Whale's upcoming screen version of *Show Boat* adapted from the Ziegfeld stage production. She negotiated for the hefty salary of $40,000 (one which Paul was certain would be rejected), travel expenses, approval of the locations, and billing among the top four actors, but (not surprisingly) had difficulty when conveying his demand for personal approval of the script and filmed takes.

The budget for *Show Boat* was set at $1 million, a sizable sum for the financially strapped Universal, which had been founded by German immigrant and film pioneer Carl Laemmle in 1914. His son, 27-year-old producer Carl Laemmle, Jr., sent a cable to Universal's London office on September 20, 1935, agreeing to all of Essie's demands save one: Not even the great Garbo, under contract to MGM, had the extravagant luxury of approving her own takes. Paul also was guaranteed time for concerts, radio performances and recording sessions, and a completion date that would allow him to return to England for a concert tour to begin on January 19, 1936.

Universal already had made a film version of *Show Boat*, based on Edna Ferber's original novel, in 1929 (released in both silent and "part-talkie" versions), but planned to produce the first all-sound *Show Boat*, based on the Oscar Hammerstein II–Jerome Kern musical adaptation, and starring Irene Dunne (as Magnolia Hawks) and Russ Columbo (as Gaylord Ravenal), in 1933. Frank Borzage was chosen to direct a screenplay by Columbia's Jo Swerling, but he eventually was moved to another project, *Little Man, What Now?* (a film originally slated for James Whale), and the musical was postponed after Columbo accidentally killed himself in a bizarre shooting accident on September 2, 1934. Laemmle Jr. didn't give up easily, however, suggesting John Boles as Ravenal, W. C. Fields as Cap'n Andy, and Jules Bledsoe, the trailblazing African American baritone who had played Joe in the 1927 Broadway production.

Jerome Kern originally conceived the stage role not for Bledsoe but for Robeson. The 1929 film, adapted from the novel, was made as a standard silent but was also released in a second version with a sound prologue including five songs, some dialogue sequences, and a concluding song, Nathaniel Shilkret and Gene Austin's "The Lonesome Road." Incredibly, "Ol' Man River" is performed in the prologue by the Magnolia Hawks character (Laura LaPlante, whose vocals were dubbed by Eva Olivetti). Though played by Stepin Fetchit, the Joe character features the dubbed voice of Bledsoe on "The Lonesome Road."

Known for his mastery of the macabre, the thoroughly English James Whale had directed four Universal horror masterpieces (*Frankenstein* [1931], *The Old Dark House* [1932], *The Invisible Man* [1933] and *Bride of Frankenstein* [1935]) in as many years. To some in the film industry, he seemed an odd choice for the new *Show Boat*, but he viewed the musical as a definite step up from the horror genre. In an interview with the *New York Post*, he said, "Because I realized how much I don't know about the Mississippi, I surrounded myself with people who knew everything."[2] A virtuoso of montage filmmaking, Whale also

used mobile camera effortlessly to maintain pace and action in his productions, and *Show Boat* is a rare example of a musical that does not *stop* when the actors begin to sing. Known for his (often bizarre) theatricality, Whale sought to create a more naturalistic milieu for this film, keeping the events in the background moving along during the musical performances.

Oscar Hammerstein wrote the final version of the screenplay, updating some of the material for a 1935 audience, and he collaborated with Jerome Kern on three new songs that would survive in the finished film. Whale wanted to cast veterans from the stage productions of *Show Boat*, including Tess Gardella, a white actress known for her blackface characterization of "Aunt Jemina," as Joe's wife, Queenie. Gardella already had played the part in blackface opposite Paul in the 1932 run at the Casino Theater in New York.

Fortunately, the Queenie role eventually went to Hattie McDaniel, who had played a small (uncredited) role in Whale's Universal film *The Impatient Maiden* (1932), starring Mae Clarke and Lew Ayres. She also was intimately acquainted with Queenie, having portrayed her in a 1933 David Belasco–Homer Curran production of *Show Boat* first staged in San Francisco and then moved to Los Angeles following a buyout by Howard Lang, a Seattle businessman, and his partner, Hollywood agent Ivan Kahn. Before the company went on tour in January 1934, McDaniel, literally worn out by the role, decided to remain in Tinsel Town to seek further film work, appearing in no less than 38 major films (including John Ford's *Judge Priest* [1934], Tay Garnett's *China Seas* [1935] and George Stevens' *Alice Adams* [1935]) prior to the release of Whale's *Show Boat* two years later.

Ironically, McDaniel landed the part in the Universal film due to racism. The Production Code Administration absolutely forbade screen depictions of an intimate relationship between an African American and a Caucasian; so, opposite Paul, Queenie *had* to be played by a black actress. Referred to as a "nigger" in the script (a carry over from the stage version), the Queenie role again was affected by the PCA's Joseph Breen, who ultimately nixed the offensive term.

Paul had turned down a role in Warner Bros.' proposed sound remake of *The Green Pastures*, in which Al Jolson had been announced (in blackface) for the role of "De Lawd." In a move similar to Universal's decision on the Gardella-McDaniel matter, Warners replaced Jolson with the formidable Rex Ingram when the film was actually produced in 1936.

After finishing a summer concert tour of 13 dates, Paul and Essie steamed for the United States on September 25, 1935, giving him ample time for rehearsals and live performances with Lawrence Brown (including concerts in New York, Montreal, Chicago, Milwaukee, Portland and Seattle) prior to beginning the *Show Boat* shoot in Los Angeles on November 18. He also sang on the General Motors Concert Series radio program, which was broadcast nationwide.

While in New York, Paul responded to criticism from the political left regarding his film roles:

> To expect the Negro artist to reject every role with which he is not ideologically in agreement ... is to expect [him] under our present scheme of things to give up his work entirely, unless, of course, he is to confine himself solely to the Left theatre. Under such an arrangement, I might as well give up my singing, my concert work, everything. To say that I had no right to appear in *Sanders of the River* is to say I shouldn't have appeared in *Emperor Jones*— that I shouldn't accept the role in *Show Boat*.[3]

Before production began, James Whale, ever the perfectionist, gathered his cast and (according to Allan Jones, who landed the Ravenal role) said, "You have all played this

Show Boat (1936). Though the African American actors are not shown on much of the advertising material for this landmark musical, this title lobby card produced for the film's original U.S. release includes head shots of both Robeson and Hattie McDaniel (who is not billed).

before, and you all have your ideas of how it should be played. I want you to forget whatever ideas you have, because I will interpret, through you, my conception of each role."[4] This approach didn't endear him to many of the actors, including Irene Dunne, who made a perceptive comment about Whale's directorial style: "He was more interested in atmosphere and lighting and he knew so little about that life."[5]

Cast as Julie LaVerne, the mulatto actress who attempts to pass as white, Helen Morgan, who had played the role in the original 1927 stage production, the prologue of the 1929 Universal film (shorn of the interracial subplot to avoid problems with censors and Southern exhibitors), and the 1932 stage revival, was Whale's only choice, although he was fully aware of her serious problems with alcohol. The studio's front office agreed to hire her at $3,000 per week, but only on the condition that, should she appear unstable, she would be fired and made responsible for paying her replacement. Whale also cast other performers who had worked with Paul in the 1932 version, including Charles Winninger (Cap'n Andy), Sammy White (Frank Schultz) and Francis X. Mahoney (Rubber Face Smith).

Oscar Hammerstein continued to revise the screenplay through January 1936. Joseph Breen was still concerned with the inclusion of the word "nigger" in some of the songs (usage faithful to the stage production); by the time the final script was approved on February 11, "less offensive" terms such as "darkie" and "eight ball" had been substituted.

Paul's first assignment was to record the songs Joe would perform in the film. In a letter to a friend, Essie described an entire Sunday spent with the orchestra recording various arrangements of "Ol' Man River":

> Paul was in marvelous voice. When he had finished singing the song a second time, the members of the orchestra put down their instruments and applauded. They tell it never happened before. James Whale ... is really good; he knows just what he wants and how to get it. He seems to want, at least with Paul, just what we want. I think the film is going to be good.[6]

Paul's vocal artistry was equaled by his mastery of studio recording techniques. His pioneering use of the microphone (singing with less volume at a distance of only two feet, rather than following the accepted practice of standing 10 feet away and unleashing the full power of his voice) allowed him to perform each take with nearly identical timing and phrasing. While rehearsing his scenes with Whale, he mapped out each vocal performance in his head prior to laying down the track. The recording then became not just singing but *acting in song* when the soundtrack was paired with the filmed take (during which he sang mentally while flawlessly lip-synching for the camera). (This process of *acting* melodies and lyrics, through phrasing, rhythm and dynamics, was later refined into an unparalleled vocal art by Frank Sinatra on recordings, radio, stage and screen.)

Whale was an openly homosexual artist in an industry where other gay directors (George Cukor, Edmund Goulding) attempted to remain in the closet. He identified strongly with other minorities and social outsiders; he instantly became friendly with Hattie McDaniel and Paul, visualizing their characters with sensitivity remarkable in a mid-1930s Hollywood film. (This fact makes his initial choice of Tess Gardella for the Queenie role seem inexplicable.) Paul and Essie had rented a house in the West Adams district of central Los Angeles, where they threw a party for their friends. The guests included Whale and his pal Jack Latham, who played the small role of a juvenile and also doubled for Allan Jones in the film. Latham recalled a humorous incident during the filming of the "Ol' Man River" scene:

Show Boat (1936). Director James Whale (1889–1957). During the making of the film, Whale, who strongly identified with minorities, attended a party thrown by Paul and Essie at their rented house in the West Adams district of central Los Angeles.

Whale had it all worked out beforehand, and he knew exactly how he was going to photograph it ... he knew exactly where he wanted the camera — always. I remember explaining the number to a few background extras,

and they wouldn't say a thing to me. "This man is singing with his soul," I told them, "not his voice. You don't notice him, you don't hear him. Just keep on going. Any questions?" They all looked at me. "Do you folks understand?" I asked. Again nothing. Finally an assistant told me they spoke no English. "Oh," I said. "Sprechen sie Deutsche?" and they all smiled and nodded. It turned out they were all Laemmle relatives—every last one of them.[7]

Three weeks of incessant rain during February 1936 plagued the production. By this time, Paul already had returned to England to honor his concert dates. Whale concentrated on shooting interior scenes, including a war montage proposed by Hammerstein. The director protested this cheap method of depicting the passage of time but filmed the material nonetheless. Fourteen days over schedule and $400,000 over budget, he finally wrapped the film on March 11, 1936.

Serious financial problems forced the Laemmles to sell their studio, and new Universal boss Charles R. Rogers told Whale (who had landed $90,000 for his work) to have *Show Boat* ready for an April 1 premiere. The director had shot an enormous amount of footage, running a total of 55 hours, and there was no conceivable way he and his longtime editor, Ted Kent, could meet such a rushed deadline. Incredibly, they assembled a cut in only two weeks for a preview at the Alexander Theater in Glendale. After the screening, Whale wrote a letter to Paul:

> After the singing of "Ol' Man River," the house just went crazy. It seemed you were really there, and the spine-chilling effect of that one song I shall never forget. There are two completely satisfying experiences I have had in the theatre: First one was on the first night of *Journey's End* at the Savoy Theatre in London—and now comes this.[8]

Whale had told Universal about his further plans for Paul: "I hope to work with him again, and if I do, he will be billed as star"[9] (a lofty sentiment, but unattainable in the Hollywood of 1935). In fact, Paul had given Whale a copy of *Black Majesty*, C. L. R. James' new play about Toussaint L'Ouverture, in which he planned to appear after returning to London. After reading it, Whale, supported by Oscar Hammerstein and Jerome Kern, expressed interest in filming it; but after several months of discussions, the project was shelved.

In the meantime, *Show Boat*, running 130 minutes, had to be re-cut. Whale and Hammerstein collaborated closely, eliminating entire scenes and musical numbers, and tightening the rest of the material considerably. Hammerstein, using the song "You Are Love," also re-wrote the ending. Irene Dunne, Allan Jones and Sunnie O'Dea reported for retakes. On April 18, Whale completed the last of the new shots, and he and Ted Kent paired the running time down to 110 minutes for a second preview, held at the Pantages Theater in Hollywood, one week later. *Daily Variety* enthused, "Result looks as if Whale had been born on the Mississippi. His sensitive guidance of the players is mainly responsible for the excellence of the production."[10]

Show Boat opens with *movement* as an innovative credits sequence uses miniature cutouts to depict the title and names of the cast and crew during a parade along the Mississippi. Irene Dunne receives top billing on a banner also featuring the credit "A James Whale Production." A second banner lists the costars, including Paul, who is billed fourth, below Allan Jones and Charles Winninger. The opening musical theme incorporates a portion of the "Ol' Man River" melody, just before Oscar Hammerstein II is credited for the stage play, screenplay and lyrics. The remainder of the sequence, including Whale's director credit and the cast listing, features a version of the song performed by a choir accompanied by banjo and orchestra.

An establishing shot of the riverboat on the Mississippi, circa 1880, dissolves to some black dock workers moving cargo. The scene rapidly cuts to a close-up of (the uncredited) Eddie "Rochester" Anderson, who utters the film's first line: "There's the show boat!" Adults, children, and even horses and pigs frantically run to the water's edge, as Cap'n Andy (Charles Winninger) and Parthenia Hawks (Helen Westley) bicker aboard the *Cotton Palace* (renamed from the *Cotton Blossom* in the novel and play). The troupe comes ashore to put on its "Monster Parade" (a term appropriate for a James Whale film) through Natchez. The husband-and-wife acting team of Julie La Verne (Helen Morgan) and Steve Baker (Donald Cook) are also arguing as they ride on the foremost wagon. Steve has been made jealous by Pete (Arthur Hohl), whom the actor threatens to "break in two" if he continues to "look at" Julie.

At the dock, Pete and Queenie (Hattie McDaniel) are working aboard the boat. "Out of my way, *Eight Ball!*" Pete orders, trying to intimidate her, but she easily stands up to such racist insults. "Who wants to get in your way?" she asks. Pete notices that she is wearing the broche he had given to Julie, whom he accosts during the festivities, furious that she had passed it on to a "colored cook." Steve knocks him to the ground but is restrained by Frank Schultz (Sammy White).

Gaylord Ravenal (Allan Jones) strolls along the waterfront, singing "Where's the Mate for Me?" The very utterance of this musical question summons forth Magnolia Hawks (Irene Dunne) onto the deck of the *Cotton Palace*, and she strikes up a conversation with Ravenal, as he stands, top hat in hand, on the dusty street below. Supposing they "fall in love at first sight," the new friends sing a duet of "Make Believe" before Ravenal is called away by Sheriff Ike Vallon (Charles Middleton).

Whale consistently displayed moments of cinematic genius in his introductions of the most important characters in his films. The first such moment in his oeuvre occurs in *Frankenstein*, when the Monster (Boris Karloff) makes his initial appearance, shown *backing* through a doorway before his visage is revealed through a series of progressive close-ups (a strategy the director varied for the same actor in *The Old Dark House* one year later). In *Show Boat*, Whale shows at least as much artistic respect for Robeson. Thirteen minutes into the film, Joe is introduced in a long shot, his face partially obscured as he shuffles down the boardwalk, hefting a heavy sack of flour on his right shoulder. The cart carrying Ravenal and the sheriff passes by as the scene cuts to a full shot of Joe, who stands up straight and makes a slightly sneering expression at the lawman (whom the viewer soon will discover is a raging bigot), while the camera dollies in to a close-up of his face.

Whale's use of sound is also brilliant. Queenie can be heard shouting, "Joe!" while the camera still lingers on Paul's slightly scoffing visage. As he turns toward the voice, another "Joe!" accompanies a full shot of Queenie, scurrying down the boardwalk and thrusting her fists into the air. The scene cuts again, to another moving-camera shot of Queenie as she scolds Joe for being a "slow poke" and "always dragging them big feet!" This deft combination of camera movement and rapid editing is classic Whale, who then cuts to a medium close-up of Joe, still grasping the sack of flour as he slowly replies, "Take your time, Queenie."

"Take my time?" she asks. "I got to have that flour to bake the bread with."

"Day won't run away from you, Queenie," he points out, "and if it do, there's always tomorrow." (Within a matter of seconds, Joe's personality has already been solidified.) He wants to get back to his "whittlin'," but she advises him, "De'll be some taters to peel later, and when I yell for you, you come in, and *make it quick*!"

Magnolia speaks to Joe about "that young man in the sheriff's buggy," then flits off to find Miss Julie, as strains of "Ol' Man River" enter the soundtrack. "Ask Miss Julie what *she* thinks," says Joe. "Better ask the ol' river what *he* thinks. He knows all about them boys. He knows all about everything."

Joe begins to whittle a small board as the scene cuts to a medium shot of his right profile. The camera then pans 270 degrees around him and tracks in to a tight close-up of his face as he sings the first verse of "Ol' Man River." Whale holds the close-up until Paul finishes the second verse, then shifts to a montage beginning with a low-angle shot of Joe struggling on the dock with an enormous bail of cotton, then cuts to a full shot of him flexing his arms in a crucifixion pose as a riverboat steams along on the river behind him. Each line of the verse is visualized, incorporating expressionistic images of Joe staggering into the saloon and reprising his crucifixion pose while grasping the bars of a cell that recall scenes in Whale's horror films (which, in turn, were inspired by such German silent classics as *The Cabinet of Dr. Caligari* [1919] and *The Golem* [1920]). The montage dissolves back to the close-up of Paul's face as Joe sings the final verse, in which the singer, though "tired" of living but "scared" of dying, nonetheless acknowledges that the river "keeps rollin' along!"

Just as the song seems to be over, Whale repeats it, this time with an alteration of the lyrics and a shift to a long shot of workers toting baskets of goods. A long shot of Joe, with the parading workers vocalizing behind him, cuts closer to show them gathering around as they sing about toiling unto death. Joe and the chorus finish the powerful reprise of the song as a final montage shows the flowing Mississippi and shirtless blacks laboring with hoes in a field, rowing a barge and moving cotton bales down the dock (images that evoke a strong slavery overtone). This time, Whale cuts to an even tighter close-up of Paul's face as he concludes the song, adding his trademark smile for good measure as the scene fades out.

During a conversation with Magnolia in the galley, Julie begins to sing "Can't Help Lovin' That Man of Mine." Queenie sneaks up behind her. "How come you all know dat song?" she asks. "I didn't never hear anybody but colored folks sing dat song. Sounds funny for Miss Julie to know it."

"Julie sings it *all the time*," says Magnolia. At Queenie's behest, she gives voice to the entire number. Queenie moves in rhythm to the tune as she tends to her kitchen chores (naturally), and soon Joe arrives in the doorway. "Why, that's my *fave-o-rite* song," he says as he descends the stairs, grinning as he chews an apple. Queenie and Joe join in, and Magnolia begins shuckin' and jivin' as everyone (including the black folks dancing on the levee) contributes to the chorus. "Magnolia!" shouts Parthenia, who chases her up to the top deck of the river boat.

At the saloon, Pete gives a photo of Julie to Sheriff Vallon, promising to tell him the truth about her "marrying a white man," as the scene dissolves to a rehearsal aboard the boat. Ellie May (Queenie Smith) interrupts to whisper the news to Steve, who slices Julie's left hand with a pocket knife and sucks blood from the wound before the sheriff, accompanied by Frank, arrives. Joe watches from the balcony as Vallon tells Andy, "I understand that you have a miscegenation case on board. Case of a Negro woman married to a white man — a criminal offense in this state."

"You wouldn't call a man a white man that had Negro blood in him, would you?" asks Steve.

"No I wouldn't — not in Mississippi," Vallon replies. "*One drop* of Negro blood makes you a Negro in these parts."

"Well, I've got more than a drop of Negro blood in me, and that's a fact," Steve tells him. "Look at all these folks here. Every one of 'em can swear that I've got Negro blood in me this minute. That's how *white* I am."

Vallon insists that Steve "tell that to the judge," but old Mississippi salt Windy McClain (J. Farrell MacDonald) steps up to inform John Law, "Now, *I'm tellin' you* ... that that there white man's got Negro blood in him," an oath supported by Andy, though Parthenia remains silent.

Whale cuts to a close-up of Joe as the sheriff warns, "If these folks around here ever get wind that you've got Negroes acting with whites, they'll ride you out of town on something that won't set so easy as a boat," and then chases away all the black folks peering in the windows.

Parthenia orders Julie and Steve off the boat, scolding Magnolia as she tries to follow. "Well, Hawks," she says to Andy, "you see what your show boat's done to your daughter?"

"I think my show boat's made a *darn fine gal* out of my daughter!" he counters, suggesting that Magnolia fill the now-vacant leading-lady spot in the show.

"Over *my dead body!*" announces Parthy. "There never was an actress in my family, and there ain't going to be!"

Andy ignores her, wandering aloud who will become the new leading man. Queenie scampers in, reporting that a "powerful fine lookin' fellow" has requested a ride south on the river. Ravenal strides toward the stage, offering to pay for one night's lodging as far as Fort Adams. The Cap'n's counteroffer is to pay him $15 per week and "a chance to see the world" in return for his services as a "juvenile leading man."

Magnolia returns, pleading with Parthy to let the Bakers remain on board. She threatens to leave with them but changes her mind after seeing the new leading man. "Nola's" offer of a kiss is rejected by Julie, Andy slips Steve some money, and Joe is pained to say goodbye as they depart. After they walk down the gangplank, Whale uses a crane shot (executed by his longtime cinematographer John J. Mescall) to track up and across the faces of the black observers on the levee, and then lingers on Joe holding onto the upper-deck rail with both hands, before the scene cuts back inside to Andy and Ravenal discussing the script for the show.

In only three weeks, the new leading couple takes the locals by storm, arousing jealousy in the veteran comics, Frank and Elly May. From the window of his upper-deck cabin, Ravenal talks to one of Magnolia's nylon stockings prior to singing "I Have the Room Above Her" (a new song written for the film and replacing "I Might Fall Back on You," a Frank and Elly May duet from the original play). Magnolia answers by singing her own verse, and they both hum a duet to end the mutual serenade before running up to the top deck to meet for a secret kiss. During subsequent stage performances, they continue to court each other with whispered romantic remarks.

The era of minstrelsy is represented by what Cap'n Andy describes as "a little Southern song, solo with banjo, by Miss Magnolia Hawks." Irene Dunne, decked out in blackface, black wig, and black arm-length gloves, pretends to strum a banjo while singing "Gallivantin' Around" (another new number for the film, replacing the instrumental "Olio Dance" performed by Frank in the play). Recently, a half-black performer was forbidden to perform on the boat, but now nine whites impersonating blacks shuck it up for an appreciative audience. In his biography of Whale, Mark Gattis perceptively points out, "During Dunne's blackface routine, Whale cuts from the gaiety of the theatre to a shot of the blacks-only section of the auditorium, as if to emphasize the isolation of an entire race by their white masters."[11]

Magnolia and Ravenal again meet secretly on the top deck. "Gay" tells her that Andy has suggested they marry after the upcoming parade in Natchez, and the couple breaks into "You Are Love" (a song Jerome Kern unsuccessfully attempted to have cut from the film). During the parade, Joe and Queenie pilot the wagon carrying the bride and her father. Whale incorporates one of his trademark montages of rapidly edited facial close-ups as the black folks mug and dance up a storm in the street outside the church. In the nick of time, Parthy speeds up behind them in a brougham, shouting, "He's a murderer! Andy Hawks, are you just going to stand there and let your only child marry a murderer?"

"Oh, don't be so narrow-minded, Mrs. Hawks. I killed a man meself once," he admits. "Now, are you comin' with us, or ain't ya? They're going to be married." Everyone is pleased when Parthy passes out cold in the sheriff's arms. "Good, now we'll go on with the wedding," adds Andy. Joe and Queenie must remain in the doorway during the ceremony, but Whale gives them each a major close-up. Paul's voice, singing, accompanies a brief montage showing the newlyweds gazing out at the Mississippi as a storm stirs up the waters.

Thunder crashes and rain pours down, while Joe shells peas and Queenie scolds him for throwing them on the floor. Joe blames it on "the river," then defends his do-nothingness by explaining, "I could do a lot of things, if it was necessary."

"Then why don't you?" asks Queenie.

"It ain't necessary," he replies, then segues into "Ah Still Suits Me" (a duet written for the film specifically to give Paul and Hattie more screen time). McDaniel raps the majority of her part, while Paul (in what is perhaps his most "effortless" film acting) is perfectly at ease popping peas into his mouth in between the vocals. This charming sequence (an inspired musical performance that further develops the relationship between these characters) is a true high point of the film.

Some time has passed since the wedding, and Ravenal and Frank are away from the boat. Magnolia is ready to give birth, and Joe (moving faster than Queenie has ever seen) rushes into the storm to summon the doctor. In a hotel room, Frank is sleeping off a drunk while Gay wins a bankroll in a poker game. The rainstorm rivals those in Whale's *Frankenstein* films and *The Old Dark House* as Joe sings and rows the doc across the river. The medico, complaining about Joe's bogus weather report, calls him a "lying son of Satan."

He sings a reprise of his earlier performance for Queenie.

Andy names the baby girl "Kim": "K for Kentucky, I for Illinois, and M for Missouri, being how she was born on the river in sight of three states." Gay and Frank return, and Parthy informs the profligate husband about the exhausted wife's condition. (True to the conventions of a 1936 film made under the Production Code, Ravenal had known nothing of the pregnancy.) "A baby! A baby!" he exclaims, hurrying to her bedside.

After Magnolia recovers, Ravenal, making good on his promise to show her the exciting life of a Northern city, transports his family to Chicago. Several years pass, and Kim is enrolled in a convent school. "Give my regards to Joe and Queenie," writes Nola in a letter to her parents, just before running into Frank and Elly May in a cheap boarding house. A messenger arrives with a letter and $200 from Gay, who explains that he is leaving to spare them further hardship. He visits the convent, to tell Kim (Marilyn Knowlden) that he will be away "on business," and then briefly reprises a bit of "Make Believe."

Prolific African American actor-songwriter Clarence Muse plays the small role of Sam, the doorman at the Trocadero, where Frank attempts to land Magnolia a spot as a "coon shouter." Apparently, everyone who left the show boat to travel north has ended up in this Chicago dive. The resident vocalist drinking, smoking and "feeling like going off on a tear"

Show Boat (1936). Queenie (Hattie McDaniel) and Joe (Robeson) in the charming "Ah Still Suits Me" scene.

is none other than Julie LaVerne, who performs "Bill" for manager Jim Green (Charles C. Wilson). Heartbroken after being abandoned by Steve, her earnest interpretation of the song captivates every worker in the joint. "Use it tomorrow night," Green orders. "And, listen, *be sober.*" (Helen Morgan's performance as the drink-sodden singer is an eerie example of art closely imitating life.)

In her dressing room, Julie overhears Nola's straight audition of "Can't Help Lovin' That Man of Mine." Green judges her performance as "rotten," and Julie walks out, leaving the singer's spot open for her former friend. Jake (Harry Barris), the pianist, "rags" the arrangement of the song, to which Frank works up a frantic tap dance.

On New Year's Eve, Magnolia's parents arrive in Chicago, where Andy sneaks out and then meets Frank while celebrating with some local girls. A patron (eternal drunk Arthur Housman) begins to heckle Nola even before she takes the stage to sing "After the Ball," but she is inspired by the sight of her father in the crowd.

In New York, Magnolia headlines at the Knickerbocker Theatre, where she receives an offer from "Sir Arthur" (Whale favorite E. E. Clive) to appear on the London stage. Time passes quickly, and Nola hands her mantle to Kim (Sunnie O'Dea), who is making her debut at the Knickerbocker, where Ravenal now is secretly working as the stage-doorman. The performance has already begun when Magnolia and her parents speed up to the curb

in a taxi. While trying to get a glimpse of the show, Gay is fired by the theater manager (Forrest Stanley). He then comes face to face with Nola, and the two are reunited after Kim inspires their duet of "You Are Love."

Having disappeared from the film at the 70-minute mark, Paul gets the final word in the film. His voice, singing the concluding line of "Ol' Man River," accompanies one last image of the calm Mississippi and "The End: It's a Universal Picture."

When *Show Boat* finally was released in May 1936, white audiences across the nation cheered both Robeson and McDaniel, who also were lauded by the critics. En route to London for the English premiere of the film, Whale told a reporter for the *New York Post* that Paul was "one of the finest gentlemen and most magnificent actors I have ever been privileged to direct."[12] The reviewer for the *New York World Telegram* wrote, "James Whale has done a beautiful job of direction and the cast responds to him with a perfection that at times is astonishing, notably in Paul Robeson's superb singing of 'Ol' Man River.'"[13]

Indeed, the "Ol' Man River" sequence is one of the strongest examples of how Whale keeps the film moving from the first scene to the last, even maintaining his admirable pace during all the musical performances. The last film required by his Universal contract, *Show Boat* also proved the final studio production bearing the name of Carl Laemmle, who had championed Whale's work since the 1931 shooting of the groundbreaking *Frankenstein*. Though the director entered negotiations with both MGM in the U.S. and Alexander Korda in the U.K., he returned to Universal to make four more pictures between 1937 and 1940, but the acceptance of his unconventional lifestyle he had experienced under the old regime was gone. He also directed one film each for Warner Bros., MGM, United Artists and Columbia before retiring from the cinema in 1941. He later referred to *The Invisible Man* and *Show Boat* as his best work (a fact dramatized in the excellent, Oscar-winning independent film

Show Boat (1936). The art on this U.S.–release insert poster provides an effective visual representation of the film, which director James Whale referred to as one of "two completely satisfying experiences I have had in the theatre."

Gods and Monsters [1997], starring Ian McKellen [who was nominated for the Best Actor award] as Whale). Debilitated by a stroke and unable to pursue his love of painting, Whale tragically drowned himself in his swimming pool in 1957.

The entire cast of *Show Boat* is top-deck, with Charles Winninger standing out for his nimble, easygoing comic abilities. Hattie McDaniel, who considered working with Paul a milestone in her career, quickly became Hollywood's top black actress. Surpassing the mighty Louise Beavers in popularity, she appeared in 23 films during the next two years, and won the Best Supporting Actress Academy Award (the first Oscar ever awarded to an African American) for her scene-stealing performance as "Mammy" in *Gone with the Wind* (1939).

While working on *Show Boat*, Paul admitted that McDaniel "was one of the best actresses he ever met."[14] Following the success of the film, he began to receive lucrative offers from the Hollywood moguls, whom he stunned by rejecting them in favor of remaining in England for his concert tours and more film work with the brothers Korda.

Though Allan Jones proved effective under Whale's direction, his acting career was short-lived, while Irene Dunne (who had not enjoyed working with Whale) earned an impressive list of film credits and five Best Actress Oscar nominations before retiring in 1952. *Show Boat* proved to be the cinematic swansong of Helen Morgan, who, after struggling in stage roles for another five years, tragically died of cirrhosis of the liver at age 41 on October 9, 1941.

During the 1940s, *Show Boat* disappeared from public view when MGM, intending to produce a Technicolor remake, bought the rights. (The studio had pulled the same maneuver

Show Boat (1936). This herald, including images of Robeson and Hattie McDaniel, was included in Universal's official pressbook sent to U.S. theaters exhibiting the film.

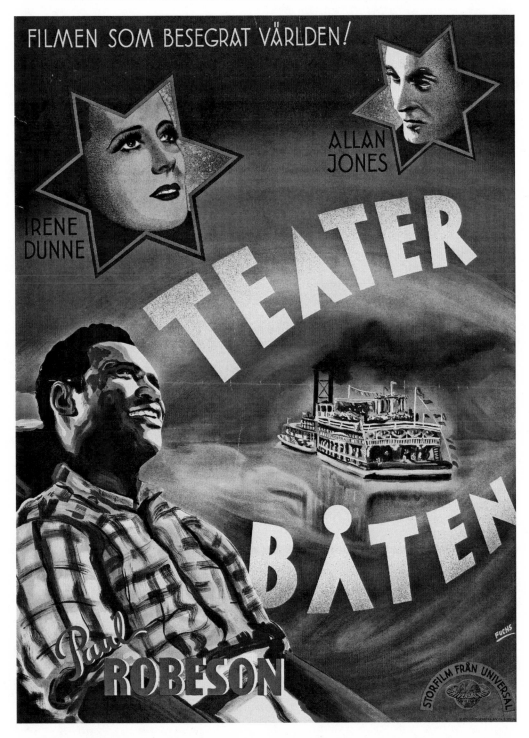

Show Boat (1936). Though romantic leads Irene Dunne and Allan Jones dominate the U.S. publicity materials, this poster produced for the Swedish release suggests that Scandinavian filmgoers recognized the true star of the film: Robeson, who boldly appears in the artwork as Joe, about to sing "Ol' Man River."

with Paramount's 1931 *Dr. Jekyll and Mr. Hyde*, exiling it to obscurity when they released an inferior remake of the Robert Louis Stevenson classic in 1941.) MGM didn't begin production on their *Show Boat* for several years, finally releasing it in 1951. Again the studio had shelved a masterpiece in order to replace it with a second-rate imitation.

Due to the political climate of the Cold War, Whale's *Show Boat* remained obscure until after Paul's death, and enthusiasts finally were able to see the film when it premiered on cable television in 1983. In recent years, the film has been reevaluated in a primarily positive light. In 1996, the Library of Congress added it to the National Film Registry as a "culturally, historically, or aesthetically significant" work worthy of preservation. In 2002, African American film historian Donald Bogle wrote:

> *Show Boat* was a film Robeson might not have cared for, but, curiously, today he seems more relaxed and less stagey in this movie than in any other.... Robeson and Hattie McDaniel ... went through stereotype routines, but Robeson never fully demeaned himself, and when he sang "Ol' Man River" and "Ah Still Suits Me" (with Hattie McDaniel), he lifted the entire movie onto his massive shoulders and carried it to moments of eloquence and greatness.[15]

In 2009, director John Landis, who cited *Show Boat* as one of his favorite films, said:

> A lot of it is written in dialect that is kind of demeaning and embarrassing, but ... the plot of the movie is surprisingly advanced in race relations. There is a kind of shocking, to contemporary eyes, blackface number that Irene Dunne does. However, this is a case where, I really think, *one*: you have to see it as a period piece; and, *two*: when you watch the performance of ... Paul Robeson, he elevates it so highly, and he's clearly so respected by the filmmakers. His entrance is very subtle, but you'll notice he's carrying something heavy as the bad guy goes by. As soon as the bad guy has passed, he stands up straight as a rail and gives him a look. His character, as written, is lazy ... and yet, the charm and *power* of Robeson overwhelms any cliché, any stereotype there. And, in fact, if you listen to the words of "Ol' Man River," with the white folk playing and the blacks breaking their backs, it's quite *up front*.[16]

Chapter 7

Singing King of Casanga
The Song of Freedom (1936)

After several trips back and forth, I decided to stay in Europe and make my home in London. My reasons were quite the same as those which over the years have brought millions of Negroes out of the Deep South to settle in other parts of the country. It must be said, however, that for me London was infinitely better than Chicago has been for Negroes from Mississippi.

— Paul Robeson[1]

Credits: Director and Assistant Art Director: J. Elder Wills; Producer: William Hinds; Screenplay: Ingram D'Abbes, Fenn Sherie, Michael Barringer, Philip Lindsay; Based on the story "The Kingdom of Zinga" by Major Claude Wallace and Dorothy Holloway; Directors of Photography: Eric Cross, Thomas A. Glover, Harry Rose; Editor: Arthur Tavares; Art Director: Norman G. Arnold; Musical Score: Eric Ansell; Song Lyrics: Henrik Ege; Additional Music: Jack Beaver; Production Supervisor: Henry Fraser Passmore; Assistant Director: Arthur Alcott; Sound Engineer: Harold V. King; a British Lion Film Corporation, Ltd.–Hammer Productions, Ltd., Picture; British Board of Film Censors Certificate "U"; Released by Exclusive Films (U.K.) on August 17, 1936; Length: 7,225 feet; Running Time: 80 minutes.
Cast: Paul Robeson (John Zinga), Elisabeth Welch (Ruth Zinga), George Mozart (Bert Puddick), Esme Percy (Gabriel Donizetti), Joan Fred Emney (Nell Puddick), Arthur Williams (Endobo, the Witch Doctor), Ronald Simpson (Mr. Blane, the Pianist), Jenny Dean (Marian), Bernard Ansell (Sir James Pyrie), Robert Adams (Monty), Cornelia Smith (Queen Zinga), Sydney Benson (Gate-Keeper), Will Hammer (Potman), Alf Goddard (Alf, the Bartender), Ambrose Manning (Trader), James Solomon (Native Leader), Ecce Homo Toto (Mandingo), Johnnie Schofield, Arthur Elliott (bits).

James Whale was still captaining *Show Boat* when Paul and Essie steamed back to England on January 12, 1936. Before departing, during an interview with African American U.S. Communist leader Benjamin J. Davis, Paul made a rare public statement about the political philosophy: "In England they call me a 'Communist' because of my views, but I'm certainly not a member of the Communist Party."[2]

Paul and Lawrence Brown toured Britain from January through April, also taking time to record five traditional songs at Abbey Road on March 24. Accompanied only by Brown's typically unobtrusive piano, Paul demonstrates tranquil virtuosity on "Shenandoah." Arranged as duets by Brown, "Ezekiel Saw de Wheel" and "Joshua Fit de Battle of Jericho," with their brisk, rocking tempos, provide quite a rhythmic contrast to the superlative ballad.

Back at their Buckingham Street flat, Paul and Essie welcomed their eight-year-old son, Paul Jr., who witnessed his father (who called him "Chappie") hard at work "studying and writing, rehearsing his music, and preparing for his roles."[3] Essie continued her role as official agent for prospective film offers, including another "African" picture to be made

71

with either Zoltan Korda or King Vidor (both of which were abandoned in favor of a concert tour of the Soviet Union), and Paul's continuing interest in a film adaptation of C. L. R. James' *Black Majesty*, to be directed by either Korda or Eisenstein.

During March, Paul starred in the Stage Society's production of the James play, staged as *Toussaint L'Ouverture*, at the Westminster Theatre. Also appearing in the cast was Robert Adams, a prolific black British actor born in Guyana, who had an unbilled bit part in *Sanders of the River* and would soon play major supporting roles opposite Paul in *The Song of Freedom* and *King Solomon's Mines*. Later, Adams founded the Negro Repertory Arts Theatre, one of the first black actors' groups in Britain, and followed in Paul's footsteps by portraying the leads in a live BBC television broadcast of *The Emperor Jones* (1938) and an N.R.A.T. stage version of *All God's Chillun Got Wings* (1944). *Toussaint L'Ouverture* ran for only two performances, but James, a socialist born in Trinidad, remained Paul's close friend and political confidant throughout the 1930s. Despite his Trotskyite opposition to Stalinism, James overlooked his disagreements with Paul, whose personality he summed up as a "combination of immense power and great gentleness."[4]

Incredibly, Paul was visited by Republican national chairman John Hamilton, who asked him to return to the U.S. to recruit blacks to campaign for presidential candidate Alf Landon in his effort to defeat FDR in his 1936 re-election bid. Paul recalled:

> My reward would be that as an actor I could write my own ticket in regard to future Hollywood contracts and starring productions, since the big film magnates were staunchly Republican and hated the man in the White House. I declined the offer and today I can smile at the thought that anyone could imagine me stumping the country, urging Negroes to turn against the New Deal and return the party of Herbert Hoover to power![5]

When Paul received word that Lillian Bayliss, manager of the Old Vic, was interested in pairing him with Laurence Olivier (as Iago) in Shakespeare's *Othello*, he turned down the offer. He mentioned the upcoming Soviet tour as the reason, but inwardly he believed that six weeks would not provide enough time to prepare for this monumental role.

Essie successfully negotiated starring roles for Paul in three major films, including contracts that allowed his personal approval of all versions of the scripts and final takes of his songs. All three projects would be completed prior to his departure for Moscow in October 1936. Paul Jr. elaborated:

> [T]he main problem continued to be the unavailability of commercially viable film stories based on black characters. In this context, he made a conscious decision to settle for mediocre but commercial stories with a relatively weak social message in order to portray powerful black male images that could deliver a positive cultural message. He had already come to the conclusion that this was possible in England but not in Hollywood.[6]

The Song of Freedom, based on the Claude Williams–Dorothy Holloway story "The Kingdom of Zinga," was an alliance between two companies, British Lion Film Corporation, Ltd., and the fledgling Hammer Productions, Ltd. Shooting began in early April under the direction of J. Elder Wills, who had been working in the British film industry, primarily as an art director and production designer, since 1927. Paul teamed with revue and radio performer Elisabeth Welch for the interior scenes shot at British Lion's Beaconsfield Studio in Buckinghamshire, which were augmented with location footage shot by a unit headed by Wills and T. A. Glover during a five-week trip to Tasso Island, off the coast of Sierra Leone, where they captured many shots of tribal customs never previously filmed. Enormous sets were constructed at Beaconsfield, and 400 extras were hired to play audience members in

the theater sequences. As reported in the official British Lion–Hammer pressbook, this "mighty drama of a primitive continent, the background for a sweeping story with the world's greatest singer and actor ... was five months in the making."[7]

On May 18, Welch joined Paul at an Abbey Road session, at which he cut new versions of his two *Show Boat* songs with an orchestra and chorus conducted by Clifford Greenwood. A familiar arrangement of "Ol' Man River" (with the term "darkies" substituted for "niggers") was followed by Welch ably handling Hattie McDaniel's duet part on "Ah Still Suits Me." Composer Eric Ansell took over on May 20 and 21, to conduct the orchestra and chorus on his *Song of Freedom* numbers co-written with lyricist Henrik Ege: "Sleepy River," "Lonely Road," "The Black Emperor" and "Song of Freedom" (called "The King's Song" in the film).

The Song of Freedom was groundbreaking in its depiction of a black married couple and an integrated working-class culture, elements that could not have been included in a production made in Hollywood. Paul's approval of the final cut, ensuring that the African scenes would not be reworked to his disadvantage during post-production, avoided any repeat of the *Sanders of the River* fiasco. When the film was released in the United Kingdom on August 13, 1936, the official publicity billed him as "THE MIGHTY PAUL ROBESON: The World's Greatest Singer in the Finest Film Production of His Career."

The Song of Freedom opens with an orchestral version of "Lonely Road" as the credit "PAUL ROBESON in" is superimposed over clouds as they move across the sky. The names of the supporting actors do not appear until the rolling "players" credit arrives at the close of the titles sequence.

The story begins in Africa, on "The Island of Casanga, off the West Coast — in the year 1700 A.D." Though slave trading in this particular region lies in the future, the inhabitants of the island currently suffer from the oppression of "their hereditary Queen Zinga — tyrant, despot, mistress of cruelty."

The unpleasant Queen Zinga (Cornelia Smith) deals with her insubordinate brother, whom she has trussed to a stake as punishment for allegedly conspiring with slave traders. "You *shall* be king, for one minute, *before you die!*" she announces, placing a medallion around his neck. The unfortunate man is slain, and she tears the medallion from his body. She and a male companion quickly run into the jungle, with a mob of spear-wielding tribesmen at their heels. They reach a small boat on the beach and row out to sea as the scene fades out.

A ship is anchored off shore as the couple lands their craft, seeking passage with a Caucasian captain who happens to be on a slaving mission. They are placed in the ship's hold with a group of shackled slaves, as a montage depicts the Zinga medallion being passed from one generation to the next. Decades of slavery grind on, until the practice is abolished in Great Britain. The sound of chains being broken on an anvil accompanies the year "1838" as it is superimposed over an image of shackles being tossed onto the ground.

A shot of Tower Bridge brings the story into the present day, as John Zinga (Robeson), wearing the now-weathered medallion around his neck, helps unload cargo from a ship at the London docks. When the workers knock off for the day, Zinga gives voice to a portion of a song that, he explains, "has been in the back of my head since I was a little fella."

Gabriel Donizetti (Esme Percy) walks down the gangplank of a passenger ship into a crowd of waiting journalists, while Zinga strides down a sidewalk, entertaining his colleagues with "Joshua Fit de Battle of Jericho." Donizetti overhears the performance while passing in his car, but Zinga and his Caucasian friend, Bert Puddick (George Mozart), duck

The Song of Freedom (1936). British Lion–Hammer Productions proudly heralds "The Mighty Paul Robeson: The World's Greatest Singer" on the front cover of the studio's official British-release pressbook. Paul's approval of the film's final cut avoided any repeat of the *Sanders of the River* fiasco.

The Song of Freedom (1936). "The Greatest Singing Star of the Age," Robeson commands sole billing on this stunning poster, the centerpiece of the British-release pressbook.

into a pub for a pint. A sailor bound for the West Coast of Africa asks Zinga, "What part do you come from, then?"

"I don't know," replies Zinga. "Wish I did."

"He's at it again," comments Bert to Monty (Robert Adams), another black companion. "Same old subject: Africa." When Zinga isn't looking, Bert casually drinks the remainder of the ale from his friend's glass. (Only 12 minutes in, *The Song of Freedom* includes content that wouldn't be seen in an American film for decades.) The camaraderie between Bert and his two black pals continues as he is summoned home by his wife, Nell (Joan Fred Emney). Zinga puts his huge arm around the small white man's shoulders, informing him, "You're just like the rest of us. When women start talkin', we just got to do what they say."

At home, John and Ruth (Elisabeth Welch) discuss his yearning for Africa, which he calls "my home. That's where we come from. I wonder which part?" Pointing to different locations on a map, he adds, "What wouldn't I give to know."

Ruth mentions their current situation in England: "But you're happy here. The people are kind."

"Oh, I know," John agrees. "They're grand people: Bert and Nell and the fellas down at the docks; but, somewhere in those parts, are *our* people, Ruth! And I've got a feeling they're grand people, too — the people we belong to."

John, embracing Ruth at the window, serenades the neighborhood with "Sleepy River," while children, black and white, slumber peacefully in their beds; Bert, Nell and Monty

The Song of Freedom (1936). Dock worker John Zinga (Robeson, center) and his closest pals on the job, Bert Puddick (George Mozart, left) and Monty (Robert Adams) [from the British pressbook].

mess about around the dinner table; and night falls on Tower Bridge and the docks as a barge floats down the river. This soothing sequence is followed by the cacophony of the over-the-top Donizetti shouting as Blane (Ronald Simpson), his pianist, pounds out some maddening, dissonant chords. The maestro raves about the "once in a lifetime" voice he has heard.

"After all, he's a mere *colored man*," babbles Blane.

"*Only* a colored man," counters Donizetti. "What does it matter, the color of his skin, when he has color in his *voice*? *Power*! *Beauty*!" The maestro rushes out of the room, declaring, "I must find *that man*! I cannot *live* until I find him!"

At the Crown and Anchor pub's "Go-as-You-Please Saturday Night Sing Song at 7:30," Zinga sits at the piano, playing the tune that haunts him. "That reminds me of Africa," remarks a sailor. "They go on like that for hours and hours."

Blane and Donizetti question a man in the street about a "colored singer," just as the bartender introduces "your old friend, Johnny Zinga!" He performs "Lonely Road" (to the accompaniment of a full orchestra on the soundtrack) for the appreciative patrons, who all sing along, until Donizetti arrives. The maestro wishes to hear only *one* voice, informing John, "You'll see no more of the docks. With me, you'll have a great future!" Greeting Ruth, he adds, "I congratulate you both. You have the world before you, with a voice like that!"

At 11 A.M. the following day, John and Ruth, dressed to the nines, call at Donizetti's flat. The pretentiousness of the operatic maestro, who greets them in Italian and attempts to "teach" John to sing with lengthy voice exercises, is cut down to size by the annoyed singer's terse admission, "I came here to sing, not to make these *noises*." At one point, when the diminutive Donizetti instructs him to voice an "ah," he lunges forward with a ferocious "Aaaahhh!" (giving Paul a prime opportunity to display his musician's innate sense of comic timing). Zinga cannot be fettered, neither by physical attire nor formal technique: "I like to be comfortable. I'm not a tailor's dummy! If they want me to sing, I've got to be *free*, not trussed up like a chicken! Can't I sing you a song instead of '*la, la, la*'?"

Donizetti's promises of a career and wealth don't faze him, until the possibility of "travel" is mentioned: "Someday, even Africa, perhaps," says the maestro. Now the "la la la's" come much more easily, and soon John Zinga, the *artiste*, is the toast of concert stages in Paris, Berlin and Budapest. (A medium close-up of Paul, wearing the Zinga medallion as he sings "Stepping Stones," is superimposed over a montage of travel and performance images.) Soon he is starring in "The Black Emperor: A Negro Opera" at London's Theatre Royal in Covent Garden. His success is proven by Monty, who now works as his valet.

Backstage in his dressing room, John tells Ruth, "It's strange that I should be playing this part: a black ruler who built an empire of slaves." (As John dresses in his costume for the finale, Paul works in his obligatory shirtless, "beefcake" scene.) The concluding scene of "The Black Emperor," clearly patterned after *The Emperor Jones*, is one of several "autobiographical" elements in *The Song of Freedom*.

Emerging for his curtain call, John honors Bert's request for one more vocal performance: "I'd like to sing you a fragment of a song which I've never sung in public before. I really don't know it, but I'll try and put some words to it." Summoning the voice of his "people" calling from "the south," he sings of their call for "freedom."

John ends abruptly, as a bespectacled patron (Bernard Ansell) tells his companion,

"I've heard that song before somewhere, but I *can't* think where." Backstage, champagne is being downed by Bert and Nell, who shakes Ruth's hand and then makes a comment about the high-class supporters crowding the dressing room: "Blimey, they're around him like a lot of rats."

John embraces Bert, and they mention the "old docks," just as Monty pops his head through the door, announcing, "Gentleman to see you, boss: Sir James Pyrie — very important." The aristocrat with the spectacles introduces himself, and Bert, addressing, "Your Lordship," declares that they had "better be off."

Pyrie, an "explorer and somewhat of an anthropologist," examines the medallion, telling John about the island of Casanga, where he heard "the King's Song — the sacred song of freedom of their people." Coincidentally, he's "probably the only white man who's ever heard it!" He informs John, "This disc is the symbol of kingship in Casanga. You know, you're probably a direct descendant of Queen Zinga." The all-knowing British scholar explains:

> When Queen Zinga died and her son disappeared, the witch doctors gained ascendancy over the island. They sold their trees to the unscrupulous slave traders, and, ever since, the island has suffered terrible droughts, because there's nothing to attract the clouds.

At this point, the film becomes a bit like *Sanders of the River* when Sir James works in a pro-colonialist comment: "The people still dominated by these witch doctors will never allow the *white man* to come near them, and so they are still *backward, uncivilized, impoverished.*"

"But if I am their king," John speculates, "they would let me help them, wouldn't they?"

"If you could prove you *are* their king," replies Sir James. "Heaven knows they need *someone* to help them in their *ignorance.*"

Donizetti is not pleased that his star wishes to abandon a New York contract for the primitivism of Casanga: "You're mad, *crazy*, insane!"

Ruth explains, "Something bigger than his success has come to him tonight. He may come back later, but he's *got* to go, *now.*"

On Casanga, drummers send word of Zinga's approach. On the beach, John, Ruth and Monty are met by a welcoming party, one of whom glances at the medallion. "Stranger, what do you want with us — you who call yourself 'Zinga'?" asks another.

"I am no stranger," replies John, claiming to be their king.

"You think you are a king, because you come to us dressed up in white man's clothes," counters the one who examined the medallion.

Ruth explains, "But he brings you knowledge from the great countries over the sea. It's not for *himself* that he wants to be king."

Some authentic shots from Sierra Leone are inter-cut with footage filmed in Buckinghamshire featuring native actors speaking a West African dialect. John apologizes to Ruth for transplanting her to an archaic culture, but she remains positive: "This is only the beginning. You'll be able to change *all* this in time."

"Everything is so different from what I expected," he admits. "It's all so *primitive.*"

"The worse things are, the more you can help them," she advises.

"It's *got* to be changed," he insists.

The tribesmen laugh heartily at the antics of Monty, who wears a French Navy cocked hat as he drags their luggage from the beach into the village. One of the loincloth-clad

The Song of Freedom (1936). As John Zinga, hereditary King of Casanga, Robeson dominates this U.S.–release title lobby card juxtaposing the two cultures depicted in the film. As Zinga's wife, Ruth, Elisabeth Welch shares her husband's status as the Toast of London (bottom right) as well as braving the dangers of the African island (bottom left).

tribesmen purloins the hat, dancing for the amusement of his brothers as the valet dodges chickens to take the bags into the hut commandeered by the Zingas.

Another tribesman, stricken by "the sickness, which is death," is carried into a hut, "where nothing can be done." Even Endobo, the witch doctor (Arthur Williams), cannot save them; but John, recognizing "the fever," sends Ruth and Monty to fetch plenty of boiled water and quinine. "I don't want to interfere with your customs, but a lot of these lives can be saved," he explains. Later, one of the men, Mandingo (Ecce Homo Toto), brings a bowl of fruit, accepts John's ancestry, and warns, "While Endobo rules, there can be *no king.*"

The witch doctor, frightening the people with "superstitious nonsense," tells them that the spirits want Zinga driven from the island. Wearing the medallion, John boldly enters Endobo's circle of skulls, shoves him to the ground, and kicks the heads around in the dust. This shattering of a taboo is followed by the sight of a dead man, killed by the fever, carried in a funeral procession of drummers and chanting tribesmen. "Does all of your magic end in this manner?" asks Endobo.

"I did what I could for him, but I was too late," John rationalizes. When he describes creating sanitation and health care, the tribesmen, incited by Endobo, laugh.

John breaks another taboo during the Night of the Full Moon, when he interrupts another of Endobo's primitive rituals, claiming that false "magic" cannot help the people with the false promise of bringing much-needed rain to end a prolonged drought. In the hut, Ruth, whose optimism has faded, confesses, "If I stay in this place, I'll go mad!" to Monty, who (continuing to provide comic relief) grabs his head and declares, "I'm just *plum crazy* already!"

Tribesmen dance in a circle around John, and then point their spears as Endobo orders him to lead them in "The King's Song." Ruth witnesses the scene, screams, and John is knocked unconscious by the witch doctor.

The village lies quiet during the night as the Zingas, each incarcerated in a separate "jail," remain wide awake. John sadly peers out his barred window as Ruth, in a reprise of his earlier joyful performance for their London neighbors, sings a melancholy version of "Sleepy River."

Ruth, who has "looked upon that which is forbidden," is scheduled to be executed. John believes he is responsible, but Mandingo, beholden to the law, refuses to help him escape. Spear-toting tribesmen lead her out, with a hood placed over her face, and John is

The Song of Freedom (1936), produced in Britain, was groundbreaking in its depiction of a black married couple, John and Ruth Zinga (Robeson and Elisabeth Welch), a progressive element that could not have been included in a Hollywood film at the time. This U.S.–release lobby card shows them flanking Endobo, the Witchdoctor (Arthur Williams), and their faithful sidekick, Monty (Robert Adams).

ordered to witness the event. Enbodo places him in the "King's Seat," telling him that the law must be obeyed, and he begins to muse on his London "Black Emperor" curtain-call performance as Ruth screams. The words begin to come to him, and he startles the blood-thirsty band: "The 'King's Song'! He knows it!" The new King and Queen of Casanga embrace as he continues to stir the hearts of the people by remembering the sacred song.

Wills incorporates an effective montage that alternates images (including oddly angled close-ups) of the Zingas with several shots of the captivated tribesmen. As John concludes his performance, the camera tilts up from a group of men to the sky above; then, through a dissolve, it moves down to the most iconic of London landmarks: Big Ben. Another familiar sight in the English capital (a flock of pigeons) provides a (rather bizarre) segue to the final performance of "A Return Visit of John Zinga in Three Short Musical Plays."

A considerable amount of time has passed. Inside the packed theater, seated in a private box, are Donizetti, Blane, and Sir James Pyrie, who remarks, "I suppose he's just as popular everywhere. He's a grand fellow; and, Donizetti, he hasn't let you down, after all."

"No, he's splendid," echoes the maestro. "He makes a lot of money for me, but for himself—*nothing*. It all goes to help those people of his." Providing a set-up for John's concluding number (and Paul's final vocal performance), Donizetti declares: "Every season, he

The Song of Freedom (1936). Zinga (Robeson) is threatened with the supreme penalty by Endobo, the witch doctor (Arthur Williams, far left), and the tribesmen when he is unable to prove his hereditary claim as King of Casanga [U.S.–release lobby card].

returns to sing. Tomorrow, he goes back again. Until next time...." A swish pan from the theater box to the stage holds on Zinga (shirtless, with the medallion around his neck) as he sits beside two African statues on a dais, merrily singing "Lonely Road." The camera tracks backward to a long shot, before the scene cuts to a medium shot of John (giving the viewer a good look at the medallion set against Paul's impressive physique), a reaction shot of the smiling Ruth, and back to John for the "beefcake" finale.

Paul and Elisabeth Welch give naturalistic performances throughout *The Song of Freedom*; but, aside from George Mozart as the working-class Bert, the British actors, who overplay their upper-crust characters with histrionic gusto, border on insufferable. (As Sir James, Bernard Ansell is the most credible; and Esme Percy *finally* abandons his feast of ham during the denouement.) In making this film, the African American artists contributed a more believable acting style, as well as an innovative cultural element, to Anglo cinema. The film is marred by some cultural clichés and exaggerations (the depiction of the Casanga women, for example, who are consistently segregated and treated in an overly chauvinistic manner[8]); but, due to Paul's input at every stage of the production, the result was a distinct improvement on *Sanders of the River*.

The Song of Freedom was an international success, drawing praise from journalists in Britain, India and the United States, where Langston Hughes wrote to Paul that the film was a big hit with Harlem audiences. London's Ardath Tobacco Company included a Paul Robeson and Elisabeth Welch cigarette card in their "From Screen and Stage" series. Reflecting the actors' decisions to seek work in Britain, the write-up on the verso of the card is free from any mention of race:

> Paul Robeson, a brilliant scholar, gave up a position in a legal firm to take up theatricals in his home town, Princeton, New Jersey, where he was born in 1898. His rich, melodious voice and dramatic acting quickly brought him to the top of the profession. Robeson appeared in many London stage productions before making his film debut in "Emperor Jones." [*sic*] "Song of Freedom," his latest production, provides some fine singing from Robeson and Elisabeth Welch. Born in New York, in 1904, Elisabeth Welch first appeared on the stage at the age of twenty. Previously she had been engaged in social work among children. Three years ago she crossed the Atlantic to make her London debut and earn the plaudits of a critical public.

Just prior to the release of *The Song of Freedom*, Paul wrote an article titled "Primitives" for the British journal *The New Statesman and Nation*, in which he delineates his concept of black culture and how it differs from the values of the Western world. The very essence of his remarks, made in 1936, would prove chillingly prophetic during succeeding decades rife with nuclear development and proliferation, commercial environmental disasters and global warming:

> The man who thinks in concrete symbols has no abstract conception of such words as "good," "brave," "clever." They are represented in his mind by symbolic pictures. It is not only the African Negro, and so-called primitive people, who think in concrete symbols— all the great civilizations of the East have been built up with this type of mind. It is a mentality which has ... given us the full flower of all the highest possibilities in man — with the single exception of applied science. That was left to a section of Western man to achieve, and on that he bases his assertion of superiority. The cost of developing the kind of mind by which the discoveries of science were made has been one which threatens the discoverer's very life. The result is that, as Western civilization advances, its members find themselves in the paradoxical position of being more and more in control of their environment, yet more and more at the mercy of it. One recoils from the Western intellectual's idea that,

having got himself on the peak overhanging the abyss, he should want to drag all other people up after him into the same precarious position.[9]

The Song of Freedom was only the third film produced by Hammer Productions, Ltd., which had been founded by comedian William Hinds (whose stage name was Will Hammer) in 1934. (Hinds, credited as Will Hammer, also plays the small role of "Potman" in the film.) Hammer made only two more films before Hinds filed for bankruptcy in 1937, but his distributor, Exclusive Films, headed by Enrique Carreras, managed to breathe new life into the company after Carreras' son, James, came on board the following year. (Nearly two decades would pass before Hammer became world-renowned for its stylish Technicolor horror films, often directed by Terence Fisher and starring Peter Cushing and Christopher Lee.)

Paul had considered traveling to South Africa, but local authorities, supported by the British, objected to his well-known anti-colonialist views. Instead, Essie and Paul Jr. (sponsored by Max Yergan, winner of the 1933 NAACP Spingarn medal for improving the education of black South Africans) made the trip, lodging with members of the antiapartheid movement before moving on to British East Africa. Paul remained in England, where he narrated the prologue (which he rewrote) and performed two songs for a five-reel antiapartheid documentary produced by Joseph Best, originally titled "Africa Looks Up" but eventually released as *My Song Goes Forth*.

On September 30, 1936, George Campbell, a journalist for *The Bystander*, published a review highly critical of Paul's film roles:

> Nine out of ten white stars are dwarfs alongside of him. And yet he has never made one first-class movie, and it looks as if he never will. The trouble lies in the unimaginative commercialization of the screen, and in our fundamentally mischievous attitude toward the whole negro [sic] race. If he could just forget he is a negro [sic], and make producers forget it too, he would be one of the great actors of the world, instead of a tantalizing possibility. *Song of Freedom* has its points, but as art it is sentimental and unreal.[10]

Paul Jr. later responded:

> Campbell failed to comprehend that Paul was consciously choosing to assert his blackness, rather than to "forget" it (assuming that was possible), and that his purpose was to impart authenticity to black characters upon whom an unreality had been imposed by even the most well-meaning white producers. This concept seemed beyond the imagination of even the most liberal whites.[11]

Further planning the Soviet trip, Paul anticipated meeting with Eisenstein to discuss *Black Majesty* and other potential film projects, including *Othello* and *Sons*, Pearl Buck's sequel to her Pulitzer Prize–winning novel *The Good Earth*. In the U.S.S.R., Eisenstein again accompanied Paul as he visited various urban and rural locales. The director had received permission to make a new film about the Russian countryside, *Bezhin Meadow*, and Paul often observed the location shooting. Though Paul realized that the Stalinist regime was "rigid and puritanical," he chose not to "publicly articulate any of his criticisms and misgivings."[12]

Paul Jr. who attended a Soviet "model school" (the equivalent of an exclusive private institution in the U.S.) whose other students included the children of Stalin and Molotov, recalled his experiences during the first public purge trial of 1936: "While I was in school in Moscow, I kept hearing about the disappearances of my classmates' parents. It was not something that my father talked about."[13]

Paul gave a total of 12 concerts in Moscow, Leningrad, Kiev and Odessa during October 1936. Eisenstein praised his performances in the Soviet press, suggesting that the lyrics of his Negro folk songs be translated into Russian for publication in the concert programs. Soviet censors were concerned about the religious content of the songs, but Eisenstein stressed the "unusual" nature of the blacks' interpretation of the Bible, stating that "our concert-goers should be able to evaluate the full power of the new class content in the folk tradition of Negro song."[14] During his performances, Paul echoed Eisenstein by explaining the meaning of the spirituals in Russian.

Chapter 8

Down in the Ditch
Big Fella (1937)

Paul Robeson ... enjoyed a unique position at the juncture of popular arts, high culture, and politics.... Robeson's theatrical activities ranged from serious modern and classical plays to musical comedy, and whatever role he played became stamped with his name.

— Edward R. O'Neill[1]

Credits: Director, Producer and Art Director: J. Elder Wills; Producer: Henry Fraser Passmore; Screenplay: Ingram D'Abbes, Fenn Sherie; Based on the Novel *Banjo* by Claude McKay; Directors of Photography: Cyril Bristow, George Stretton, H. A. R. Thomson; Editors: Brereton Porter, Douglas Robertson; Musical Score: Eric Ansell; Additional Musical Numbers: Will Grosz (a.k.a. Hugh Williams), G. H. Clutsam; Production Supervisor: A. W. Osborne; Assistant Director: Arthur Alcott; Sound Engineer: Harold V. King; a British Lion Film Corporation, Ltd.–Hammer Productions, Ltd., Picture; British Board of Film Censors Certificate "U"; Released (U.K.) on June 16, 1937; Running Time: 73 minutes.

Cast: Paul Robeson (Joe), Elisabeth Welch (Amanda), Roy Emerton (Spike), James Hayter (Chuck), Lawrence Brown (Corney), Eldon Gorst [a.k.a. Eldon Grant] (Gerald Oliphant), Marcelle Rogez (Marietta), Eric Cowley (Ferdy Oliphant), Joyce Kennedy (Mrs. Oliphant), Dino Galvani (Gendarme), Anthony Holles (Gendarme), Eslanda Robeson (Barmaid), Margaret Rutherford (Nanny).

Filmed on the heels of *The Song of Freedom* by the British Lion–Hammer co-production team, *Big Fella*, loosely based on the Claude McKay novel *Banjo*, gave Paul his first serio-comic characterization free from prevalent black stereotypes. Elisabeth Welch again costarred opposite Paul, who was pleased to welcome Lawrence Brown to the set for his first film role. Essie also was hired to play the small role of a barmaid. Ingram D'Abbes and Fenn Sherie's screenplay for this musical comedy incorporates several elements from Charles Chaplin's silent masterpiece *The Kid* (1921), in which the Little Tramp cares for an abandoned child (Jackie Coogan) who grows to love his accidental guardian.

Born in Jamaica in 1889, Festus Claudius McKay was a militant socialist and pioneering author in the Harlem Renaissance. His book of poetry, *Harlem Shadows* (1922), was one of the first literary works published during the movement. *Banjo: A Story Without a Plot* (1929) was the second of his three novels, book-ended by *Home to Harlem* (1928), which won the prestigious Harmon Gold Award for Literature, and *Bananas Bottom* (1933). His short stories were collected as *Gingertown* (1932), and his two autobiographical volumes, *A Long Way from Home* (1937) and *Harlem: Negro Metropolis* (1940), were the last works published during his lifetime. Prior to his death of a heart attack in 1948, he became disillusioned with communism and was baptized in the Catholic Church.

Banjo is noted for McKay's perceptive portrait of working-class blacks living on the

Marseilles waterfront (in an area known as "the Ditch") during the 1920s. Although the environment in McKay's Marseilles is an integrated, multicultural one, the black characters experience what he refers to as a "universal attitude, which, though the method varied, was little different anywhere."

The novel's protagonist, the African American sailor-musician Lincoln Agrippa Daily, is nicknamed "Banjo" after the instrument he plays so well. Although Banjo and his mates (including West Indians, Senegalese and fellow Americans from the South) enjoy the lifestyle of the carefree, hell-raising vagabond, the novel deals seriously with issues of race, class and poverty. McKay's satirical depiction of black petty bourgeois attitudes (specifically toward less fortunate brothers and sisters) eventually generated some controversy among the emerging black middle class in the United States.

At one point, when describing the brutality waged by the Marseilles police against Banjo and his boys, McKay addresses what he calls "the happy irresponsibility of the Negro in the face of civilization":

> For civilization had gone out among these native, earthy people, had despoiled them of their primitive soil, had uprooted, enchained, transported, and transformed them to labor under its laws, and yet lacked the spirit to tolerate them within its walls.
>
> That this primitive child, this kinky-headed, big-laughing black boy of the world, did not go down and disappear under the serried crush of trampling white feet; that he managed to remain on the scene, not worldly-wise, not "getting there," yet not machine-made, nor poor-in-spirit like the regimented creatures of civilization, was baffling to civilized understanding. Before the grim, pale rider-down of souls he went his careless way with a primitive hoofing and a grin.
>
> Thus he became a challenge to the clubbers of helpless vagabonds—to the despised, underpaid protectors of property and its high personages. He was a challenge of civilization itself. He was the red rag to the mighty-bellowing, all-trampling civilized bull.

There are no overt examinations of race or class in the primarily lighthearted *Big Fella*, in which Paul's character, Joe (shortened from "Banjo"), is a comic variation on his dock worker in *The Song of Freedom*. But Joe does become entangled with the Marseilles police (who set the major plot in motion) and an upper-crust British couple who eventually witness the effect this carefree, working-class black man has on their unhappy son, who is thoroughly fed up with repressive, aristocratic commandments.

Again working with director J. Elder Wills at the Beaconsfield Studio in Buckinghamshire, Paul developed a capable yet sensitive character who cares for the runaway boy on the streets of Marseilles. The film runs a brisk 73 minutes and features an excellent score by Eric Ansell, with additional numbers by Will Grosz (billed as Hugh Williams) and G. H. Clutsam. Paul recorded the Ansell songs "Lazin'" and "Roll Up, Sailorman" at Abbey Road on May 3, 1937.

As in *The Song of Freedom*, Paul receives top billing, above the title:

<div align="center">

PAUL ROBESON
in
BIG FELLA
with
ELISABETH WELCH

</div>

Lawrence Brown is billed fifth in the list of players, but Essie receives no screen credit for her cameo appearance.

Atmospheric establishing shots of the Marseilles docks are accompanied by Paul singing

"Lazin'" on the soundtrack. Joe's pals (one black, Corney [Lawrence Brown], and one white, Chuck [James Hayter]) can be seen, literally lazing around on the dock, as the Big Fella continues to serenade his colleagues, some of whom are actually working, mending nets for further fishing expeditions. The sound recording (by Harold V. King) is superb for a mid–1930s British film, and the transition from Paul's concluding note (graced with subtle, well-controlled vibrato) to the blast of a ship's horn is quite startling.

Aboard the *Ville d'Oran*, two gendarmes meet with a distressed British couple, Mr. and Mrs. Ferdy Oliphant (Eric Cowley and Joyce Kennedy), whose young son, Gerald (Eldon Gorst), has gone missing. The mother, who assumes the lad has been kidnapped, is assured by the skipper that paying a ransom will keep him "from any harm." Cowley and Kennedy histrionically portray the stereotypical, stiff-upper-lipped and stoop-shouldered upper-class Brits of the period. "Oh, why can't they speak *English*?" whines Mrs. Oliphant, referring to the Marseilles police.

"Lost Child" posters, announcing a 50,000-franc reward, are plastered all over the city. Joe is still seated at the docks, giving voice to "All God's Chillun Got Wings," but he finally is forced to communicate with mere speech after two gendarmes arrive to take him to the prefecture. Joe is briefly waylaid by the (obviously British) local conman, Spike (Roy Emerton, who uses an obnoxious, bogus laugh throughout the film), before being questioned about the missing boy. The police commissioner asks Joe to infiltrate the street gangs "down in the Ditch," but he is reluctant until Mrs. Oliphant makes an impassioned appeal.

"Well, there's one thing I thought I'd never be: it's a policeman," he admits. "Mind you, I wouldn't do this in the ordinary way, but if it's a *kid*, that's different." Reminded about the 50,000 francs, he adds, "Don't you worry. *I heard*." Corney and Chuck, assuming their friend is in trouble, are waiting outside. Though he can't reveal the details, Joe claims that the police have "called him in" on "somethin' that's got 'em beat," and then orders his pals to "keep your eyes and ears open."

"What for?" asks Chuck.

"Well, I told you, I can't tell you!" says Joe.

"Oh, I see," Chuck replies. "Well, if we hears about something what we don't know nothing about, we'll let you know."

"I don't quite understand this," mutters Corney. (Paul's characterization is free of the usual stereotypes, but Brown is saddled with the familiar black sidekick who speaks in broken "Negro dialect"; however, his shtick is balanced by that of his equally obtuse Caucasian counterpart.) The trio combs the city by streetcar, then on foot; and Joe's constant scrutiny of every boy he sees reveals the truth to his pals, who aren't quite so dimwitted after all.

At the Café Cosmo, the chic Amanda (Elisabeth Welch) sings a romantic number for the appreciative patrons. (Essie can be seen working behind the bar during Welch's performance.) Spike rushes in, orders milk from the bartender, thrusts the bottle under his vest, and sneaks out. Joe and his pals, noticing this strange behavior, follow him home.

"What the hell do you guys want?" Spike snarls, slamming his apartment door. They overpower him, tumble into his room, and find only a cat drinking the milk from a saucer, a discovery the intrepid trio finds very amusing. While relaxing at the café, Chuck inadvertently informs Spike about Joe's "police" assignment.

"Howdy, Big Fella!" says Amanda, who refers to Spike as Joe's "boyfriend." When Spike is angered by a mention of the cat incident, Joe calms him by waving him off and taunting, "Alright, *Sista*!" Amanda laughs, pats Joe on the back, and walks back toward the bar as the vanquished Spike sits back down. (This episode, genially played by Paul and Elis-

Big Fella (1937). This one-sheet poster produced for the film's U.S. release bills Robeson as "The World's Greatest Singing *and* Dramatic Star." Also featured are Elisabeth Welch (center inset and bottom, second from left), Lawrence Brown (bottom, fifth from left) and Roy Emerton (bottom right inset).

abeth Welch, appears to have been partially improvised and is an extraordinary cultural moment in a 1937 film.) Everyone in the café joins in the fun: some "meow," the violinist annoyingly scrapes his instrument with his bow, and Amanda serves Spike a large mug of milk, while bringing beer for the others.

Spike exacts his revenge, announcing Joe's project to the crowd, asking, "Any of you gentlemen kidnap a little boy?"

The shenanigans continue until the barmaid (Essie, delivering her first lines in the film) haughtily scolds the amused Joe:

> What have you got to laugh at, you Big Bozo? The boys were peaceful enough until you came in! What sort of a cop do you think you are? Every time you and Spike get friendly, something gets broken! If it's roughhousing you're looking for, come to me! I'll give you all you want.

This amusing incident with Paul being dressed down by his real-life wife culminates with Amanda guiding Joe away from the bar, declaring, "Say, if he wants to make a noise, I'll fix him. This way, Big Fella." Turning toward the crowd, she asks, "Hey, boys, what do you want to hear?"

"Roll Up, Sailorman!" they all shout, joining in on the final chorus of the sea ditty as the scene fades out.

Big Fella (1937). This U.S.–release title lobby card features Robeson and most of his supporting cast, including his wife, Eslanda (bottom left), who plays the small role of a barmaid.

Back at the docks, Corney and Chuck attempt to fish, Joe casually works on a "ship in the bottle," and some young boys splash away in the water below. One of the lads climbs the ladder, scampers down the pier, and stomps directly on Chuck, nearly smashing his "blinking buttock!" Joe threatens to spank the boy, whom they quickly identify. He attempts to escape, and the other three ragamuffins (including a black child called "Darky") join in a furious melee ending with Gerald's clothes being tossed into the river. Joe wraps him in a sailor's rain slicker and bundles him off to Amanda's apartment, where the boy amiably reveals that he "wasn't stolen. I *ran away*." Fed up with the stifling upper-crust British lifestyle, he longs to be "like other boys" and grow up to become a sailor.

Dressed in "girl's clothes," Gerald blackmails the gang into *not* returning him to an oppressive environment. "Oh, come on, be a sport!" the plucky child urges Joe. Realizing he'll be caught again if he returns to the street "Arabs," he chooses to stay with Joe, admitting, "I think I could have some fun with you." When he assumes that Amanda is Joe's wife, she suggests, "You can just *lay off* that," as Corney and Chuck laugh. The lad again uses blackmail to get his way, and all five join a "secret society" by stacking their fists and chanting, "*Bumpjee*, I swear!"

In a charming domestic scene, Joe teaches Gerald to box, while Amanda sees to their comfort. The lad sits on Joe's lap, and the Big Fella, calling him "Son," cautions him about growing up too quickly: "It's only when you're a man that you know how grand it is to be a little boy." Explaining the figure of speech "reaching for the moon" used by his "Mammy," Joe reveals, "She used to sing me a song about it," then launches into "My Curly Headed Baby."

Gerald remains on Joe's lap for the first verse and chorus (during which Wills includes some cutaway shots of Amanda preparing a bed for the boy), then gets up to stroll onto the balcony, where he spots a black woman bathing her baby in the apartment across the alley. Joe joins the lad before beginning another verse and chorus (which Paul ends by singing the last "Lulla, lulla, lulla, *luuulla — bye*" at the higher end of his vocal range, smoothly ascending the scale and beautifully sustaining the final three notes), followed by the curly-headed baby's mother closing the window and pulling the curtains shut. The lullaby leads to Gerald donning one of Amanda's nightgowns and asking Joe to join him in prayer, during which he asks God to bless his new friends and keep the police away. The child feels perfectly safe in such a relaxed setting, simply overjoyed to be tucked in by Joe, who retreats to his own apartment, and Amanda, who leaves to sing at the café.

Police Headquarters receives a series of envelopes from the various Marseilles sub-stations, all of which have "nothing to report." Two gendarmes visit Joe as he teaches the French song "Peanuts" to Gerald, who crawls into a hiding place behind the curtains. Having bamboozled the law, the Big Fella and his little pal laugh heartily as they shake hands.

At the café, a tap dancer burns the floor as Spike and Marietta, a shady mademoiselle, stroll in to be insulted by the barmaid (Essie's final appearance), who then threatens to fire Amanda for being late. Amanda finally arrives, only to inform Joe that the lad and his clothes have disappeared. Corney and Chuck attempt to devise a plan of action, but Joe orders them to be quiet while Amanda performs her number! A few lines into "Harlem, You're Still in My Heart," the scene cuts to a medium close-up of Gerald, under a table, crawling across the barroom floor toward Joe.

During a performance of the Can-Can, Marietta kills the lights, and Spike kidnaps the boy, with Joe and company in hot pursuit. At the prefecture, Spike lies about battling with "a bunch of dagoes" who had imprisoned Gerald "in a cellar." The boy attempts to expose

the conman as "nothing else but a big fibber!" but his father orders him to be quiet as he hands Spike 50,000 francs. Joe bursts in, only to be dismissed by the commissioner and called a "Big Bozo" by Spike. Outside the station, Spike offers to split the dough "fifty-fifty" back at his apartment, and Joe is persuaded to go out on the town.

Strolling down the street, Joe sings "River Steals My Folks from Me" for Spike and Marietta. (The scene is realistically grounded by Wills' use of an actual set [rather than opting for back-screen projection, which was commonly used in Hollywood films of the period], tracking the camera backwards as Paul sings while walking with the other actors.) Corney and Chuck accompany Amanda home, but Joe stays out, downing champagne with the dishonest duo at the Montevideo. A rapid montage literally drowned in drink leads to a close-up of Joe's unsteady legs as he shuffles toward Amanda's door.

The following morning, Amanda applies cold towels to Joe's aching head and then orders, "Now, get the heck out of here!" He attempts to reason with her about Marietta's presence at the party, but she shoves him out the door.

Back on the *Ville d'Oran*, Gerald is subjected to the same restrictive regimen, including a nanny (an unbilled Margaret Rutherford, in her fifth film appearance) who tries to feed him porridge. He gazes out a window, asking to "go down and see the boys," while his conventional, clueless parents attempt to fathom the cause of his sullen mood and loss of appetite.

Following a visit from the doctor, Gerald's hunger strike ends when the folks ask the equally dejected Joe to accompany him back to England. Joe gladly accepts but then discovers that he can't leave his life on the docks and — Amanda. Performing a final song, "You Didn't Ought to Do Such Things," Joe exacts *his* revenge on Spike by pressing the conman into service in his stead. (The film, which is progressive in so many ways, unfortunately con-

Big Fella (1937). **This impressive poster art produced for the film's Australian release exaggerates Robeson's physical prowess, casting the singer of "six magnificent songs" in a delightfully menacing light!**

cludes with a shot of the shanghaied rogue, decked out in *blackface*, protesting as the ship leaves the harbor.)

Though working with less ambitious material than he had explored in *The Song of Freedom*, J. Elder Wills (this time wearing *three* hats, as director, art director and producer) created an amiable atmosphere and admirably brisk pace for *Big Fella*. The excellent musical sequences feature consistent yet relaxed movement achieved through a spare use of editing and credible performances (from the supporting cast to the bit players). Carefully tailored for the Robeson persona, Ingram D'Abbes and Fenn Sherie's screenplay retains little of McKay's *Banjo*, but no filmmaker, on either side of the Atlantic, could *really* have adapted this novel for the consumption of the movie-going public of 1937.

The ensemble acting of Paul, Elisabeth Welch, Lawrence Brown, James Hayter and young Eldon Gorst (billed as Eldon Grant in the credits) in the domestic scenes provides some of the most believable and entertaining moments in *Big Fella*. The relationship between Gerald and the care-giving, nascent Joe-and-Amanda couple provides quite a contrast to any white and black involvement exhibited in Hollywood films produced during the mid- to late 1930s: the typical "contented house slave" roles in popular antebellum and Civil War fare, from 20th Century–Fox's *The Littlest Rebel* (1935), with Shirley Temple and Bill "Bojangles" Robinson (as "Uncle Billy"), to Vivien Leigh and Hattie McDaniel (as "Mammy") in Selznick's *Gone with the Wind* (1939); scores of various genre films featuring top stars amused (or annoyed) by the "comic relief" of such reliable, often infantile sidekicks as Stepin Fetchit, Willie ("Sleep 'n' Eat") Best and Fred ("Snowflake") Toones; and, ranking as one of the ultimate racist cinematic indignities, (the usually delightful) Allen Jenkins referring to mighty jazz genius Louis Armstrong as "Uncle Tom" in Warner Bros.' *Going Places* (1938), in which "Satchmo" serenades a *horse* with Harry Warren and Johnny Mercer's "Jeeper's Creepers."

In *Big Fella*, after spending only a brief time with Joe and Amanda, Gerald experiences a newfound happiness that is admirably played with subtlety by Eldon Gorst; but, as soon as the boy is returned to the pompous British parents, he reverts to childish overacting. Gorst, who was 14 when playing the pre-teen Gerald Oliphant (his second screen role), appeared in only four more films (all of them in Hollywood) over the next decade. The practice of casting him as much younger boys continued, culminating with his performance as 16-year-old Sandy MacFadyen in the MGM Lassie series entry *Hills of Home* (1948), when he was approaching his *26th* birthday. Tragically this role proved his last, and he committed suicide in Los Angeles on March 2, 1950.

In April 1937, Joseph Best released *My Song Goes Forth*, in which Paul directly addresses the camera as he voices his desire for equality between Africans and the inhabitants of Europe and North America. Known for his documentaries about the British Empire, Best, benefiting from the suggestions of both Paul and Essie, had chosen to depict South Africans in a non-stereotypical manner, showing them as seeking higher education and positions in modern industry while enduring the inequalities of everyday life. While the film received positive reviews, its release ultimately was limited by the objections of white South Africans who opposed the progressive political content. Conversely, the U.S. Communist Party considered it "not ... militant enough."[2] In an attempt to secure a wider release the following year, Best heavily edited the film, reducing it to two reels and re-titling it *Africa Sings*.

Enough Here for All
King Solomon's Mines (1937)

And Solomon finished all the work that he made in the house of the Lord, and
brought in the things that David his father had dedicated, the silver and the gold,
and the vessels, and laid them up in the treasures of the house of the Lord.
—III Kings [7:51]

Credits: Director: Robert Stevenson; Screenplay: Charles Bennett, Michael Hogan, Roland
Pertwee, A. R. Rawlinson, Ralph Spence; Directors of Photography: Glen MacWilliams, Cyril
J. Knowles (African exteriors); Camera Operator: Bernard Knowles; Editor: Michael Gordon;
Musical Score: Mischa Spoliansky; Musical Director: Louis Levy; Song Lyrics: Eric Maschwitz;
Art Director: Alfred Junge; Assistant Directors: Slim Hand, Geoffrey Barkas (African exteriors);
Sound Recordist: A. Birch; Wardrobe: Marianne; a Gaumont British Picture; British Board of
Film Censors Certificate "U"; Released by General Film Distributors (U.K.), June 17, 1937, and
by Gaumont British Picture Corporation of America (U.S.), July 26, 1937; Running Time: 80
minutes.

Cast: Paul Robeson (Umbopa), Cedric Hardwicke (Allan Quartermain), Roland Young
(Commander John Good), Anna Lee (Kathleen "Kathy" O'Brien), John Loder (Sir Henry Curtis),
Arthur Sinclair (Patrick "Patsy" O'Brien), Robert Adams (Twala), Arthur Goullet (Sylvestra
Getto), Ecce Homo Toto (Infadoos), Makubalo Hlubi (Kapse), Mjujwa (Scragga), Sydney Fair-
brother (Gagool), Alf Goddard (Red), Frederick Leister (Diamond Buyer), Ben Kubeka (bit).

The much-anticipated Gaumont British adaptation of H. Rider Haggard's novel *King
Solomon's Mines*, costarring Robeson with Cedric Hardwicke, Anna Lee, Roland Young and
John Loder, began shooting at Shepherd's Bush Studios in London during the autumn of
1936. Standing alongside *King Kong* (1933) as one of the decade's great fantasy-adventure
pictures, it offered Paul another "royal African" role, though shorn of the sticky political
problems that had followed his *Sanders of the River* experience.

Published in 1885, *King Solomon's Mines* was touted as "The Most Amazing Book Ever
Written!" In actuality, the story was the result of a five-shilling bet between H. Rider Haggard
and his brother to determine if he could write a "novel half as good" as Robert Louis Steven-
son's 1883 adventure masterpiece *Treasure Island*. Born in Bradenham, Norfolk, England,
Sir Henry Rider Haggard (1856–1925) was a scholar, reformist, and successful novelist who
created the "Lost World" genre (eventually spawning Sir Arthur Conan Doyle's *The Lost
World* [1912] and Edgar Rice Burroughs' *The Land That Time Forgot* [1918]).

At age 19, Haggard was sent to Africa, where he worked in the office of Sir Henry Bul-
wer, Lieutenant-Governor of Natal. In 1876, he was transferred to the staff of the Special
Commissioner for the Transvaal, an area comprising the majority of the Boer South African
Republic. In April 1877, Haggard was in Pretoria when the British annexed the colony, and
he attained the position of Registrar of the High Court of the Transvaal the following year.

He remained in Africa until the autumn of 1881, logging his firsthand experiences of the colonial conflicts that uncovered the ruins of ancient civilizations and veins of precious metals and stones ripe for British plunder. In particular, he became fascinated by the exploits of explorer and big-game hunter Frederick Courtney Selous (1851–1917), a pal of President Theodore Roosevelt and Lord Cecil Rhodes, who provided the inspiration for Allan Quartermain, the protagonist of *King Solomon's Mines*.

Both the Hebrew Bible and the Islamic Koran include tales about Solomon, the former identifying him as King of Israel and the latter as a mere prophet. The biblical version is the most familiar, depicting Solomon as the son of King David and his queen, Bathsheba; Solomon becomes famous for his wealth, wisdom, and dalliance with the Queen of Sheba. Haggard had heard about possible locations of Solomon's "mines," including a site at the Timna Valley in southern Israel (which later was proved false).

The novel begins in the city of Durban, where Allan Quartermain is engaged by Sir Henry Curtis and his associate, Captain Good, to locate Curtis' brother, who went missing during a quest to discover the legendary mines. Possessing a map allegedly showing the way to the location, Quartermain agrees to lead the expedition in return for a share of the treasure (to be passed on to his son in the event of his death). They are accompanied by Umbopa, a native guide whose well-spoken demeanor suggests a regal heritage. After braving the dangers of deserts, wild animals, warriors, and the wrath of the evil hag Gagool (who discovers that Umbopa is actually Ignosi, King of the Kukuana tribe), the adventurers find Curtis' brother, laid low by a broken leg, and return to Durban and then England, loaded down with the treasures of Solomon.

Taking the *Treasure Island* challenge seriously, Haggard wrote the novel as a first-person narrative, capturing some of the fast-moving, conversational style of Stevenson's sinuous prose. Rejected by several publishers as a "novelty" with little to interest readers, the 320-page novel became a best-seller for London's Cassell and Company, who labored to keep up with popular demand.

Remarkably, although the novel includes colonialist "native" stereotypes typical of Victorian literature, Haggard was ahead of his time in integrating positive depictions of black African characters, particularly Umbopa/Ignosi and Foulata, a Kukuana woman who has an interracial romance with Good (a potentially controversial element nixed by her premature death, though gently in the captain's embrace). In one "progressive" passage, Quatermain refuses to use the word "nigger," explaining that many black natives are more deserving of the title "gentleman" than their white colonial counterparts.

King Solomon's Mines was first adapted for the screen in 1919 as *Allan Quatermain*, a feature directed by Horace Lisle Lucoque for South African Film Productions, Ltd. In the title role, Hal Lawrence was supported by Ray Brown (as John Good), Halford Hamlin (as Henry Curtis), and a black actor, Umpakayiboni (as "Umslopogaas").

Surrounded by some of Britain's finest actors, Paul passed time with good company during the making of *King Solomon's Mines*. At the dawn of his acting career in 1913, Sir Cedric Hardwicke (1893–1964) toured with Frank Benson's Shakespearean company in South Africa and Rhodesia, prior to serving with the British Army in France during World War I. He had appeared in seven films, both in England and Hollywood, prior to signing for the role of Allan Quatermain (which is expanded to *Quartermain* in the film).

Twenty-four-year-old Anna Lee (1913–2004), the goddaughter of Sir Arthur Conan Doyle, was married to director Robert Stevenson during the making of *King Solomon's Mines*. During the course of her lengthy career, she appeared in seven films (and one tele-

vision episode) directed by John Ford, who was godfather to her children. In 1989, she recalled, "I costarred with some wonderful leading men in my career: Boris Karloff, Edward G. Robinson, John Wayne — and, you know, I worked with *Paul Robeson*."[1] Interestingly, her most widely known character, the matriarch on the daytime soap opera *General Hospital*, on which she appeared for 25 years, was named Lila *Quartermaine*.

London-born Roland Young (1887–1953) served with the U.S. Army during World War I, made his film debut as Dr. Watson opposite John Barrymore as a romantic variation on Conan Doyle's *Sherlock Holmes* (1922), and gave a series of critically acclaimed comic performances while under contract to MGM (1929–1932) before achieving resounding success as a freelance film and stage actor on both sides of the Atlantic. Having played the title role in Alexander Korda's production of *The Man Who Could Work Miracles* (1936), a brilliant comic fantasy adapted by H. G. Wells from his own story, Young was at the top of his game when he signed with Gaumont British to play Commander John Good.

Handsome leading man John Loder (1898–1988), the son of General W. H. M. Lowe (the British officer who accepted the surrender of Patrick Pearce at the end of the 1916 Rising in Dublin), was born William John Muir Lowe in London, and was well educated at Eton and the Royal Military College. Following service in World War I (including a stint in a POW camp), he remained in Germany, where he acted in a few films before seeking better roles in England (including two 1936 classics, *The Man Who Changed His Mind*, with Boris Karloff, and *Sabotage*, directed by Alfred Hitchcock) and Hollywood. (After appearing in *King Solomon's Mines*, he made another big score by marrying Hedy Lamarr in 1943, but the marriage lasted only four years.)

Production on *King Solomon's Mines* began during the early autumn of 1936. Gaumont British sent assistant director Geoffrey Barkas and cinematographer Cyril J. Knowles to South Africa to shoot authentic exterior footage at several locations, some faithful to those described by Haggard in the novel. Hundreds of Zulus (including Ben Kubeka, brother-in-law of the regent chief) were hired to perform native rituals, dances and battles, which come across with realistic ferocity on the screen. Most of the dialogue sequences were filmed with the major cast at Shepherd's Bush in London, but Robert Stevenson and editor Michael Gordon made an admirable effort to integrate seamlessly hundreds of shots (many of them featuring rousing action) filmed on two separate continents.

The screenplay, credited to Michael Hogan and Roland Pertwee (but also including contributions from Charles Bennett, A. R. Rawlinson and Ralph Spence), follows the basic framework of the novel but alters the motivations and activities of some of the major characters. In the film, Kathleen O'Brien provides the impetus for the entire harrowing adventure, hiring Umbopa, then asking the "Great White Hunter," Quartermain, to help her track down her father, Patrick, who has struck out alone to find King Solomon's mines.

Though Haggard's original Umbopa is not a singer, Paul breaks into song at several points in the film. British audiences always turned out to hear him *sing*, and he continued to be employed by film companies primarily as a vocalist who also could act. To create Paul's songs, Eric Maschwitz wrote lyrics that were set to the melodies of Mischa Spoliansky, who composed the musical score. (Maschwitz, a screenwriter and broadcaster, later penned the lyrics for the 1940s standards "A Nightingale Sang in Berkeley Square" and "These Foolish Things.") On May 1, 1937, Paul and Eric Ansell recorded versions of "Ho! Ho! (Wagon Song)" and "Climbing Up (Mountain Song)" at Abbey Road. Spoliansky, who also had written the score for *Sanders of the River*, benefited from Paul's performances of his songs, which became some of the composer's most memorable works. When the production

King Solomon's Mines (1937). Neither Robeson nor Sir Cedric Hardwicke is anywhere to be seen on this U.S.–release one-sheet poster, though the romantic subplot involving lovely Anna Lee and (someone *slightly* resembling) John Loder is featured prominently.

wrapped, Paul requested that a grand piano be delivered to the set, where he and Lawrence Brown performed an impromptu concert for their studio colleagues.

Part of the magic of *King Solomon's Mines* is that Paul's singing is a natural component of the Umbopa character. Unlike *The Song of Freedom* and *Big Fella*, in which he either sings professionally or as an amateur in a tavern (with the other characters openly referring to his talent), *King Solomon's Mines* presents him as slightly superhuman, and his inherent vocalizing (which is never mentioned) both comments on and improves the environment he and his companions endeavor to explore.

As in his earlier British films, Paul receives top billing, above all the Caucasian actors. The original Gaumont British print, released by General Film Distributors, opens with a credits panel listing Paul above Cedric Hardwicke and Roland Young, which then dissolves to the film's title and a credit for Haggard's novel, followed by "with Anna Lee and John Loder."

"The Diary of Alan Quartermain, White Hunter, 1881-1882" provides first-person commentary throughout the film. (The opening credits spell his surname *Quartermain*; now the diary misspells his forename as *Alan*.) The journal (being written as the film unfolds) begins, "Every word of this story is true, stamped on my memory for ever." Cedric Hardwicke's mellifluous voice also narrates the beginning of the tale, as the diary dissolves to the map showing the way to King Solomon's mines: "Like many others, well, I didn't believe in them. In those days, Africa was a land of many romantic legends and had a vast unexplored interior."

Quartermain speaks of diamonds being discovered in Kimberley, as Hardwicke's narration fades into the South African mine where hundreds of natives are toiling to extract the precious stones for the colonials who sell them to the "Cameron Brothers, Licensed Diamond Buyers." Patrick O'Brien (Arthur Sinclair), pistol in hand, bursts into the shack, accompanied by his daughter, Kathleen (Anna Lee exchanges her own Kentish accent for an Irish one; just as she would slip into Welsh for John Ford's splendid *How Green Was My Valley* four years later). The energized Irishman's hopes are dashed, however, when his "diamond" is judged a mere crystal. (Anna Lee is beautiful, believable, and a bit brazen as she stands up to any possible competitor, even a braying jackass, to which she gladly responds with a fully extended tongue!) "Kathy" and "Patsy" exit the shack, with "less than a pound" in the family kitty.

Regardless of their desperate financial situation, Patsy drapes a new shamrock necklace around the neck of his daughter, who then does the same for him, as "there were two in Mulligan's store."

"*Sure*, with a shamrock apiece, there's nothing on Earth can hold us down!" he enthuses.

"Look!" Kathy exclaims and points into the distance. Stevenson cuts to a long shot of an ox-drawn wagon, introducing Quartermain in profile as he loads in supplies. Approaching the wagon, Kathy asks for a lift, but Quartermain, pipe in mouth, doing his best to ignore them, tersely responds, "*No.*" The plucky lass explains that her father is "Bachelor of Arts, Trinity College, Dublin," but the savvy adventurer suspects he is "a down-and-out from the diggings, eh?"

"Oh, so you don't approve of us?" Kathy inquires.

"I don't approve of anyone who tears up the face of the country for greed," replies Quartermain. (The film immediately sets Haggard's protagonist apart from the colonial herd. He is in Africa for some reason other than plunder.) He remains steadfast in his refusal

until Kathy (putting on a performance that amuses him), offers, "Me father's own sister is dyin' in Kilkenny. Well, if they never meet this side of the Gates, 'tis you that will have prevented them."

During a four-week journey northward, Quartermain writes in his journal, "In spite of myself I have come to like my Irish companions who utter no complaint on this weary task." They are now "on the edge of country that has never known the foot of Man." (We must assume he actually means "White Man.")

Around the campfire one evening, Quartermain admits to Kathy that he dislikes hunting, an activity he pursues only to make "a living." A wagon bearing two unconscious passengers rolls in. Umbopa, weary from an unsuccessful trip to the north, receives water from Kathy, while a seriously ill man, Sylvestra Getto (Arthur Goullet), lies inside. Prior to meeting his maker, Getto stirs long enough to reveal that he knows the way to King Solomon's mines. On the ground beside the wagon, Patsy picks up a map, "three hundred years old," and tells Kathy that he "will seek the treasure." Quartermain's warning against such a folly goes unheeded.

The next morning, the wagon has disappeared. Quartermain offers Umbopa a job, which he refuses. "I do not work for money," he says, "and you do not go my way." Patsy has left his abandoned daughter nothing but a note, stuffed into one of her shoes. She attempts to talk Quartermain into going after him, then threatens to go "on me own two feet." Umbopa, offering to guide Kathy across the river, is accused by Quartermain of being "after diamonds."

"*White men* care for diamonds," replies Umbopa, and he is tossed out of the camp for his trouble. "That fellow is up to no good," Quartermain tells Kathy.

At Kitsfontein, Quartermain stops to collect his two big-game hunting clients, Sir Henry Curtis (John Loder) and Commander Good (Roland Young). As Kathy merrily offers the tongue she earlier had extended toward a braying ass, Umbopa sneaks up behind her, making an offer she can't refuse.

Roland Young immediately displays his subtle comic abilities as Commander Good is introduced in the nude, wearing a monocle while bathing in a section of culvert pipe. Sir Henry tips it over just before Kathy arrives, announcing that the hired hands won't carry out her orders (which she lied had been issued by Quartermain) to send the wagon "back north." Good peeks out of the pipe, only to be greeted by Kathy's assertion, "I thought it was a pig."

"Commander Good, Royal Navy," counters Sir Henry.

"*Retired*," Good adds, ducking back inside the culvert, as his companion prepares to aid Kathy in speaking to "the boys."

Later, Quartermain discusses the proposed hunting expedition with Sir Henry and Good, who explains that his companion is "the victim of a woman's wiles." Quartermain takes the news calmly, noting, "She has three hours' start, and it will be two days before I can get another team together," but then writes in his journal that he and his clients "cannot allow her to die in the desert."

A stunning long shot of the renegades' wagon climbing a steep slope cuts to a medium, low-angle close-up of Umbopa, singing as he leads the oxen along. (More than 21 minutes pass before Paul offers his first song in this charming scene. Stevenson juxtaposes the close-ups of Paul, filmed at Shepherd's Bush, with some effective footage, using a double, shot on location in Africa.) One of Umbopa's coworkers plays a harmonica and the rest hum a chorus. Kathy, stripped down to her undergarments inside the wagon, happily makes some

alterations, first to a pair of trousers, and then to her long, blonde locks, before climbing out into the driver's seat to scrutinize the map. Umbopa's final, sustained note trails off as the wagon heads down the other side of the hill.

That evening, the hunters catch up with Kathy, who is "heading for the desert in a *stolen wagon*" and, as pointed out by Commander Good, "wearing what's left of *my* trousers." She refuses to return with Quartermain, insisting that she, assisted by Umbopa, cross the desert on foot. Quartermain again orders the guide to leave, but Sir Henry steps up, offering to join them on their journey.

"I won't have it!" interjects the stubborn, independent Kathy.

"Nobody's asking you," replies Sir Henry. Blessed with the truly heroic spirit of adventure, he and Good are more than willing to strike out across the murderous sands with the girl and her quietly courageous African comrade.

"Well, I happen to be a man who respects a contract," admits their equally fearless leader. "I'm lining up with the rest of you."

"You're a good fellow, Quartermain," declares Sir Henry, extending his hand.

Following suit, Quartermain responds, "On the contrary, I'm a *fool*."

Stevenson builds the desert scenes by combining long shots filmed on location (using

King Solomon's Mines (1937). The five major players in this treasure-hunting epic (left to right): Allan Quartermain (Sir Cedric Hardwicke), Umbopa (Robeson), Sir Henry Curtis (John Loder), Commander John Good (Roland Young) and Kathleen "Kathy" O'Brien (Anna Lee) [U.S.–release lobby card].

doubles filmed at effective angles) with montages of medium shots and close-ups staged in the studio (and smoothly blended through a judicious series of dissolves). The desert vistas, against which the weary but determined characters trek (almost silently, speaking only in whispers), while accompanied by Spoliansky's atmospheric musical score, create a hypnotic quality similar to that achieved by John Ford and composer Max Steiner in the equally mes-merizing *The Lost Patrol* (1934), which depicts the travails of a doomed British army unit (commanded by Ford favorite Victor McLaglen) cast adrift in the deserts of Mesopotamia (Iraq) during World War I.

Quartermain and Umbopa discover O'Brien's abandoned wagon, with the oxen lying dead in the sand, and a note, tacked to the driver's seat, indicating that his feet are taking him northward. Kathy remains determined, refusing to believe that her father is dead; but, after 11 days in the scorching desert heat, she and her comrades are down to their last ration of water. A sudden sandstorm complicates matters further, and Umbopa orders them to lie in a cluster, face down in the sand. When the cloud of sand subsides, Umbopa raises his head and announces, "I smell *water*." Stevenson incorporates a powerful, rapidly edited montage of tight close-ups as they all frantically dig in the sand, and then thrust their faces into the dirty water for relief. Lifting his head from the sand hole, Good spies a mountain in the distance.

Refreshed from their drink, the now-hearty band climbs up the rocky slopes. Umbopa favors the group by giving voice to "Climbin' Up." The renewed vigor of his companions is multiplied by his enchanting behavior, and the scene achieves a near-spiritual quality when he stops at a summit, with a range of towering peaks as his backdrop, to sing, "Mighty mountain!" and then wait to hear his majestic voice echoed back. This sequence alone, with its gracefully achieved, quasi-biblical nuances, makes *King Solomon's Mines* a unique film, casting Paul in a somewhat mystical light.

Camping at the base of a waterfall, they rest and feast on melons. Good again enjoys an opportunity to practice physical hygiene (and Roland Young enacts the second of his two "partial-nudity" scenes), parading about sans trousers as he shaves. A group of tribes-men, armed with shields and spears, approaches, instantly contradicting Sir Henry's asser-tion that the adventurers are in "uninhabited country." The natives are stopped in their tracks, however, by an unexpected power, as Umbopa explains: "They say, 'What manner of man is this with the beautiful white legs, and grows hair on one side of his face, and can pluck his eye from his head and replace it where it grows'?" Quartermain addresses them in their own language, while Umbopa tells Good, "He's telling them you are 'white god from the skies.'"

"You mean, on account of my legs?" Good asks, modestly adding, "I never thought they were as good as all that" before playfully gesturing with his monocle.

Referring to Quartermain's performance, Kathy observes, "He couldn't have done that better if he'd been an Irishman!"

Recalling similar moments in *Sanders of the River*, these scenes contain some expected cultural clichés (and, like the earlier film, the location footage includes some female nudity during the village sequences). When Quartermain points out the soldiers' quarters and the king's hut ("Buckingham Palace and Wellington Barracks"), Good facetiously responds, "So unlike the home life of our Dear Queen, isn't it?"

Twala, the king (Robert Adams), approves of meeting "the strangers who've come to his land and claim to be gods." Garbed in a white outfit topped off by an enormous feather headdress, he humiliates a water-toting minion and then laughs loudly. Observing the inci-

King Solomon's Mines (1937). The intrepid band (left to right: Roland Young, Sir Cedric Hard-wicke, Robeson, Anna Lee and John Loder), among the Kukuana tribe, including the feather-clad King Twala (Robert Adams, background), in Robert Stevenson's rousing fantasy-adventure classic.

dent, Good asks Quartermain, "Would it do any good if I ripped off my trousers, do you think?"

Carried atop a litter by several of his men, Twala leads them to the location of the "white stones," where the ancient Gagool (Sydney Fairbrother) guards the entrance. "Through that door," Quartermain explains, "slaves brought jewels to the Queen of Sheba thousands of years ago." Umbopa warns them about becoming trapped inside the mine, and Sir Henry resorts to punching out the enraged Twala, inciting the warriors. "They've never seen a gun fired before," says Quartermain, who blasts a spear from Twala's upraised hand, sending all the tribesmen scurrying back to the village.

That evening, the tribe performs ritualistic chants and dances, while the interlopers, held in a small hut, plan their next move. Quartermain doubts that O'Brien survived, but Umbopa, quietly handing Kathy a small shamrock necklace, proves that her father did indeed reach the mines. Quartermain, insisting that he is "in charge," recommends that they leave during the night, but Umbopa orders them to stay. Quartermain possesses no authority in a country where "Gagool will put her mark upon the enemies of the king. They die like cattle." Umbopa points out, however, that "the people are weary of wickedness and blood. If there was one to lead them, they would rise up."

Towering over Cedric Hardwicke and bathed in the low-angle, chiaroscuro lighting of cinematographer Glen MacWilliams (whose impressive, five-decade career began in Hollywood in 1918), Paul makes the most of this dramatic moment as Umbopa reveals his true identity. As MacWilliams slowly dollies in to a close-up of his face, Paul (in a long take, with no edits) draws on his Shakespearean abilities to deliver a striking (yet admirably nuanced) speech:

> Once there was a king in this land, Imotu, the Loved, but he fought the wicked Gagool, who was older than the memory of the oldest man. For that, she made his brother, Twala, the One-Eyed, kill him while he slept. The wife of Imotu and the son of Imotu were driven into the desert. It is *said* they died.

Stevenson cuts to a close-up of Quartermain, who responds, "And if they didn't, the son of Imotu should be king, and *not* Twala." The scene cuts back to the close-up of Umbopa, who nods affirmatively, then to a two-shot of the men. Looking up at Umbopa, Quartermain adds, "*You* are the son of Imotu."

"*I* am the son of Imotu," he admits, drawing off his sash to reveal a large tattoo of a snake on his torso. (Stevenson now incorporates a close-up of Paul, who finally unleashes a subtle version of his trademark smile.) Outside the hut, an eavesdropper reports what he has heard to a fellow tribesman, and the chanting and dancing continues.

Several tribal elders, including Infadoos (Ecce Homo Toto, who had worked with Paul on *The Song of Freedom*), report to the hut, where Umbopa briefs them before unveiling the artwork on his belly. (This scene contributes the requisite Robeson beefcake to *King Solomon's Mines*.) The elders bow, Umbopa proudly stands before them, and Good wittily comments, "The committee seems unanimous. I always thought that fellow had a spot of royal blood in him. You don't get a snake on your stomach for nothing, you know."

With the Robeson physique lit for maximum effect by MacWilliams, Umbopa informs the adventurers, "It is agreed. Tomorrow, at the smelling out of the evildoers, they will lead the people of the Kukuana against Twala. But I need your help. And, in return, I offer you your lives, and the freedom of the mines." He promises each member of the group what he seeks, and then assures Kathy, "If your father is alive, he is in the mine." In order to succeed, Umbopa tells Quartermain that he must perform some "magic" more powerful than that of Gagool, whose killers will be sent to beat them to death.

In his next journal entry, Quartermain reveals his thoughts about the "all-powerful" Gagool, who "strikes greater terror than our guns can ever do." Apparently, Umbopa isn't superhuman, after all; hence Quartermain's assertion that "Only God can save us!"

Stevenson incorporates location footage into the scene depicting Twala's warriors readying themselves for the king's command. The sound recording by A. Birch is seamlessly blended with Michael Gordon's editing to make it appear as if the white "evildoers" are really present during the ritual. Forever cracking wise, Good asks Sir Henry, "Funny to think it's Derby Day back home, isn't it? I had a bet on Manitoba." Pulling a diary from his jacket, he turns to the entry for "Wed. 2nd June 1882," which conveniently notes that a total eclipse of the sun will be visible over South Africa at 11:15 A.M. (This device resembles a memorable event in Mark Twain's novel *A Connecticut Yankee* [1889], published four years after Haggard's *King Solomon's Mines*.)

Tension mounts as Twala watches Gagool order the savage executions of several members of the tribe, and Gagool then slowly advance toward Quartermain and company. She points to Umbopa, but, as masked, spear-wielding warriors run toward him, Quartermain

buys time by firing a shot above their heads. He leaps onto a rock, points to the sky, and, in their native tongue, explains the forthcoming "magic." The entire chanting assemblage of tribesmen surrounds him, but the sky darkens, sending them fleeing fearfully in all directions. Umbopa takes center stage at Twala's throne, raises his arms, and boldly sings, "Kukuana! Kuku-a-na!" which eventually is taken up by the tribesmen, who add their voices and drums to the chant. Soon, the sky reopens and the sunlight pours back down.

On a nearby mountainside, Twala rallies reinforcements from the Kouaki and Kukami tribes. Situated behind wooden fortifications, Quartermain, Good and Sir Henry, backed by Umbopa and his men, attempt to stave off a hail of spears from Twala's army. (Shades of the Alamo, with its small band of volunteers holding out against an enormous, vastly superior force, permeate this rousing battle scene. The outcome, however, is quite different.) Twala's forces trample down the wall of wood, and brutal hand-to-hand combat ensues. Sir Henry emerges victorious from an axe duel with Twala, bringing an end to the slaughter.

Kathy has fled to the mine in search of her father, whom she discovers, resting his broken leg atop a peninsular formation beside a river of molten lava. Quartermain props open the entrance, and the three Englishmen rush into the steamy, volcanic cavern. Gagool sets fire to the wooden pillars supporting the mountain but is crushed to death in the ensuing

King Solomon's Mines (1937). Sir Henry Curtis (John Loder) emerges victorious from an axe duel with King Twala (Robert Adams), bringing an end to the slaughter [U.S.–release lobby card].

King Solomon's Mines (1937). Though top-billed in the film, Robeson falls beneath Sir Cedric Hardwicke and Anna Lee on much of the advertising. He does at least *appear* on this U.S.–release insert poster, however.

avalanche. Lamenting the loss of the diamonds, Good is corrected by a grateful O'Brien, who discloses, "I've a fortune here in me pocket. There's enough here for *all* of us."

Trapped by the rockslide, they quietly accept their fate, until the voice of Umbopa, echoing through the cavern, signals their valiant rescue. With the volcano "burying for all eternity beneath a mountain of fire and stone the secrets of King Solomon's mines," they just escape with their lives and O'Brien's pocketful of diamonds. Quartermain writes, "I am glad. There is nothing to keep us here and tomorrow we must set forth — never to return."

Umbopa, now garbed in kingly clothes, provides a retinue of 100 men to lead them back across the desert. "Go, now my friends," he tells them, "and, in time, remember how we stood, shoulder to shoulder, in the Great Battle." Two powerful images (a two-shot of Umbopa and Quartermain, and a long shot showing them with the entire assemblage) feature the warm handshake between African and Englishman. With his people standing behind him, Umbopa sings "Climbin' Up." The scene dissolves to the parade of men and one woman ascending the mountainside, as he concludes his powerful performance. The film ends with images of the trekkers silhouetted against the sky, Umbopa raising his shield and spear, and his people faithfully following suit.

Actor James Earl Jones said:

> Paul Robeson was a gorgeous singer, so that's what they had him do a lot of the time. The movie would *stop*. [They] are huffing and puffing in the desert, and he's singing like he's entertaining them ... but he did it with such a *game face*."[2]

Perhaps Paul's "game face" was his *knowing* that *King Solomon's Mines* was something more than a fantasy-adventure intended merely to entertain. The film (like its literary source) contains sociopolitical elements (subtle undertones that blend with the narrative) that set it apart from his previous, more straightforward screen efforts. Paul's performance style, too, is more understated than in many of his other films (an

impressive achievement, considering that he delivers treacherously difficult, archaic, literary dialogue in a perfectly natural manner). To preserve Umbopa's mysterious persona, he consistently uses subtle facial expressions and gestures and doesn't fully unleash his charismatic smile until late in the film. (Had conditions existed for Paul to make more adventure films during the Golden Age, he may have become the more physically powerful, African American equivalent of Errol Flynn or Tyrone Power.)

Cedric Hardwicke's sensitive portrayal of the tolerant Quartermain created one of the most admirable white men in the entire Robeson cinematic canon. As the capable Kathy, Anna Lee interpreted one of 1930s cinema's most competent heroines (the antidote to the ultimate damsel-in-distress scream machine, Fay Wray, in *King Kong*). In Britain, Paul received top billing; but in the United States, he was listed third, behind Hardwicke and Lee, on the advertising materials.

One of Golden Age cinema's most adept directors of adventure tales, Robert Stevenson, aided by a witty script and Michael Gordon's sharp yet unobtrusive editing, created a brisk pace to match the sparkling performances of his excellent cast. Though his combination of authentic African location footage and staged studio material is obvious, this strategy was unavoidable, given the constraints of a limited budget and the technical facilities available in the British film industry at the time. These limitations are more than offset by the raging battle scenes and impressive special effects during the closing mine sequence.

King Solomon's Mines was also adapted for the screen in 1950 by MGM, a studio known for its high-budget remakes that prove popular with the public but stray radically from the original source material. Starring the romantic duo of Stewart Granger as Quartermain and Deborah Kerr as the wholly non-literary "Elizabeth Curtis," MGM's Technicolor version (a forerunner to the studio's equally inferior *Show Boat* remake of 1951) greatly diminishes the role of Umbopa (Siriaque), making the original all the more significant for Paul's presence.

Greener Pastures
Jericho (1937)

Of all his films, *Jericho* was always my father's favorite.

— Paul Robeson, Jr.[1]

Credits: Director: Thornton Freeland; Producer: Walter Futter; Screenplay: George Barraud, Robert N. Lee, Peter Ruric; Based on a story by Walter Futter; Director of Photography: John W. Boyle; Editor: Edward B. Jarvis; Musical Score and Direction: Van Phillips; Original Songs: Michael Carr, Jimmy Kennedy; Art Director: Edward Carrick; Assistant Director: Donald Wilson; Sound Recordist: A. S. Ross; Presenter: Max Schach; Sound System: Western Electric Noiseless; Musical Publishers: Peter Maurice Music Co., Ltd.; a Capitol Buckingham Film Production; British Board of Film Censors Certificate "U"; Released by General Film Distributors (U.K.) on August 23, 1937, and as *Dark Sands* by Record Pictures (U.S.) on August 16, 1938; Length: 6,996 feet; Running Time: 77 minutes.

Cast: Paul Robeson (Corporal Jericho Jackson), Henry Wilcoxon (Captain Mack), Wallace Ford (Mike Clancy), Princess Kouka (Gara), John Laurie (Hassan), James Carew (Major J. R. Barnes), Lawrence Brown (Private Face), Rufus Fennell (Sergeant Gamey), Ike Hatch (Private Tag), Frank Cram (Colonel Lake), Frank Cochrane (Agouba), George Barraud, Frederick Cooper, Henry Aubin (Explorers), Eugene Cozier (Mick Jackson), Charles Farrell (Sergeant on Guard), Peter Gawthorne (Court-martial President), Danny Green (Sergeant), Eslanda Robeson (Tribal Princess, footage deleted).

Essie, once again acting as her husband's manager, negotiated a contract for a major dramatic role in a film set in Africa; but this time, like his character in *The Song of Freedom*, Paul's work would actually take him to the continent of his ancestors. Capitol Buckingham Film Corporation and director Thornton Freeland cast him as Jericho Jackson, an African American medical student drafted into the U.S. Army during World War I. After accidentally killing a sergeant during his rescue of men trapped aboard a troop ship, Jackson is court-martialed and sentenced to death.

Born in Hope, North Dakota, Thornton Freeland (1898–1987) was involved in show business on both sides of the Atlantic, first as a child actor on the stage, then as an assistant cameraman at Vitagraph before working his way up to director on United Artists' *Three Live Ghosts* (1929), starring Robert Montgomery and Joan Bennett. For the next two decades, he directed 26 films in the United States (including the classic RKO musical *Flying Down to Rio* [1933], featuring the first screen pairing of Fred Astaire and Ginger Rogers) and Britain (*Brewster's Millions* [1935], costarring Sydney Fairbrother, who went on to play Gagool in *King Solomon's Mines*; and *Accused* [1936], costarring Douglas Fairbanks, Jr., and Dolores del Rio).

Paul's involvement in the production of *Jericho* included his many suggestions for rewrites, including transforming the original tragic ending into the vindication of the black

hero, making Jericho Jackson a non-stereotypical, triumphant character. To add to the "progressive" content of the film, the screenplay provided a comical white sidekick (Wallace Ford) to assist Paul's black protagonist. Paul Robeson, Jr., recalled:

> He had enormous control of all aspects of the film when he did *Jericho*. It was shot in Egypt, where they really had control over what they were going to do. Why [did] my father believe that *Jericho* was the best film he ever did, bar none? Well, number one, the *image*. This is a black soldier in World War I who was portrayed as a genuine hero, because at the time, in 1937, it was forbidden in American film ... to portray a black male as a hero. Forbidden, period. There was no law, but there *was*. This was a wise, good, self-sacrificing black male image, who kept the troops' spirits up. Then, in a great crisis, he rescues two dozen trapped men from drowning. The second [reason] was that it had a really solid series of messages. There are these really peacenik lines about "Here I am, in this army, which is about killing people, and I'm out saving people's lives." And he has this white sidekick, and throughout the film ... there is this wonderful exploitation of the white man's stereotype of a black man *reversed*.[2]

Location work was done in the Egyptian Sahara, where five crew members trekked 2,500 miles into the desert to shoot footage of the Great Salt Caravan for one of the film's most important scenes. Home to the Kanuri, Toubou, Hausa and Taureg tribes, the oasis village of Bilma was the destination of the Saharan route traveled by the caravan of men and 15,000 camels. The completed sequence, edited to a length of 500 feet, became the first filmed record of this annual trans–Saharan event.

Another scene required a shot of a flock of sheep grazing contentedly at the foot of a cluster of palm trees. After transporting fresh sod from Cairo to the desert location and purchasing three dozen sheep from a local village, Thornton Freeland, making certain that the animals had only been fed a minimal amount the previous day, turned them loose on the thick turf and rolled the cameras. According to General Film Distributors' official press-book, "The sheep looked round at each other in a dazed and doubting way — they had never seen grass like that before and they weren't risking it! They filed slowly off the emerald turf to the more familiar sand and fell ravenously on a few yellow and withered blades."[3]

While scouting potential village locations in the Sudan, producer Walter Futter discovered Princess Kouka, a native of El Fasher, where her father reigned as chieftain. Futter, captivated by her beauty, explained to the chief that he wished to cast her in a leading role opposite Paul Robeson in a film to be completed in England, but the concerned father initially was against allowing his high-born daughter to leave her native environment. Kouka, who had gone to the cinema during a previous trip to England, was fond of imitating people and excited enough by the offer to threaten a prolonged fast until her father relented. Though fluent in her native dialect and French (which she had learned from a governess brought to El Fasher from Cairo), Kouka spoke no English. However, Futter was so impressed by her personality and talent for mime that he decided to take the risk of casting her as Gara, a Taureg shepherdess who becomes Jericho's wife, hoping that she could convincingly deliver the dialogue phonetically.

Lawrence Brown landed a small role, Private Face, who appears in the opening troopship sequence with Jericho, but his footage was shot in the studio, precluding him from joining Paul and Essie on the African trip. Essie was excited to be cast in another small role, as the wife of a Taureg chief (but her footage apparently ended up on the cutting-room floor during post-production).

During the Egyptian shoot, which began in February 1937, Paul and Essie lodged in

Cairo, only a few miles from their major desert location. Two months earlier, the Anglo-Egyptian Treaty of 1936 had been ratified, resulting in a British withdrawal that left only 10,000 troops and auxiliary personnel behind to protect the Suez Canal and environs. This agreement between His Majesty, George VI, King of the United Kingdom, and 17-year-old King Farouk I of Egypt and Sudan was intended to last for a period of 20 years. Paul and Essie enjoyed the local autonomy created by this indirect colonial rule, a situation that set the region apart from other African nations under European control. *Show Boat* had been a hit in Cairo, so Paul was welcomed wherever he went.

While touring the Great Pyramid of Giza with costar Henry Wilcoxon, Paul walked into the center of the inner tomb, which had been constructed by the ancient Egyptians nearly 4,500 years earlier. As Wilcoxon coughed, they noticed the incredible reverberative qualities of the structure, prompting a musical experiment during which Paul sang each note of a harmonic triad in quick succession. The resulting echoes created a full chord that Paul followed up (in German) with the stunning aria "O Isis and Osiris" from Mozart's *The Magic Flute.* The pressbook reported, "Henry Wilcoxon says that that was one of the most thrilling moments of his life — standing there in the heart of the Great Pyramid listening to the world's grandest bass voice — singing for his exclusive benefit."[4]

Back in England, the company completed the remaining scenes at Pinewood Studios in Buckinghamshire. Most involved interior shooting, but one additional exterior sequence required fabricating a desert settlement. A circus in Southend-on-Sea in Essex supplied the camels, while Arabian extras were hired at the East End docks.

Paul recorded three original songs written for *Jericho* by Michael Carr and Jimmy Kennedy. At Abbey Road on April 29, 1937, he cut "My Way" and "Golden River" with an orchestra and chorus conducted by Clifford Greenwood, while Van Phillips took up the baton on July 2 for "Deep Desert."

During an interview with a reporter for the *Philadelphia Tribune,* Paul revealed:

> I'm sick and tired of caricatures.... I know where I'm going. Each picture progresses toward my ultimate goal. Hollywood wouldn't do anything but *Show Boat* for me ... [but it] is responsible for my present role ... in *Jericho.* I refused a fortune for *Uncle Tom's Cabin* after that, and if I did another *Show Boat* I would deserve any amount of criticism.[5]

(If actually planned by one of the Hollywood studios, the version of *Uncle Tom's Cabin* mentioned by Paul was never produced.) Capitol Buckingham Film's official publicity, referring to him as "the most outstanding success story in the entertainment world — and most other spheres of life," declared:

> Paul Robeson: his career carries with it implications unique among film stars. He is today the most famous Negro in the world. The position is an honourable one, but it is burdened with responsibilities. His own people look upon him as an example — his success reflects honour on his race; in the same way any failure he might have would be keenly felt by them. Gifted with an infinite capacity for study he has compared the Greek, Latin, Hebrew and Chinese languages with two African dialects he has learned, to satisfy himself that the African Negroes had a language that compared in structure, subtlety and intellect with other ancient tongues. This proved to him that the Negroes had behind them a cultural background. One day he wants to devote the whole of his time to research work in this cause.[6]

It seems natural that Paul, in seeking heroic characterizations for black actors, eventually would fall into a World War I role. Following the success of Universal's *All Quiet on the Western Front* (1930), the first major anti-war epic of the sound era, the 1930s cinema,

Jericho (1937). The front cover of General Film Distributors' official British-release pressbook features Robeson as the powerful Jericho Jackson in both his incarnations: World War I soldier, saluting his superior officer (Henry Wilcoxon), and Chief of the Taureg tribe.

in both Hollywood and Europe, became saturated with films, both dramatic and comic, about the Great War and its aftermath.

No stranger to World War I roles, Wallace Ford (1898–1966), born Samuel Jones Grundy in Bolton, Lancashire, suffered through a harrowing childhood in England and Canada, including brutal stints in an orphanage and 17 foster homes. At age 11, young Grundy ran away to join a vaudeville troupe in Winnipeg, where he remained for three years, until he and a friend, actually named Wallace Ford, tramped and rode the rails into the United States. When his pal was tragically killed by a railroad car, Grundy assumed "Wallace Ford" as his stage name while seeking acting roles with repertory companies. He eventually became a versatile and prolific character actor, primarily in Hollywood, where he was a favorite of John Ford, who cast him in 13 films, including the classics *The Lost Patrol* (1934), *The Whole Town's Talking* (1935) and *The Informer* (1935). Back in his homeland in 1937, he reported to Pinewood, where he enjoyed working with Paul during the *Jericho* shoot. Like Paul, Ford had a personal crusade of his own, as reported by the studio:

> It is the strangest ambition you would expect to find in the man who has built up an enviable reputation as a screen "tough guy." He feels that religion has been allowed to lose its significance and importance the world over. He would like to devote all his time to propagating a general recall to faith. "I don't root for any particular religion," he explained. "I root for them all. I simply believe that everyone would feel happier and would get more out of life if they had something to believe in implicitly."[7]

(Considering the hellish reality of Ford's early life, his adoption of this philosophy had a positive effect in his specific case. Every year at Christmas, he mailed a large donation check to the Dr. Barnardo's Homes, a British charity organization for orphaned and needy children, where he had lived briefly before being sent to Canada.)

Born in Dominica, British West Indies, Henry Wilcoxon (1905–1984), following film extra work and a four-year stint with the Birmingham Repertory Company, became a close friend of Cecil B. DeMille, who cast him in "historical" leads (Marc Antony in *Cleopatra* [1934] and King Richard the Lionheart in *The Crusades* [1935]) and supporting roles in six major epics. (Wilcoxon later served as associate producer on the Oscar-winning DeMille extravaganzas *The Greatest Show on Earth* [1952] and *The Ten Commandments* [1956].) At age 31, he brought his classically handsome, to-the-epic-born charisma to *Jericho*, in which he gives a performance reminiscent of Laurence Olivier (with whom he would costar in London Films' *The Lady Hamilton* [1938], directed and produced by Alexander Korda, the following year). When interviewed on the set of *Jericho*, he said:

> Obviously, one can't go on playing youthful and romantic parts all one's life and every actor should have something to fall back on. I have always been interested in the process of making films and never missed an opportunity of learning something about directing. Eventually I want to concentrate on this work.[8]

(On December 8, 1941, just 20 minutes after President Franklin Roosevelt declared war on Japan, Wilcoxon enlisted in the U.S. Coast Guard, earning the rank of Lieutenant during a five-year hitch.)

Wilcoxon had the demeanor of a cool-headed, gentlemanly military officer, whether in *reel* or real life; but in the opening credits of *Jericho*, he is billed below the title, while pacifist Paul, with his name in larger type, towers above it. Customary for a supporting sidekick, Wallace Ford lands third in the cast listing.

At the film's start, aboard a troop ship bound for France, a group of African American

Jericho (1937). This advertisement included in the British pressbook features Robeson and his costars, Henry Wilcoxon, Wallace Ford and Princess Kouka.

soldiers are below decks, relaxing in their bunks, crying over Dear John mail, shooting dice, and requesting tunes from the harmonica player. Private Face (Lawrence Brown) has an anxiety attack, just as Captain Mack (Henry Wilcoxon) descends from the deck to cheer up the troops. A far better mood enhancer reaches their ears when Private Jericho Jackson launches into a song.

In an innovative introduction, Paul is not seen but *heard*, as the sequence cuts from Mack to a position between two rows of bunks. The camera smoothly tracks between the bunks, as the men lean forward to hear "Green Pastures" (and the viewer is literally led to Jericho). Private Jackson is just taking it easy, lying flat on his back in his bunk as he happily sings, beaming that big Robeson smile as he hits the line, "Brother, are you walkin' my way?" (Paul's ebullient performance here is quite an emotional shift from the reserved one he had just given during the majority of *King Solomon's Mines*.) All the brothers collectively answer by joining in on the chorus; after they repeat the lyrical question, Jericho rises from his bunk to sing the bridge, walking down the aisle toward the camera as it tracks back to its original position. Jericho sits next to the troubled Private Face, concluding the song as Mack (unnoticed by the men) smiles and walks back up to the deck.

Mack promotes Jericho to corporal, claiming, "Much as I'd like to keep you with me, I'll try to get you transferred to the medical corps, where you belong — make some use of that three years' training." A German submarine is spotted off the port bow, and a torpedo strikes them broadside. As sea water floods in, many of the soldiers panic, and Private Face jumps overboard. Jericho attempts to free a group of trapped men but is ordered to vacate by the troublesome Sergeant Gamey (Rufus Fennell), whom he shoves out of the way. Falling to the deck, the sergeant accidentally strikes his head on a steam valve. Jericho frees the men and drags the injured Gamey topside before noticing that he has died.

At the A.E.F. Camp Genicourt in Bordeaux, Major J. R. Barnes (James Carew) testifies about the torpedo incident, claiming, "I don't exactly know how the sergeant lost his life." Private Tag (Ike Hatch), however, innocently describes in great detail how Jericho "popped Gamey right in the kisser."

"Corporal Jackson, is Private Tag's evidence substantially correct?" inquires the Court-martial President (Peter Gawthorne).

"Yes, sir," responds Jericho, "but...." Quickly interrupted, he is not allowed to offer his own explanation, and is accused of being "guilty of two of the most heinous offenses known in the army: disobedience of orders and striking your superior officer." Captain Mack stands up to support Jericho (accurately describing the character *and* the actor):

> At college he had an excellent record as a scholar and athlete. And as a soldier, his conduct has always been exemplary. Another thing is, sir, he is very popular with the men. So the moral effect on the Negro troops in prosecuting Jackson for an essentially heroic act would be — well, would be very bad, to say the least.

Accused of bias, Mack is ignored, and Jericho is arrested for murder and condemned to death. During a YMCA Christmas concert held on December 24, 1917 (at which "the gang" curiously performs the Stephen Foster plantation song, "My Old Kentucky Home," originally titled "Poor Uncle Tom, Good Night"), Mack and Barnes discuss their futile attempt to free Jericho. "Headquarters turned down our appeal for clemency," Mack reveals, "although every officer in the battalion signed it."

In a last-ditch effort, Barnes agrees to cable the Secretary of War. "We'll try it," he says. "They can't no more than break us." (The 47th U.S. Secretary of War, Newton D. Baker, served Woodrow Wilson from 1916 until the end of the president's second term in 1921 and was responsible for creating the first national military draft.)

Locked in his cell, sitting with his head in his hands, Jericho gladly stands to attention and salutes Mack, thanking him for his efforts (and dramatically delivering dialogue obviously crafted for Paul):

Did I want to learn how to kill? No, but they taught me and taught me, until my arms ached, with sticking steel into sand bags. These hands that I want to use to heal, to *save* life, to *give* life, turned into hands for killing. I didn't want to kill that rat, Gamey. I only wanted to help.

Mack accepts personal responsibility for allowing Jericho to join his comrades at the concert. Wartime and clichéd ethnic elements blend as a tap-dancing troop's routine to "It's a Long Way to Tipperary" precedes Jericho's performance of "Holy Night" (an alternate version of "Silent Night"). The concluding lyric, "Sleep in heavenly peace," and the beginning of a preacher's prayer provide effective counterpoint as Jericho seizes a guard's pistol and escapes into the streets of Bordeaux, where he overpowers a tall African resident and steals his clothes. Dressed in overcoat and fez, the incognito Jericho speaks French to a search party and then sings as he calmly walks away. Demonstrating cunning inventiveness, he quickly commandeers a small fishing boat, rows out to a schooner, tosses a drunken sailor into the smaller craft, raises the mainsail, and weighs anchor for wherever the wind will take him.

Accused of gross negligence and collusion, Mack is arrested and confined to his quarters. In the wide-open sea, Mike Clancy (Wallace Ford), an American deserter, climbs out of a hatch, calls Jericho "Froggy," and asks about the fate of the captain. Framed in a full two-shot, against the background of the sea, Paul impressively stands a head taller than Ford as Jericho appoints himself skipper. "I guess you're right," replies the slightly stunned Clancy.

While sharing bread the next morning, Jericho admits he's "that tough murderer the MPs were looking for." As to their unknown destination, he tells his new companion, "The chaplain said that the wise men found truth and righteousness in the desert." Meanwhile, Mack is "dishonorably dismissed" from military service and sentenced to five years in prison.

Jericho and Mike beach their sinking craft on the North African coast, happily sharing dates and munching bananas as they ride mules through a desert village. "Well, we're on our way, *boy*," Jericho tells him. (While the diminutive Ford is well matched to his brown animal, Paul looks like a giant atop his white one.) Soon, they are reduced to traveling on foot. In a clever series of close-ups, their army-issue shoes dissolve to sandals and then to bare feet as they continue to tramp across the burning sands.

The two American entrepreneurs open a "free" sideshow featuring "the world's most famous strongman, The Mighty Jericho!" but beat the retreat when an official inquires about their papers. The two fugitives quickly mount camels and head back into the desert. (In a glaring lapse of continuity, Paul's robe changes from white to black when the scene cuts to the camel bazaar. This time, however, Paul rides a brown animal; and Ford, a white one.) The ensuing escape on camelback is a novel twist on the classic adventure-film chase.

At a Taureg oasis, they encounter the lovely Gara (Princess Kouka), tending to her flock of sheep. (Though the scenes involving "camel behavior" are very realistic, there were obviously several animal changes during the filming of the journey, which lasts only 45 seconds on screen. By the time they reach the oasis, Paul's animal is white.) Gara is a bit puzzled about Mike, who agreeably bears the brunt of his companion's attempts to impress the lady. "Take care of the camels, *boy*!" orders a grinning Jericho.

Gara's brother, Hassan (John Laurie), rides in with two other men, speaking of their search for a physician to examine the chief, who was thrown from a camel. Mike talks up Jericho as "The World's Greatest Doctor," which Hassan declares "may be the will of Allah."

At the fortress of the Taureg chief, the "doctor" tends to his broken leg. At this point, Mike considers himself one half of a couple, using the plural pronouns "us" and "we." Should Jericho's medical attention allow their host to walk again, they will be given unlimited "shelter and sustenance."

"Atta boy, Sheikh!" proclaims Mike, enthusiastically slapping the injured man's wooden leg splint before telling his friend, "You hear that, *Jerry*? We're going to settle down for once."

Jericho and Gara tend to the tribe, using quinine to treat malaria and dreaming of building a hospital, while Mike has the time of his life enacting military "maneuvers" with Hassan. On November 11, 1918, the Great War ends with the signing of the armistice between the Allied and German forces. A montage of newspaper articles dissolves away the years, and on June 15, 1922, ex–Captain Mack, "a model prisoner," is released from Leavenworth Prison in Kansas. Before he exits the prison, the warden informs him that "Jackson vanished completely. Not a trace of him has ever been found."

Having earned his freedom, Mack vows, "I'm going to get that man if it takes me the rest of my life." Another montage of news stories shows the obsessed ex-soldier tramping endlessly, eventually to New York, where a local headline reports, "Ex–army Captain's Search for a Negro in the World's Hay Stack Takes Him to Europe." (This line, probably unintentionally, reads uncomfortably close to "a nigger in the woodpile.") Similar articles in London, Berlin and Paris fail to aid Mack, who returns to Bordeaux, to conduct research in the local newspaper archives.

Jericho has added the role of diplomat to his many responsibilities, calling a summit of tribal chiefs to form "one mighty caravan, safe, at least, from *each other*" while obtaining their yearly supply of salt. Too old to make the trip, the Taureg chief appoints Jericho as the "brave and strong leader." A stunning desert location shot, including thousands of men and camels amidst the dunes and palm trees, opens "The Gathering of the Great Salt Caravan," as proclaimed by an on-screen title. Jericho watches as Mike, using a nanny goat as an incentive, conducts a series of races between two of its offspring. Soon, a sentry arrives to report the approach of three white men "in petrol wagons" (Frederick Cooper, Henry Aubin, and screenwriter George Barraud) who are on a scientific expedition. Jericho, now called "Chief" by Mike, gives them permission to join the caravan.

While encamped that evening, the English explorers spin a Big Band recording of "Green Pastures." Jericho is attracted by the music, sees a newspaper story marking the sixth anniversary of the armistice (November 11, 1924), and his conscience begins to weigh on him. Instinctively humming along with the tune, he realizes that he may have blown his cover and returns to his own tent. The next morning, he climbs to the summit of a high sand dune to perform the song (accompanied by a full orchestra).

Paul strikes a dashing figure in his full chief's regalia, as Ford continues his shtick with the kid goats. A scout rides in to report enemy raiders in the desert, prompting Jericho to order 200 horses and fighting men assembled for action, "to clear the way" for the caravan. The film reaches epic proportions as impressive footage of the raiders on camelback, riding through a desert canyon as Jericho's men fire from the dunes on either side, is inter-cut with closer shots of him gesturing orders, his troops blasting away, and reinforcements emerging from hiding places in the sand to attack the enemy from within their circle of camels.

When one of the raiders sneaks up to stab Jericho in the back, Mike lunges at him, causing the knife to penetrate the enemy's chest. "Hey, that was a close shave," he reports

to his friend, just as he is shot in the back by another raider, who is quickly dispatched by Jericho. The little white man, attired in full Taureg regalia, says, "I'm okay" as he dies, clasping hands with the black man whose life he has just saved. (This is a unique and significant scene in Paul's cinematic career, a powerful solidification of the racial role reversal depicted by the two characters throughout the film.)

The explorers, equipped with a camera and tripod, stand atop a high cliff, filming the spectacle in the canyon below. Cinematographer John W. Boyle executes a slow, leftward pan to show the sweeping expanse being traversed by the caravan as it continues on its way, now unhampered by raiders. The next scene opens with a train of camels, impressively silhouetted against the sky as they trek down a sandy slope, dissolving to a close-up of Jericho running the sand through his hands as he sings "Deep Desert." The camera pulls back to a medium shot, showing him, in full dress, surrounded by tribesmen, with the trekking camels still visible in the background. (This is one of the most memorable Robeson cinematic images.) This striking, soothing sequence fades out as Jericho concludes his serenade and the camels continue their march into the setting sun.

In London, Mack enters the Vogue Theatre, where he watches a newsreel about the Great Salt Caravan (a "documentary" consisting primarily of the authentic footage shot on

Jericho (1937). Corporal Jericho Jackson ("Singing Star Supreme!" Paul Robeson) cradles his dying white sidekick, Mike Clancy (Wallace Ford), after the faithful little man saves his life. This interracial role-reversal relationship, a seriocomic highlight, was cinematically groundbreaking [British-release lobby card].

location in Egypt). In a fine example of narrative economy and cinematic novelty, Thornton Freeland, rather than depicting the explorers at work during the actual caravan event, saved this subplot to use as a plot revelation, a "film within the film" to be witnessed simultaneously by both the newsreel-watching Mack *and* the viewers of *Jericho*. The typically "witty" commentary of the British narrator includes references to "the leader of the trek, a giant Negro ... attended by a white lieutenant, an American" as Jericho is seen, riding happily atop his white camel, and then accepting the "portable gramophone" from the adventurer-filmmakers. Mack walks out of the theater, while the narrator concludes, "And it seems incredible that the outside world would have known nothing of this epic journey across the limitless desert but for this photographic record." (Interestingly, the medium Paul used in an attempt to improve real-life conditions has the opposite effect on his character in the film.)

Mack seeks out his old army buddy, J. R. Barnes, now employed by London's Norwood American Aircraft, to secure a plane for a flight to the Sahara, his only chance for gaining a "complete pardon and honorable discharge." At this point, Jericho and Gara have a baby son, whom Daddy regales with "Short'nin' Bread." (Favored by Paul Robeson, Jr., during childhood, and often mistakenly identified as a plantation song, this composition by James Whitcomb Riley was first published in 1900.) His lullaby is interrupted by the sound of an aircraft, which lands just outside the desert fortress.

"Captain Mack!" shouts Jericho as he runs to meet his old commanding officer, but his extended hand is refused.

"I've come to take you back!" Mack replies, but his attempt to draw a pistol is halted by Jericho's guards.

Told the truth about the court-martial and imprisonment, Jericho expresses his regret for circumstances he didn't foresee and then introduces Mack to Gara and their son, Mike (the namesake of his departed, heroic pal), whose appearance begins to melt away the ex-captain's years of obsessive hatred. While Mack sleeps, a group of tribesmen conspires to kill him, but Jericho helps him escape to the plane. As the frantic mob runs out to stop them, Jericho insists on going back to "take what's coming" to him, but Mack deliberately stalls the engine, asking his former comrade to get out and swing the prop. With the prop engaged, Mack shouts, "So long, Jericho!" as he speeds toward his takeoff into the desert sky. An orchestral version of "Green Pastures" fills the soundtrack as the happy couple returns to put their baby to bed.

The ending posed an enormous challenge to Paul's editorial control. Paul Jr. revealed:

> He had one step short of final cut, which was *veto* of a final cut which was intolerable to him. Unprecedented in film at that time, anywhere. No film star, not even Greta Garbo, ever had that much control of a film — and it came into play in only one part of the film, and that was the ending.
>
> Now, the rule was if a black man kills anybody, he's got to die in the end. He cannot go off into the sunset. The ending that the director wanted to get past the American censor had Dad being talked into going back to stand trial with this lieutenant. Dad looked at the ending and said, "No way." He helped the guy escape but he stayed there and lived "happily ever after." So they shot that, and the director came back and said, "I can't get it past the censor."
>
> Dad said, "Okay, I've got a solution." So, they're hightailing it out to the plane and so, since the lieutenant has to pilot it, Dad has to start up the propeller and then jump in. Of course, the chief's people get wind of this, and so they're out to just take this guy and kill him, and get their chief back. At that moment, the lieutenant has second thoughts and

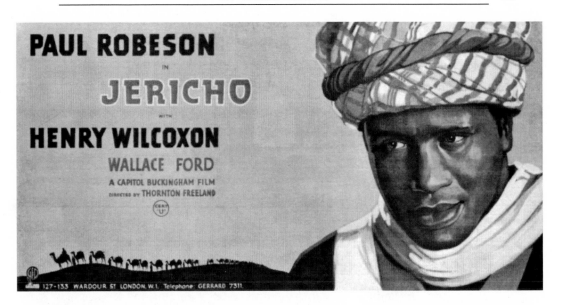

Jericho (1937). This billboard-size, 48-sheet poster from the original British release attracted many a London filmgoer to see the performer General Film Distributors referred to as the "most distinguished representative of a world-scattered ancient race" [from the British-release pressbook].

takes off, leaving Dad there, and you don't know, whose decision was that? And that's the ending, and it got by.[9]

General Film Distributors' publicity campaign included several large posters with striking artwork of Paul, Henry Wilcoxon and Wallace Ford. The pressbook encouraged exhibitors to promote, "first and foremost ... the value of the star, whose brilliant singing and acting talent has brought him fame throughout the world." The enormous, billboard-size 48-sheet, graced with a huge head shot of Paul in his Taureg regalia, also featured a silhouette of camels crossing a desert vista during the Great Salt Caravan, which "could be cut out and placed above the entrance to [the] theatre where they cannot fail to attract great attention and interest." To top off the exploitation, theater owners were also prompted to have their "attendants ... dress in flowing white robes, easily improvised out of sheets, and have their skins slightly darkened."[10]

Aside from Paul and Wallace Ford, the *Jericho* cast is a mixed bag. Though it was a common practice for Caucasians to portray all sorts of "ethnic" characters, the British actors playing Saharan nomads alongside Princess Kouka (who struggles valiantly with her phonetic English) are decidedly out of place. Even the dependable Henry Wilcoxon cannot disguise his graceful British diction while playing an American officer.

Paul was delighted with the opportunity to play an epic black character, but critics faulted the "average" story and the unrealistic use of the song sequences. At this point, he vowed to avoid any further roles that depicted blacks as simple caricatures, taking his acting career in a more political direction as he sought exclusively to portray characters with only positive qualities. He also began to voice his preference for performing on film, rather than on recordings and the stage.

Paul soon changed his mind, however. Back in London, he wasn't receiving the types of film offers he sought, so he returned to the stage by joining the founders of the Unity

Theatre, a British trade union project located at St. Judes Hall, near the St. Pancras district in the borough of Camden, where he trod the boards without pay to further the workers' cause. Originally formed in London's East End as the Workers' Theatre Movement, Unity staged "documentary pieces" based on current social and political issues for a working-class audience. The actors' improvisational performances eventually came under fire from the Lord Chamberlain's Office, which had the legal right, under the Theatres Act of 1843, to approve all scripts.

World events (racist and anti-labor violence in the U.S.; fascist aggression waged by Hitler in Europe, Mussolini in Africa, Japan in China, and in the Spanish Civil War; and independence movements in Africa and India) spurred Paul further toward the communist-led left, as represented by the Soviets' support of the anti-colonialist cause. Paul addressed the U.S. race problem in the New York publication *Sunday Worker*:

> If other young Negroes got the chance, they'd outstrip me a thousand times. But how can they with this damned system of discrimination plugging up every hole of opportunity? And then after they get it, they can't get any recognition for what they really achieve.[11]

Paul, with Essie and Paul Jr., returned to the U.S.S.R., hoping to become involved in film adaptations of *Othello* and *Stevedore*. He also revealed that he had turned down an offer from David O. Selznick to play a supporting role as a slave in the pro–Confederate soap opera *Gone with the Wind*. He spent more time with Sergei Eisenstein at the director's country home, where they discussed cinematic ideas in a makeshift studio. *Bezhin Meadow*, a film about rural collectivism, had been suspended by the Soviet government, so Eisenstein, speculating that he was now "semi-retired," informed Paul that their film collaborations might not materialize as planned.

Eisenstein actually was secretly continuing the *Bezhin* shoot, under the cover of a new title, "Pavel Morozov," on his estate. Young Paul Jr. observed the cast and crew while his father continued his discussions with the director. The lad later watched Paul and Sergei perambulating the grounds, apparently talking about the events in Stalin's latest purge.[12]

On May 1, President Franklin D. Roosevelt's signing of the 1937 Neutrality Act forbade loans and the sale of arms to both sides in the Spanish Civil War. Francisco Franco's fascists, supported by Hitler and Mussolini, were gaining ground against the Republicans, who were not equally backed by Stalin, a fact ignored by Paul as he jotted down his thoughts of the situation: "This is OUR STRUGGLE, and if we allow Republican Spain to suffer needlessly, we will ourselves suffer as deeply."[13]

On June 24, Paul took the stage of London's Albert Hall in a benefit concert for the Spanish Republic. His performance for 6,000 patrons was broadcast worldwide and raised $8,000 in only 20 minutes. When he sang "Ol' Man River," he received enormous applause for abandoning the defeatist concluding lyrics for his own powerful improvisation: "I keeps laughin' instead of cryin'; I must keep fightin' until I'm dyin'." Three days later, when he attended a meeting at London's Kingsway Hall welcoming Indian National Congress leader Pandit Jawaharlal Nehru back from a visit to Spain, he said:

> We in black America and other parts of the world have closely watched the Indian struggle and have been conscious of its importance to us. The struggle for an enlightened and progressive European Democracy and the Colonial struggle for Democratic Freedom are interdependent and inseparable. The emergence of leaders like Nehru give the lie to tales of a backward people, of a decayed culture. We peoples of long oppression must remember [that] we must not be talked out of our heritage.[14]

Though he was placing less emphasis on his cinematic career, Paul remained popular on screens across the world during 1937, when *Show Boat, The Song of Freedom, King Solomon's Mines, Big Fella* and *Jericho* all were playing to enthusiastic audiences. He also remained a solid presence on radio, and his records (particularly the songs from his films) continued to sell. At Abbey Road on October 18, 1937, he tackled some impressive compositions with the aid of conductor Ronnie Munro. Franz Gruber's Yuletide classic "Silent Night" was followed by "All through the Night" (an English translation of the 18th-century Welsh folk song "Ar Hyd y Nos") and two Duke Ellington masterpieces, "Solitude" and "Mood Indigo."

Paul strengthened his ties with black performers in the U.S. by joining the Negro Actors Guild, which held its first meeting in New York on December 4, 1937. Noble Sissle was unanimously elected President by a small group of members, who also chose Bill Robinson as Honorary Vice President, the Reverend Adam Clayton Powell as Chaplain, Fredi Washington as Executive Director, W. C. Handy as Treasurer, Muriel Rahn as Recording Secretary, J. Rosamond Johnson as Chairman of By-Laws, Cab Calloway as Chairman of the Executive Board, Elmer Carter as First Vice Chairman, Leigh Whipper as Second Vice Chairman, and Simon S. Feinstein as Counsel.

Paul was elected Ninth Vice President among a group of 10, including Ethel Waters (First), Duke Ellington (Fourth), Louis Armstrong (Seventh) and Marion Anderson (Eighth). All members suggested names of African American performers who should be asked to join the Guild.

At two Abbey Road sessions on January 14 and 21, 1938, Paul recorded four songs from George Gershwin's opera *Porgy and Bess.* He previously had turned down two offers to play Porgy in the operatic version: one from the composer himself, and a second that would have paired him with Josephine Baker. Backed by an orchestra conducted by Carroll Gibbons, he cut "Summertime," "It Takes a Long Pull to Get There," "It Ain't Necessarily So" and "A Woman Is a Sometime Thing."

One week later, Paul and Essie prepared for a trip to war-torn Spain by first traveling to Paris. On January 29, 1938, newsreel cameramen filmed Paul at the Madrid barracks speaking with and singing for the soldiers, who enjoyed Spanish versions of "Joshua Fit de Battle of Jericho," "Singin' with a Sword in My Hand" and "Ol' Man River." Director Juan Manuel Plaza included the footage in *Canciones de Madrid* (1938), a 10-minute film produced by Estado Mayor Comisariado del Ejercito del Centro and distributed by the Film Popular company.

Scholar Ralph Bunche had borrowed Essie's 8mm home movie camera to document a trip to South Africa, where he attempted to retrace her previous steps. In January, he wrote to Paul, assuring him that he was "an idol of the Bantu," who, when mentioning African Americans who impressed them, ranked him with "Joe Louis ... Jesse Owens and Duke [Ellington]."[15]

When Paul's concert manager, Harold Holt, wrote a letter criticizing his decision to perform for members of the British labor movement at a stadium in London, he instead sang on the stages of the city's cinemas and in halls where working-class audiences could hear him for affordable ticket prices. He followed these performances with a grand return to the Albert Hall, where he kicked off his 1938 Celebrity Concert tour that took him throughout the provinces of England and into Scotland, where he sang to a record number of patrons at Glasgow's Exhibition Hall. Joining die-hard concertgoers were working-class fans Paul had gained through his recordings, radio performances and, especially, his cinematic appearances.

Ignoring criticism of his abandonment of the traditional concert format, he included folk songs and popular film numbers in his set lists. On April 13, 1938, he represented the connections between Celtic and African American music by recording Marjory Kennedy-Fraser's arrangement of the traditional Scottish piece "Eriskay Love Lilt" with Ronnie Munro at Abbey Road. Later in the year, they re-teamed for another Celtic classic, "Loch Lomond" (with Paul appropriating the "proper" stage version of a Scottish burr).

Following the appeasement of Germany by Britain and France in September 1938, the iron fist of European fascism was given license to hammer wherever it may. On September 30, one day after British Prime Minister Neville Chamberlain declared, "Peace in our time," Hitler occupied the Sudetenland in western Czechoslovakia. Six weeks later, the Nazis launched a nationwide pogrom with *Kristallnacht*, a violent rampage of looting and destruction that left 200 synagogues burned, 100 Jews dead or injured, and 20,000 placed under arrest. Paul, viewing these events as a certain prelude to a European war, planned to return to the United States, where reviving his concert career was preferable to the demeaning roles offered by the Hollywood cinema.

Paul was careful not to make political statements during his professional concerts, and instead covertly worked in commentary by adding Negro protest songs, as well as material from Russia, Republican Spain and the German resistance, to his repertoire. Focusing on

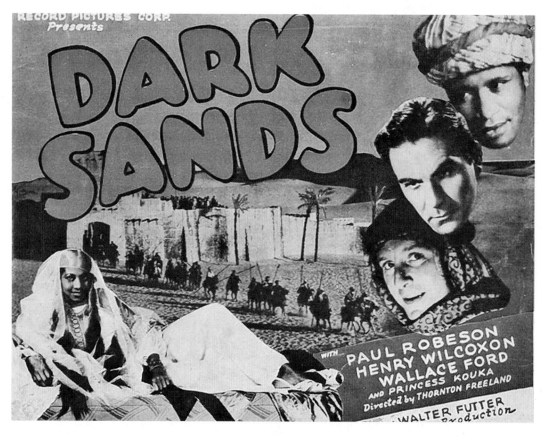

Jericho (1937), released as *Dark Sands* in the United States. This U.S.–release title lobby card features (a blue) Robeson with his costars, Henry Wilcoxon, Wallace Ford and (at bottom left) that star from the Sudan, the lovely Princess Kouka!

major singing events, he dropped his usual dates at cinemas, where he had been performing "half concerts."

His career emphasis had moved back to the concert stage, but he never gave up seeking out quality film projects that would address his political concerns. While in Spain, he and Essie had learned about Oliver Law, an African American World War I veteran and communist who became battalion commander with the Abraham Lincoln Brigade in 1937. Paul attempted to spur the production of an independent film based on Law's exploits, but (not surprisingly) he couldn't find a single investor. As a result, he became even more vocal in his criticism of the commercial film industry, stating that he would participate only in projects with "socially significant" content. Referring to the true muscle of studio employees, Paul told a reporter:

> [W]orkers in the film studios have the power and they ought to realize it. During one of my films ... everybody [was] on the set, lights burning, director waiting: [the] head of the company had just come onto the set with some big financial backer.... And what happened? Everything stopped ... because the electricians had decided it was time to go out and eat.[16]

Paul also continued his stage work as a member of the Unity Theatre group's General Council. Collaborating with producer Herbert Marshall (who earlier had met Paul in Mos-

Jericho (1937), released as *Dark Sands* in the United States. As a frantic mob approaches, Jericho (Robeson) insists on going back to "take what's coming" to him, but Captain Mack (Henry Wilcoxon) deliberately stalls the plane's engine, asking his former comrade to get out and swing the prop [U.S.–release lobby card].

cow while studying with Eisenstein), he served as acting coach, co-producer and public advocate. In mid–June 1938, Paul portrayed the lead (an Irishman, his first "white" role) in Ben Bengal's *Plant in the Sun*, an award-winning play about a sit-down strike in a U.S. factory. The play, directed by Marshall, enjoyed a two-month run, culminating with a special performance on July 23 for a packed house that included many Members of Parliament who had been invited by Paul and other celebrities during a session at the House of Commons nine days earlier.

Paul asked Essie to travel to New York, to assess the potential of his making a personal appearance tour of cinemas in the United States. She met with William Morris and other theater and film promoters, actors John Gielgud and Maurice Evans (whom they considered for a possible U.S. production of *Othello*), and many prominent artists in the African American community. Encouraged by the growing leftist presence in Hollywood, she thought Paul might more easily find work in "socially conscious" film productions. Talk even began to circulate about Ernest Hemingway's possible authorship of a screenplay for Paul's proposed film about Oliver Law.

Jericho was re-edited as *Dark Sands* for its August 16, 1938, U.S. release. The African American press called the film "good entertainment" with "exceptional photography," and lauded Paul as "magnificent." The fact that mainstream white reviewers considered it lackluster didn't hurt its success with black filmgoers, who were looking forward to the star's return to the United States.

A People's Film
The Proud Valley (1940)

Deep River.
My home is over Jordan.
Deep River, Lord,
I want to cross over into campground.
— African American spiritual

Credits: Director: Pen Tennyson; Producer: Michael Balcon; Associate Producer: Sergei Nolbandov; Screenplay: Louis Golding, Jack Jones, Roland Pertwee, Pen Tennyson; Based on a story by Herbert Marshall and Alfredda Brilliant; Directors of Photography: Glen MacWilliams, Roy Kellino; Editor: Ray Pitt; Musical Score: Felix Mendelssohn, Evan James, Mai Jones, H. T. Burleigh, James James, Lyn Joshua, Thomas John Williams; Musical Arrangements and Direction: Ernest Irving; Art Director: Wilfred Shingleton; Makeup: Heinrich Heitfeld; Production Manager: Frederick James; Assistant Director: L. C. Rudkin; Sound: Eric Williams; Sound Recordist: Stephen Dalby; Production Manager: Frederick James; Camera Operator: Jeff Seaholme; Still Photographer: Wilfrid Newton; an Ealing Studios Production; British Board of Film Censors Certificate "A"; released by Associated British Film Distributors, Ltd. (U.K.) on April 6, 1940, and (as *The Tunnel*) by Supreme Distributing Company (U.S.) on May 16, 1941; Length: 6889 feet; Running Time: 76 minutes.

Cast: Paul Robeson (David Goliath), Edward Chapman (Dick Parry), Simon Lack (Emlyn Parry), Rachel Thomas (Mrs. Parry), Dilys Thomas (Dilys), Edward Rigby (Bert), Janet Johnson (Gwen Owen), Charles Williams (Evans), Jack Jones (Thomas), Dilys Davis (Mrs. Owen), Clifford Evans (Seth Jones), Allan Jeayes (Mr. Trevor), George Merritt (Mr. Lewis), Edward Lexy (Commissionaire), Noel Howlett (Company Clerk), Roddy Hughes (Lloyd), Mike Johnson (Cage Operator), Harry Terry (Miner), Ben Williams (Will Morgan), Babette Washington, Grant Sutherland, Edward Keyes (bits).

The Spanish Civil War ended in tragedy with the fall of Madrid on March 27, 1939. Paul and Essie, along with antifascists everywhere, were appalled by the subsequent mass executions of 200,000 Spanish Republicans. Paul was especially disillusioned by the failure of Britain, France and the United States to stem the rising tide of fascism. "Because support was not given," said Paul, "many more Americans, Englishmen and Frenchmen will have to die."[1]

In the midst of this sociopolitical cataclysm, Paul and Lawrence Brown began a concert tour of Scandinavia. During a Copenhagen benefit for Spanish refugee children, they performed a set list of folk songs, spirituals and antifascist anthems. Considering the tour an artistic and political success, Paul returned to London at the end of April, poised to leave Britain and pursue his concert career in the U.S., where he also planned to star in a stage revival of *The Emperor Jones*. Continuing to use the African American press as his vehicle

for social commentary, he emphasized, "I won't let people forget I'm a Negro.... It should be the mission of Negro artists to earn respect as Negroes."[2]

Many black intellectuals were becoming involved with the Harlem Communist Party led by Benjamin Davis. Writers such as Ralph Ellison and Richard Wright were attracted by the U.S. Communists' championing of African American rights, especially the Party's recognition of the importance of the arts and the black church in the struggle for equality. Paul maintained a cordial distance from the Party but addressed his apparent espousal of communism (which to him was not a political but a *social* support), stressing that, although he wasn't a communist, he admired Russia for its racial egalitarianism. He "didn't care" about "what goes on in the upper circles of the [Soviet] government."[3] He later wrote:

> I have publicly expressed ... my deep conviction that for all mankind a socialist society represents an advance to a higher stage of life — that is a form of society which is economically, socially, culturally, and ethically superior to a system based on production for private profit.... The development of human society —from tribalism to feudalism, to capitalism, to socialism — is brought about by the needs and aspirations of mankind for a better life.[4]

In June 1939, *The Emperor Jones* enjoyed a week-long run at the Ridgeway Theatre in White Plains, New York, where Paul garnered stunning reviews for a performance during which he eliminated all usages of the word "nigger" from Eugene O'Neill's original text. He also received several offers to appear in productions by Langston Hughes, Duke Ellington and Margaret Webster, who pitched *Othello* to costar Maurice Evans. In a cable to Paul from London, Essie wholeheartedly supported the *Othello* proposal, including her (beneficently objective) mention of casting Paul's former paramour Peggy Ashcroft as Desdemona.

On June 15, MGM released the 138-minute compilation feature *Land of Liberty*, which recounts a "patriotic" history of the United States through newsreel footage and clips from 125 Hollywood films featuring such stars as John and Lionel Barrymore, Claudette Colbert, Gary Cooper, Bette Davis, Henry Fonda, Clark Gable, Basil Rathbone, Randolph Scott, James Stewart and Loretta Young. Narrated by Gayne Whitman from a script by Jesse Lasky, Jr., and Jeanie Macpherson, and edited by Cecil B. DeMille, the film all but ignores "unpatriotic" material, such as the stark realities of the Great Depression. Appearing in an excerpt from *Show Boat* placed at a point in the chronology prior to the Civil War, Paul's "Joe" character of the 1890s was unwittingly transformed into a slave, lending the lyrics to "Ol' Man River" a much harsher meaning. Included without his permission, Paul was not pleased when the film opened at the World's Fair in New York.

Paul steamed back to London in early July to take a six-week vacation including an exercise regimen designed to melt away 25 unwanted pounds. By the middle of the following month, he was fit enough to go back to work, and this time in a new medium. As reported in the August 18, 1939, issue of *Radio Times*, he made his debut on British television (something he would never be allowed to do in the United States, which began regular broadcasts during the Red Scare).

The previous November, Paul had met with his Unity Theatre cohort Herbert Marshall to discuss forming a new independent film production company that would seek to "depict the Negro as he really is— not the caricature he is always represented to be on the screen."[5] Paul specifically announced his plans to star in biopics about Samuel Taylor-Coleridge, Joe Louis and (again) Toussaint L'Ouverture.

Now Herbert Marshall's name was mentioned again, by producer Michael Balcon, who made Paul a serious offer to make his first feature film appearance in two years, as the title

character in "David Goliath," a powerful story by Marshall and Alfredda Brilliant about a black coal miner with a stunning voice who labors in the Welsh collieries. Balcon had teamed with young filmmaker Pen Tennyson, a great-grandson of poet Alfred Lord Tennyson, who had just completed his first film as writer-director, *There Ain't No Justice* (1939), for Ealing Studios. Impressed with his work, Ealing had accepted "David Goliath" as his follow-up project.

Physical evidence of mining in South Wales dates back to the 13th century, but the Industrial Revolution brought a vast development of coal commerce, particularly during the early 19th century, when mine shafts began to be tunneled deep into the earth. Just prior to World War I, Cardiff, the capital of Wales, had become the world's greatest coal exporter. For nearly a century, the Rhondda Valley in South Wales, home to the largest continuous coalfield in the British Isles, produced a wealth of coal for the mining companies (reaching their peak in 1913) and much unrest among the workers. Transportation difficulties and the dangerous nature of working in coal shafts buried far beneath the valley (not a natural habitat for human beings) were two major concerns. Between 1844 and 1909, 16 mining disasters, most of them gas explosions, occurred in the Rhondda collieries, killing a total of 1,018 workers.

During the mid–1920s, economic depression led to pay cuts and longer workdays, resulting in a general strike called by the Trades Union Congress that lasted only nine days, with no gains for the workers. When the Great Depression hit in late 1929, a decline in public assistance, rising unemployment and growing health problems worsened conditions further. By 1939, 50,000 people, most of whom had no prospect of employment, had left the Rhondda Valley.

The culture of the Rhondda area has been known for its strong masculine relationships, most obviously represented by "male voice choirs," often comprised of comrades from the coalfields. Dating back to the seventh century, the "Eisteddfod" is a traditional Welsh cultural festival during which local community choirs perform.

Pen Tennyson began shooting the "David Goliath" project in the Rhondda Valley on August 23, 1939, just eight days before World War II erupted with Nazi Germany's invasion of Poland. The "10-year" German-Soviet Treaty of Non-Aggression signed in Moscow by foreign ministers Vyacheslav Molotov and Joachim von Ribbentrop during the wee hours of August 24 unleashed further anti–Soviet sentiment throughout Europe and the United States, but Paul remained unfazed as he further prepared for his role by exploring an actual working mine and lodging with local miners' families.

Paul's relationship with the people of Rhondda had begun 10 years earlier, when he joined the group of marching miners in London. Truly inspired by the event, he contributed the proceeds from one of his 1929 concerts to the Welsh Miners' Relief Fund, and then made his first visit to the Rhondda Valley to perform and spend time with the workers and their families.

While working on the film, some of the miners pointed out that Paul belonged among *them*, not with the aristocrats who attended his concerts in London and other cities. They related firsthand accounts of their struggles, experiences that further strengthened Paul's commitment to the working class, both in Europe and in the United States. While performing for an audience of miners at the Tower Colliery, he received the workers' support for his suggestion of changing the film's title to *The Proud Valley*. The screenplay, specifically tailored for Paul, includes scenes in which David Goliath sings for the local people and is invited to perform with the men's choir at the Eisteddfod (an honor Paul actually would

be granted in 1957, when, forbidden to leave the United States, he joined the Welsh singers via a telephone line). Paul later said:

> I was in the Welsh Valley, and the Welsh people sing very much like we do, the Negro people — many of our songs, *beautiful* songs. I was one of the few outsiders who has sung at a Welsh Eisteddfod, their national festival which has gone on since the time of the Druids.... I, today, feel as much at home in the Welsh Valley as I would in my own Negro section in any city in the United States.[6]

The interior scenes were shot at Ealing Studios outside London, where filming was shut down when Hitler's troops marched into Poland on September 1. All entertainment across Britain was suspended for two days, but when production resumed on *The Proud Valley*, Essie began to drive Paul to work every morning. On evenings when Paul had to work over schedule, she braved blackout conditions while driving home. Paul Robeson, Jr., recalled:

> It was a *completely* independent film. It was filmed in the mining valleys of South Wales, where he went and lived with the miners. Most of the actors were miners. There were two or three actors. The rest were miners.
> The movie was supposed to be titled "David Goliath," and he said, "I've been down in your mine. I've been here for a while with you, and I've just renamed the film, and the name I'm giving it is *The Proud Valley*. So, in every sense, this was a totally different film than anything he'd made before, literally a people's film, made with the people, for the people, by the people — I mean, all the clichés, it sounds almost corny.[7]

Production wrapped on September 25, and the rough cut of *The Proud Valley* was ready for screening only three days later, when Paul was in the midst of a four-day Abbey Road recording session yielding 20 songs that had been favorites of his British audiences over the years. On September 28, he and conductor Walter Goehr produced versions of "Oh, Promise Me," from Reginald De Koven's 1890 comic opera *Robin Hood*, and the Irish folk song "She Is Far from the Land." Returning to the studio the next day, Paul, accompanied by Lawrence Brown, recorded two songs from *The Proud Valley*, Thomas John Williams' "Ebenezer" and James James' "Land of My Fathers." Essie wrote in her dairy that the film "is beautiful ... moves well, has character, real atmosphere, sincerity, authenticity" and that Paul "is very real, very fine, and fits right into the picture."[8] The official publicity unleashed by Associated British Film Distributors, Ltd., hailed him as "THE SAMSON OF SONG!"

A choir performs "All Through the Night" as the title sequence proclaims:

<div align="center">

PAUL ROBESON
in
"THE PROUD VALLEY"

</div>

The setting is "South Wales, 1938" as the establishing shot pans left, across vacant railroad tracks to show a lone figure, dressed in a pea coat and soft cloth cap, leisurely walking down a country road. He stops to remove some stones from one of his worn shoes, as a train whistle heralds the approach of a locomotive pulling a line of coal cars. Replacing the shoe, he runs for the train and jumps into the aft-most car, landing directly on top of a fellow rail-rider,

"Here, here!" the old hobo, Bert (Edward Rigby), growls. "What the hell do you think you're doing, eh?"

"Sorry, friend," the interloper calmly apologizes. "I didn't see you." Questioned by the veteran tramp, he reveals his status as a ship's stoker, unemployed since landing in Cardiff.

The Proud Valley (1940). The cover for Associated British Film Distributors' original British-release pressbook touts, "Paul Robeson: The Samson of Song!"

Bert, however, is a self-employed "grinder," a "murderer" of well-known songs who is paid by unfortunate bystanders to "go away."

Well aware of the Welsh musical culture, the handsome black man, with a subtle grin on his face, endures some dreadful vocalizing and comments, "I'm sure the people in these valleys won't stand for that noise." When they reach the Blaendy Colliery, he tells Bert, "I worked down in the mines for five years back in the States."

As the current shift ends, a miners' argument is interrupted by Dick Parry (Edward Chapman), who demands, "What I want is more singing and less talking in the Blaendy choir," ordering the men to attend practice at "eight o'clock sharp."

A fight breaks out, and young Emlyn Parry (Simon Lack) stands up for his father during the skirmish. "Qualified postal clerk" Gwen Owen (Janet Johnson) emerges from the village post office and rushes to the scene, where she rescues her bloodied beau, "Em," from a further beating by Ben Jenkins. Back at the post office, Gwen's mother (Dilys Davies) has received the lad's manager's certificate, the result of his hard work at night school.

In the street, the two vagrants assault the ears of passersby. Mrs. Owen runs out, assuming that someone has been "run over," and orders them to "shut up," lest she bring the law down upon their heads, but Em sends them packing at the cost of a single coin.

That evening, Dick cringes at the performance of his first tenors, then deals with the absence of his "celebrated bass soloist, Mr. Ben Jenkins," whose face "ran into" the fists of his son earlier in the day. The choir master diligently drills his men, but halts upon hearing a voice, emanating from the street, singing Felix Mendelssohn's "Lord God of Abraham." The choir members join in for the finale, then dash to the windows to see who possesses the amazing pipes. Invited to the rehearsal, the unemployed stoker bids farewell to his street companion.

Seated at the Parry dinner table, the grateful guest is showered with praise as Dick tells his wife (Rachel Thomas) that the voice, which "floated in that hall like thunder from a distance," will ensure the choir's victory at the Eisteddfod. Promising his new friend a job in the Blaendy pit and a bed in their home, Dick incurs the wrath of the wife. As the couple argues outside, little Dilys (Dilys Thomas), one of their five daughters, approaches the stranger, and she (and the audience) is the first to hear his name: "I'm David Goliath," he says.

"Oh, I know," the girl replies, "same as in the story teacher told us in Sunday school." By the time the marital "tantrums" end, David is promised the sofa in the front room; when Em pops in with news of his forthcoming marriage, the guest's status is upgraded to lodger in the lad's old room.

The Proud Valley (1940). Standing in the street below their rehearsal room, David Goliath (Robeson) sings Mendelssohn's "Lord God of Abraham" to impress the members of the Blaendy Men's Choir [frame enlargement].

On the day of the Eisteddfod, a group of workers complain to Dick about David's position in the mine and the choir. "This fellow brought a *black man* to work down the pit," Seth Jones (Clifford Evans) declares.

"Well," a powerful voice, off-screen, interjects as Seth looks up to see David approaching him. (Paul registers genuine anger merely by staring straight ahead as he walks toward Clifford Evans.) "What about it?" he asks, to which no reply is given.

In a moment unique in his films, Paul, in a tight close-up, subtly depicts his character's emotional pain when being confronted by racism. He closes his eyes, hangs his head and stoops his shoulders slightly, as Dick stands up for the singer, worker and "decent chap": "Here's Seth talkin' about him bein' *black*." (Just before the word "black" is voiced, Paul opens his eyes and quickly stares back at the offender.) "Well, damn and blast it, man, aren't we *all* black down that pit?"

Laughter breaks out as one miner suggests, "Aye, take a look at your selves. This fellow's as good a pal as any of you."

"Well, anybody else got anything to say before me and my *buddy* go down the pit?" asks Dick. This bold 1939 scene concludes with the cage operator (Mike Johnson) offering the practical inquiry, "Haven't you chaps finished chewin' the fat? What about a bit of work? Keep the home fires burning?"

David speaks bitterly about the incident as they enter the mine, but his spirits are buoyed when one of the men suggests they sing "the Eisteddfod test piece." Leading the men into "All Through the Night" (Paul unleashes his smile after singing the first line), David creates a moment of complete solidarity among the men as they make their way down the shaft. (Tennyson uses no editing, instead covering the entire vocal performance with a single, 180-degree panning shot. As with the majority of song sequences in the film, this performance is completely realistic, with no off-screen music added on the soundtrack.)

A bus bearing the banners "The Eisteddfod" and "Blaendy Male Choir" pulls up to the curb outside the Parry household as the children are being readied for the journey. Meanwhile, the men of the choir toil "down the pit" in a section known as the "Klondyke." (Paul's pre-production workouts certainly paid off, as his physique, befitting his character surname "Goliath," is truly stunning here. Though he usually has one such appearance in each film, this is a contender for the ultimate Robeson beefcake scene.)

A few minutes before the end of the shift, a small pocket of gas is discovered in the Klondyke, and the family is startled by a siren from the colliery. Em rushes to join the rescue team but is prevented from entering the fiery tunnel. Soon, a miner, bearing another on his back, slowly walks out of the shaft. David is all right, but Dick, gravely injured, mentions the Eisteddfod and his wife just before he dies.

One month later, the Eisteddfod is held, on May 8 and 9, in the ruins of an ancient, castle-like cathedral, surrounded by a moat. Em addresses the gathering, thanking them for postponing the event, allowing the singers to regroup after the tragic death of their conductor. David then introduces their number by praising his fallen friend: "I didn't know Dick Parry for long, but I lived and worked with him enough to realize that he was a *man*, every inch of him. Sometimes when we were alone, I used to sing him this song, which we are now going to sing for you." Tight close-ups of the sorrowful faces of Parry's wife and daughter precede David's opening of the profoundly soulful "Deep River." (Paul, accompanied by the orchestra, sings the first verse as a solo and then is joined by the choir on the chorus. This brief but powerful scene is one of the musical highlights of his entire cinematic canon.)

The colliery closes down soon after the Eisteddfod, and the workers are forced to report to the Blaendy Labour Exchange to sign up for the dole. The only available mining jobs involve digging for whatever bits of slag can be found. While his colleagues and their poverty-stricken families understandably complain, David remains resolutely optimistic: "There's my seventeen bob dole money. I do my bit on the slag heap. I try not to eat too much." Rather than moving on to the Darden Valley or finding a ship at Cardiff, he chooses to remain in Blaendy. He explains to Em, "Your father was my friend. He took me in, gave me food and shelter, found me work. What kind of a man would I be, if I left now, when things were bad?"

When Mrs. Owen writes off Em as a penniless bum, David induces Gwen to cheer him up, a gesture that inspires the lad to visit the mine owners in London. The village stages a parade as a rousing send-off for Em, David and three other miners on their 208-mile trek to the capital. (The rather unconvincing performance of "All Through the Night" by the men's choir and marching band is overdubbed by an arrangement that includes some "off-screen" strings.) Their initial grinning enthusiasm becomes a bit dampened at the halfway mark, but they rally by singing away the remaining miles. As coins from passersby begin to fill David's cap, a montage of newspaper headlines announces the increasingly belligerent activities of Hitler, who marches into Poland on September 1. (The screenplay was constantly revised to keep up with current events.)

Three days (and many songs) later, the team of five harmonizing men reaches the offices of Blaendy Colliery, Ltd. A guard is unable to persuade the secretary to alert "Sir John," who is tied up in an important meeting, about the presence of the miners' delegation; but when she leaves to see off her soldier sweetheart at Victoria Station, David persuades the amiable guard to duck out for a smoke. Offering to "hold the fort," David (claiming, "I wouldn't be much help to you —*in there*") convinces the lads to walk right into the board room, where the owners are discussing the possibility of reopening some of the coal pits. Em claims that the men, if allowed to tunnel through a sealed section of the mine, can have Blaendy up and running within a week. The dangers involved must take a back seat to the realities of the war with Hitler, another miner claims, emphasizing that coal "is as much a part of our national defense as guns or anything else." Mr. Lewis (George Merritt), a mining engineer, agrees to accompany them back to Blaendy to open the mine.

Armed with blasting powder, respirators, and a caged canary, the valiant miners, including Lewis, venture into the sealed section of the pit. On the ground above, their families and friends harmonize a hymn. (The realistic detail of the mine sequences, filmed on location with the technical expertise of local advisors, creates a true atmosphere of uneasy claustrophobia.) David provides the muscle required for Em to set a dynamite charge, and they blast their way into the adjoining shaft. Piling their respirators onto a mine truck, they attempt to open the iron doors into the next tunnel, but are halted by a wall of flame. One of the men removes a wooden pole from the track, inadvertently causing the trucks to roll away as he struggles to close the doors. Lewis and an assistant's efforts to shore up the

Opposite: The Proud Valley (1940). **This photo collage from the British-release pressbook features David Goliath (Robeson) surrounded by his many Welsh friends, Mrs. Parry (Rachel Thomas: round insets, lower left and upper right; and bottom right corner), Bert (Edward Rigby: round inset, upper left), Emlyn Parry (Simon Lack: top left; round insets, lower right and center; and bottom left corner), Dilys (Dilys Thomas: top right), Dick Parry (Edward Chapman: round insets, center and upper right), and Gwen Owen (Janet Johnson: bottom left and right).**

passage are defeated when the speeding trucks slam into the men, crushing them to death as the mine caves in. (Tennyson, editor Ray Pitt, and sound technicians Eric Williams and Stephen Dalby collaborated to create a harrowingly suspenseful sequence. Interestingly, the event maintains a political balance by killing off one company executive and one mine monkey.)

Mrs. Parry leads the people in a Welsh hymn that also is sung by one of the miners trapped in the pit below. David's optimism appears to have been defeated (Paul, staring straight ahead this time, registers a crestfallen expression rivaling his earlier reaction to prejudice), until they discover a weak spot in one of the walls. With only an hour of air left, they decide to blast their way out; with a disastrously short cable to set off the charge, one of them must sacrifice himself to save the others. Em draws the fatal chunk of coal, but David, unable to reason with him about his mother, sisters and sweetheart, knocks him cold. (Paul, in a tight close-up, delivers a slight, warm grin before the scene cuts to show him landing a well-staged left to Simon Lack's jaw.) Moving him to safety, David grabs the plunger of the detonator; and, as the melody of "Deep River" gently crescendos onto the soundtrack, he slams it down. A close-up of David's grimacing face is dramatically inter-cut with a shot of the explosion as the blast brings life-giving air into the pit. (This final image of Paul's face is a stark contrast to the film's first glimpse of him.) The remaining men say a prayer for David before they make their way out of the mine, singing in Welsh as they go.

A montage of mining methods shows that David's sacrifice has allowed the Blaendy pit to re-open. The people line the tracks, singing to the accompaniment of their village band, as the trucks bring the coal to the surface. A series of dissolves moves the scene farther out from the colliery, to conclude in the pastoral countryside as Paul's voice segues onto the soundtrack, expressing David's undying love for his "home sweet home." The camera tilts up to the sky as the chorus crescendos and the cast listing, headed by Paul, rolls up and into the clouds.

Under the down-to-earth direction of Pen Tennyson, Paul, surrounded by a mix of fine British character actors and authentic folks from the mining communities, gives a thoroughly convincing, instinctive performance as a working man whose essential optimism culminates with his own death, a sacrifice made for the people who have accepted him as one of their own. More than six decades after the film's release, William Greaves, a director, said, "*Proud Valley* was a wonderful film. It was very encouraging to see the integration of black and white people on the screen in a role that was not condescending."9

As Dick Parry, Edward Chapman is so believable that the death of his character less than halfway into the film seems a pity. Although the plot necessarily focuses on the male characters, the females are also quite strong, headed by Rachel Thomas, whose debut as Mrs. Parry in this film began a successful acting career that stretched over the next five decades.

Tragically, the promising Pen Tennyson, who had begun his career as assistant director to Alfred Hitchcock with a successful working relationship that helped produce *The Man*

Opposite: The Proud Valley (1940). This second photo collage from the pressbook features Robeson in several key scenes from the film, including David Goliath's efforts to prevent a mining disaster (top left), his moving performance of the African American spiritual "Deep River" at the Eisteddfod (top right), his arrival in London with his colliery comrades (bottom left), and his toiling on the slag heap with his fellow miners (bottom right).

The Proud Valley (1940). Paul Robeson, "The Samson of Song," also dominates this centerpiece poster featuring his fine supporting cast: (left to right) Rachel Thomas, Simon Lack and Edward Chapman [British-release pressbook].

Who Knew Too Much (1934), *The 39 Steps* (1935), *Secret Agent* (1936), *Sabotage* (1936) and *Young and Innocent* (1937), was killed in combat when his plane crashed on July 10, 1941. A mere 28 years old, he had completed only one more film as writer-director, *Convoy* (1940), another Ealing production. His widow, Nova Pilbeam, to whom he had been married for less than two years, had costarred in the first and last of her late husband's Hitchcock assignments.

Exhibited primarily in Britain, *The Proud Valley* was re-titled *The Tunnel* in the United States, where a limited release by the Supreme Distributing Company was held up until May 1941. Five months later, John Ford's impressive film version of Richard Llewellyn's 1939 novel *How Green Was My Valley*, filmed entirely in California (with only one Welsh actor in its cast), was released, to great fanfare, critical acclaim and five Academy Awards.

Llewellyn, an Englishman, based *How Green Was My Valley*, set during the late 19th century, on conversations with local Welsh families. Though a less sentimentalized, more accurate depiction of mining life in South Wales, the independently produced *The Proud Valley*, lacking the commercial potential of a major studio picture, disappeared like so many miners "down the pit." Seven decades later, it is essential viewing, as a motion picture including a truly valid cinematic representation of the Paul Robeson ethos.

On October 1, 1939, Paul, Essie and Paul Jr. steamed toward New York from Southampton aboard the U.S.S. *Washington*. When the head waiter asked Paul to confine himself and

The Proud Valley (1940), released as *The Tunnel* in the United States. This stunning U.S.–release one-sheet poster depicts David Goliath (Robeson) deep in the Blaendy coal mine with his Rhondda Valley comrades.

his family to their quarters while eating, he defiantly took a table in the middle of the dining room, which served whites only. Eventually they were assigned a reserved table in a far corner. A steward finally approached them, offering greetings and admiration from all the crew. When the captain asked Paul to sing at an evening concert, he instead performed for the crew members in their quarters.

In New York, Paul answered many questions from reporters, voicing his intentions for his future career, including any possible film roles. Paul Robeson, Jr., revealed:

> Paul told them that, as the son of a slave, he had returned to his Southern black roots. When he was abroad he looked at the world from the point of view of Africa. But at home his outlook was that of a black worker in Mississippi. As for the much-discussed search in Hollywood and on Broadway for roles that he would not accept, there was no amount of money that could entice him to play a role that did not advance the cultural stature of his people.[10]

Paul wrote:

> I came to understand that the Negro artist could not view the matter simply in terms of his individual interests, and that he had a responsibility to his people who rightfully resented the traditional stereotyped portrayals of Negroes on stage and screen.... If the Hollywood and Broadway producers did not choose to offer me worthy roles to play, then I would choose not to accept any other kind of offer.[11]

On November 5, 1939, CBS Radio broadcast Earl Robinson and John Latouche's epic *Ballad for Americans*, sung and narrated by Paul, who became the first official black spokesman for the American way of life, ironically one which still ran rampant with segregation, lynchings (actually mentioned in the lyrics of the song) and other numerous racial inequalities. In the wake of Paul's historic performance, the network received an unprecedented number of phone calls praising one of its programs. A few months later, *Collier's* magazine named him both "favorite male Negro singer" and "America's no. 1 entertainer."[12]

We Were Brothers
Native Land (1942)

Native Land is obviously a Communist project.
— Federal Bureau of Investigation[1]

Credits: Directors and Producers: Leo Hurwitz, Paul Strand; Screenplay: Leo Hurwitz, Ben Maddow (a.k.a. David Wolff), Paul Strand; Director of Photography: Paul Strand; Editor: Leo Hurwitz; Assistant Editors: Lionel Berman, Robert Stebbins; Musical Score: Marc Blitzstein; Musical Director: Lehman Engel; Assistant in Orchestrations: Henry Brant; Sound Editors: Robert Stebbins, Ralph Avseev; Production Manager: George Jacobson; Production Assistants: Julia Milch, Ruth Miller; Associate Directors: Alfred Saxe, William Watts; Animation: Ted Ashbaugh Studios; Released by Frontier Films (U.S.) on May 11, 1942; Running Time: 88 minutes.

Cast: Paul Robeson (Narrator/Vocalist), Fred Johnson (Fred Hill), Mary George (Hill's Wife), John Rennick (Hill's Son), Amelia Romano (Window Scrubber), Houseley Stevenson (White Sharecropper), Louis Grant (Black Sharecropper), James Hanney (Mack), Howard Da Silva (Jim), Art Smith (Harry Carlyle), Richard Bishop (Spy Executive), Vaughn King (Mary, Mack's Wife), Robert Strauss (Frank Mason), Dolores Cornell (Girl with Balloon), John Marley (Thug with Crowbar), Tom Connors, Jr. (Joseph Shumaker), Harry Wilson (Eugene Poulnot), the Rev. Charles Webber (Minister), Virginia Stevens (Whitey's Widow), Clancy Cooper (Whitey's Eulogist), Tom Pedi (Harry), Bert Conway, Charles Jordan (bits).

In March 1937, a group of leftist, New York–based filmmakers founded Frontier Films, a non-profit production company, to make documentaries about current social issues. President Paul Strand was assisted by two vice presidents, Leo Hurwitz and Ralph Steiner, and a secretary, screenwriter John Howard Lawson (a prominent U.S. Communist Party member who later became one of the infamous "Hollywood Ten"). Other members included Elia Kazan (then a Group Theatre actor and CPUSA member) and documentary filmmaker Willard Van Dyke.

Since the concept of producing "realistic films of American life" was a fairly radical one in the United States at the time, the filmmakers (seeking to offer an alternative to such conservative newsreel fare as Louis de Rochemont's *The March of Time*) drew their inspiration from the political documentaries of Soviet director Alexander Dovzhenko (best known for *Earth* [1930], part three of his "Ukraine Trilogy" that also includes *Zvenigora* and *Arsenal* [both 1928]). Frontier Film's *Heart of Spain* (1937), *China Strikes Back* (1937) and *People of the Cumberland* (1938) were followed by *Native Land*, a depiction of the American people's ongoing struggle for "life, liberty and the pursuit of happiness."

The various components of *Native Land* consist of newsreel footage, Paul Strand's cinematography, and recreations of events involving civil rights violations from the mid–1930s featuring actors from New York's Group Theatre. These elements are united by the musical score of Marc Blitzstein (whose controversial 1937 musical *The Cradle Will Rock*, directed

by Orson Welles, had been shut down by the Works Progress Administration) and Paul's narration and vocals.

Hurwitz, Strand and Ben Maddow based their screenplay on the findings of the La Follette Civil Liberties Committee, a special Senate investigating commission chaired by Wisconsin Progressive Senator Robert M. La Follette, Jr., from 1936 to 1941. The Committee was established to probe the findings of the National Labor Relations Board, which had investigated specific U.S. industries that avoided collective bargaining and had published its conclusions regarding strikebreaking services, private police organizations, and industrial espionage and warfare used to disrupt legal union activities.

In 2007, Tom Hurwitz recalled his father's approach to making the film:

> *Native Land* was a film based around an idea ... of the building of unions as part of the original struggle for liberty in the United States.... It was a time of tremendous ferment and thought. People were driven by *ideas*, both on the right and the left. They thought that ideas would change the world, and *their ideas* would change the world.
> *Native Land* was one of the first political documentaries that was conceived of in the United States. The talent that was put together to produce this film was extraordinary. Almost the first thing that came to mind was that Paul Robeson would have to narrate the film. They needed Paul Robeson's voice. He *immediately* agreed ... and I think gave a certain amount of financial help as well.... His image and his quality was one of absolute rectitude and absolute support of the underprivileged and of the lower classes.[2]

The "budget" for the film (originally titled "Labor Spy") was raised throughout the production phase, which had begun in 1937. Hurwitz and Strand (having no organizational or corporate support) would shoot a sequence, put their editors to work, and then screen it for potential financial donors. Before *Native Land* was finished in early December 1941, more than 15,000 people had seen some version of the film.

Paul rehearsed with the script for several weeks, attempting to hone his narration and songs to perfection. Leo Hurwitz cast the film from the ranks of the Group Theatre, including Howard Da Silva, Houseley Stevenson, and cinematic neophytes Robert Strauss and John Marley, all of whom became successful character actors in Hollywood (aside from occasional periods of unemployment, due to their political beliefs).

The film is a striking blend of documentary footage and interpretive dramatizations of actual events. Though the "recreations" can be considered political propaganda, each incident was based on solid evidence investigated by the La Follette Committee. The action is preceded by a written prologue including a reference to the World War II home front that was intended to appeal to contemporary audiences:

> Since the founding of our country the American people have had to fight for their freedom in every generation.
> *Native Land* is a document of America's struggle for liberty in recent years.
> It was in this struggle that the fascist-minded on our own soil were forced to retreat, and the people gained the democratic strength essential for national unity and for victory over the Axis.

Prior to depicting specific incidents in which the civil rights of U.S. citizens were violated, the film begins with a general historical overview including images of "the sea, the sky and the continent." This preface to the often disturbing material that follows is deliberately positive, showing the forests and fields cleared by the settlers, but not mentioning the Native Americans who were "displaced" by "We, the People." In fact, the existence of the "Indians" is not only excluded but actually *denied* by the filmmakers. At one point, Paul

recites the completely fictitious line, "We were *alone*." (An initial fallacy such as this casts a dubious shadow on the overall historical legitimacy of the film. However, the filmmakers undoubtedly were being very careful not to offend any potential non-leftist viewers who might walk out of the theater during the first few minutes.)

This depiction of the "new kind of nation ... free of all tyranny" does include brief mentions of the Revolutionary War, slavery and the Civil War. A montage of close-ups features images of the American flag, monuments to the founding fathers and Abraham Lincoln, and the Statue of Liberty. In the comments referring to Westward Expansion, the very existence of the red man again is buried beneath a whitewash of patriotic rhetoric:

> In the name of liberty, we opened the roads to the West. We crossed the blue Alleghenies, the Ohio, the Mississippi, the last ranges of the Rockies. We took *freedom* with us. More than a word. It was an *axe* to clear the continent.

(These words in praise of Manifest Destiny [the film's true propaganda] as recited by Paul sound embarrassing six decades later, but he and his fellow artists obviously had to keep their current agenda at the forefront.)

A mere eight minutes of this "history" brings the film up to the 1930s. "More than a dream," says Paul, "more than a document, the Bill of Rights meant a way of life — a way of life for *all Americans*." The first individual incident is now recreated as Paul introduces the story of "a Michigan farmer working his own land." The images bring to mind not only the visual style of contemporary Soviet film but also the American documentaries of the Great Depression, such as Pare Lorentz's New Deal–sponsored *The Plow That Broke the Plains* (1936), which was shot by Leo Hurwitz, Ralph Steiner, Paul Strand and Paul Ivano.

Much of the *Native Land* footage was shot "silent," with the dialogue and sound effects dubbed in during post-production (certainly a cost-effective strategy for a group of political artists relying on handouts to make their film). The structure of each scene first presents the dramatized event, and then offers commentary, written by Ben Maddow (credited as David Wolff) and spoken by Paul, including the location and date of the original incident.

The "Michigan farmer," Fred Hill (Fred Johnson), plowing with two horses, is seen with his loving son (John Rennick) just before he retreats to the house to wash up. His wife (Mary George), peeling potatoes, tells him that strangers have arrived, asking if he is "the Mr. Hill that spoke up at the farmers' meeting last night."

Native Land (1942). During the "historical" prologue featuring a montage of American iconography, this image is accompanied by Robeson's commentary: "One nation, indivisible, with liberty and justice for all. The *immigrant*, hungry for bread and for liberty. The brave and the persecuted..." [frame enlargement].

Proudly, she had answered, "You bet!" unknowingly sealing his doom. (Hurwitz cleverly creates a montage juxtaposing images of Mrs. Hill's prowess with a paring knife and their young son's efforts with the plow in yonder field.) Soon after, she discovers the three strangers speeding off in their car, and her husband, with a savage head wound, dying on the bank of a nearby stream. As the camera pans into the gently flowing water, Paul comments, "A man's farm invaded, his liberty attacked, the right of free speech denied to an American. It happened in Custer, Michigan, September 1934."

Newspapers and other periodicals, newsreels and the radio were the only sources of public information available in 1942. Produced prior to the television age and the resultant explosion of the mass media, *Native Land* slowly dissolves from a farmland stream to another waterway, moving through a modern urban sprawl, with Paul pointing out:

> Never heard of it. People never heard of it. Twenty miles down the river. People in the next town, going their own way, taking the Bill of Rights for granted, unaware of what happened to one man, far away. People in American towns, busy with work, children, and what's for supper — in Hartford, or Troy, or Dallas, or Cleveland, Ohio.

He then introduces the next story, "a spring day in 1936," as a teenage cleaning girl happily scrubs the windows of an urban tenement. Unable to enter one of the apartments, she tries the doorknob, keys, furious rapping, and ramming before finally forcing her way in. (Hurwitz's rapidly edited montage skillfully incorporates discontinuity and conspicuous jump cuts to convey the girl's increasing agitation.) A shot of a dead man's feet, adjacent to handbills scattered on the floor and stained with spilled ink, incites a scream from the frightened girl. Paul interjects, "Again. It happened again. They say he was a union man. Nothing in the newspapers. It wasn't on the radio. Don't understand it. New York, Chicago, Cleveland...."

Paul moves on to "Fort Smith, Arkansas" as a dissolve transports the viewer from a teeming city street to "a country church used as a meeting place by Negro and white sharecroppers" in "midsummer 1936." The local sheriff has deputized 15 men to break up a meeting of the farmers who have demanded an additional 10 cents for a bale of cotton. The integrated sharecroppers union is further represented by two men who run for their lives through the rushes as the bullets buzz past their heads. (Rather than enhancing this sequence with a Blitzstein composition, Hurwitz instead chose the stark, violent sound of gunfire and the shouts of the shooters as the sole soundtrack.) Hiding in the brush, the white man (Houseley Stevenson) binds the leg wound of his black counterpart (Louis Grant) before exploring the surrounding area. Paul's voice surges onto the soundtrack as the black man crawls from the hedges to join his white comrade. Concealed by foliage on the adjacent ridge, a deputy cocks his rifle as the two men embrace, the white helping the black struggle down the gravel road. A remarkable series of shots depicts an intense emotional bond between the two men just before their pursuer (dressed totally in white) fires a fatal shot that drops the black man into the dust.

As the white man again embraces his fallen black friend, the scene cuts to an extreme close-up (with ambient sound) showing the shooter drawing his rifle bolt for another shot. (Though the name "Ku Klux Klan" was derived from combining the Greek word "kykolos" [circle] with "clan," a popular legend attributes its origin to the sound made by a rifle being cocked.) Shots pepper the road, and the white sharecropper must flee for his own life, which ends as he is struck by a bullet and lands on a barbwire fence. "The South in July," comments Paul. "Cotton country. Two men, dead on a road in Arkansas...." A sequence of rural images,

captured by a roving camera, is attended by Paul's summation of the events thus far:

> The rights of plain Americans destroyed. Darkness blotted out the violence of the day. The sharecroppers hunted in the Arkansas swamp. The organizer killed in a rooming house. The farmer struck down on his own farm. And night erased them all, for 130 million Americans.

Paul opens the next scene with another song, "American Day," "millions" of citizens who fail to cherish their Bill of Rights. A third into its running time, the film finally focuses on labor unions, following "the simple rhythm of millions of people, going every day to bring the machines to life," as

Native Land (1942). The white sharecropper (Houseley Stevenson) attempts to aid his black counterpart (Louis Grant) in a scene based on a union-busting lynching that occurred in Fort Smith, Arkansas, during the summer of 1936 [frame enlargement].

it shifts from staged scenes to actual documentary footage of factory workers turning out everyday commodities (including wartime armaments) and attending meetings. Stressing the need of coworkers to "think, move and act together," the scene centers on the basic concepts of "the word 'brother,' the word 'cooperative,' the word '*union*.'" However, Paul points out that these Americans, interested in "democracy" and "the pursuit of happiness," became "overconfident." As the scene cuts to the face of one particular individual, he states that "this man's name was *on file* in an office building, 600 miles away...."

Images of customer service employees in an office are identified by Paul's mention of weapons and ammunition with the designation "*entirely* confidential": "The phone rang and a man was bribed. Traps for weak men, good openings for criminals. Behind the front of everyday business, conspiracy against the lives of innocent men."

A member of "local 131," Jim (Howard Da Silva, though his familiar voice was over-dubbed by another actor), is rooted out as an informant by Harry Carlyle (Art Smith). A powerful sequence showing Jim forced to "walk slow" between two lines of his "union brothers" (including a shot from the frightened "spy's" point of view) is followed by the revelation that both Jim *and* Harry are in cahoots with the company to break the union.

Laughing at the top of his lungs, Jim compares his fellow "stool's" acting to that of Humphrey Bogart. Obviously under pressure from the bosses, Harry, ordered to provide the union's "who's who," wants to quit.

"Not bad," one of the owners remarks. "He is a good actor," while "the Chief" threatens him with potential "internal injuries."

After Mack (James Hanney), the union president, asks Harry to hide the membership list in his room, the little man is visited by a company goon, who pressures him further

into staging a mock theft and beating. With the union log in its possession, the company eventually fires all the members, "not to be rehired under any circumstances."

Returning to documentary footage of union activities, the film shows how workers "tore up the blacklist":

> We fought the secret payroll. We won back our rights as Americans. We reorganized. We went on the march. No more fear in the streets. No more meetings in the dark. We carried our names in the open air. A thousand new members a day. Two and a half million new people never organized before. Organization: a new Declaration of Independence for the People.

Union statistics are followed by the story of Frank Mason (Robert Strauss), a Memphis grocer first terrorized by a thug with a crowbar (John Marley) and who was then murdered and tossed into a ditch. Also actual footage of peaceful demonstrations that became union-busting riots in Brooklyn, San Francisco and Bainbridge, Pennsylvania, is shown. The Reverend Charles Webber appears as a minister, in defiance of threats, delivering his condemnation of "the contempt for human life, the worst sin of all" shown by authority figures in his community:

> Men with great names have hired criminals, have paid weak men to spy on their brothers, have expended secret money to set Christian against Jew, and white against colored, to brand every immigrant a dangerous enemy. Why, they would even fingerprint Jesus, the Carpenter of Nazareth, if they could.

The "forces of darkness" mentioned by the preacher are now visualized in no uncertain terms, as white-hooded members of the KKK, armed with gasoline and flaming torches, take action on "the road north of Tampa, Florida, [on] the night of November 30th, 1935." Joseph Shumaker (Tom Connors, Jr.) and Eugene Poulnot (Harry Wilson), leaders of the Modern Democrats, who "had almost defeated the Klan in the city elections," are dragged from a car to be tarred and feathered by forces who "hated one thing: the practice of democracy."

The closing scene depicts the "thunder of voices" raised nationwide and answered by the 76th Congress and the Senate Investigating Committee that uncovered the

> conspiracy [that] entangled the whole United States ... the spies of a secret war, all over the country, planted in every local ... private armies ... armed vigilantes, strikebreakers, company police paid by private corporations ... and a system of nationwide propaganda used to attack progressive legislation ... the interlocking parts of an immense conspiracy directed by a handful of fascist-minded corporations. Here was a criminal conspiracy to undermine the Bill of Rights, to weaken the strength of Americans ... exposed to the light of day.

Footage of "Memorial Day 1937" shows integrated crowds flying the flag, honoring the dead, parading through the streets, and relaxing in public parks: "a holiday of rest and play, and no thought of danger." *But*, as the scene cuts to shots of children riding on a merry-go-round, this seemingly upbeat ending is interrupted by the sound of a siren heralding images of 2,000 people marching peacefully toward the Republic Steel Plant in Chicago as they are attacked by police. Paul narrates this "act of fascism — ten killed, ninety injured — the act of a desperate minority. The dead were all shot in the back." A final dramatization depicts a grieving widow (Virginia Stevens) and her daughter as a grave is being dug at a funeral attended by a group of whites and one black man. One of the mourners (Clancy Cooper) delivers an impromptu eulogy:

He was a fine man. I'd like to say a few words, in the way of goodbye. Hard to know what to say. Never thought I'd come to carry Whitey down here. We were the same as brothers. Everybody considered we were brothers. They started firing at us. They saw him fall down. When I saw it, I didn't believe it. To take away a man's life; shouldn't get away with a thing like that. He had a right to go on that line. He was the kind of man who stood up for his rights. We don't forget that, *never.*

Native Land (1942). **Harry Carlyle (Art Smith), a member of "local 131," is forced by the bosses to rat out his union brothers, who all are subsequently fired, in a powerful scene also featuring Howard Da Silva and James Hanney [frame enlargement].**

After the eulogist drops a long-stemmed rose onto the grave, a montage of the mourners' faces inter-cut with sculpted images of Presidents Washington, Jefferson and Lincoln is accompanied by Paul's summation, a reiteration of "historical" and patriotic points, plus one last push for the labor movement:

City and farm — we organized millions, to unite the People, to make the Bill of Rights a reality, to make the nation *strong.* We pushed forward the horizons of our freedom into the 20th century. We built liberty into the beams of our houses, the House of America, which we will guard against, from within and without.... And yet, today, our liberty is in danger. The freedom we have won from enemies abroad must be saved again from enemies within. Once again, the enemy rises to threaten the four freedoms, the rights of all Americans, every creed and every color, to a job, a home, adequate food and medical care, the right to bargain collectively, to act for the greatest good of the greatest number, the right to live in peace, unthreatened — threatening no one. Today these words must become deeds, for there has never been a moment in our history when Americans were not ready to stand up as *free men* and *fight for their rights.*

The close-up of the eulogist's statement, "We don't forget that, *never*" is repeated, followed by a final image of the Statue of Liberty and a superimposed "The End — A Frontier Films Production."

Considering that *Native Land* was produced on a shoestring budget, the technical aspects are impressive. The overall pacing (slowed only by redundant content in the concluding sequences), powerful montage editing, and flowing, mobile camerawork prove Leo Hurwitz and Paul Strand's abilities as capable, innovative filmmakers. Marc Blitzstein's stirring score adds the ideal musical complement to the drama created by the use of subjective camera and Soviet-style editing.

Native Land premiered at the World Theatre in New York on May 11, 1942, a day on which many Americans were preoccupied with depressing news of their troops surrendering to the Japanese in the Philippines. Not surprisingly, the film, exhibited in only a few other select U.S. cities, fared poorly at the wartime box office. Tom Hurwitz explained:

Frontier Films had counted on the help of the [U.S.] Communist Party to reach the unions, where they could screen this film. But, instead, the Communist Party was involved in the popular front against fascism. That was their program. The Soviet Union had been attacked. The whole world was different now, and the *class struggle* had to be subdued in favor of fighting fascism.

It got shown in art houses. It ran in New York City for quite some time. It got excellent reviews, and then it disappeared. And it *really* disappeared.

And, after the war, there was the Red Scare, and the people who had made *Native Land* joined the ranks of the blacklisted. And the film itself wasn't distributed. In filmmaking circles, it's thought of as a milestone in the American documentary, but it did not have the social effect that it could have had, had it been brought out in a more timely manner. So it sat, almost unseen, until the Sixties, until my father bought it back.[3]

Shantytown Shake-Up
Tales of Manhattan (1942)

He abandoned being a superstar....

— James Earl Jones[1]

Credits: Directors: Julien Duvivier, Malcolm St. Clair; Producers: Boris Morros, Sam Spiegel; Associate Producer: Samuel Rheiner; Screenplay: Harry Blankfort, Alan Campbell, Ladislas Fodor, Laszlo Gorog, Ben Hecht, Samuel Hoffenstein, Robert Katscher, Buster Keaton, Ferenc Molnar, William Morrow, Donald Ogden Stewart, Lamar Trotti, Laszlo Vadnay; Director of Photography: Joseph Walker; Editors: Robert Bischoff, Gene Fowler, Jr.; Musical Score: Sol Kaplan; Orchestrations: Charles Bradshaw, Hugo Friedhofer, Clarence Wheeler; Vocal Arrangements: Hall Johnson; Musical Director: Edward Paul; Art Directors: Richard Day, Boris Leven; Set Decorator: Thomas Little; Costume Designers: Irene, Bernard Newman, Dolly Tree, Gwen Wakeling, Oleg Cassini; Makeup: Guy Pearce; Unit Manager: Joseph H. Nadel; Assistant Director: Robert Stillman; Sound: W. D. Flick, Roger Heman, Sr.; Dialogue Directors: Don Brodie, Alan Campbell; Premiered August 5, 1942; Released by 20th Century–Fox Pictures (U.S.) on September 24, 1942; Running Time: 127 minutes.

Cast: Charles Boyer (Charles Orman), Rita Hayworth (Ethel Halloway), Ginger Rogers (Diane), Henry Fonda (George), Charles Laughton (Charles Smith), Edward G. Robinson (Avery L. "Larry" Brown), Paul Robeson (Luke), Ethel Waters (Esther), Eddie "Rochester" Anderson (Reverend Lazarus), Thomas Mitchell (John Halloway), Eugene Pallette (Luther), Cesar Romero (Harry Wilson), Gail Patrick (Ellen), Roland Young (Edgar), Marion Martin (Squirrel), Elsa Lanchester (Elsa Smith), Victor Francen (Arturo Bellini), George Sanders (Williams), James Gleason ("Father" Joe), Harry Davenport (Prof. Lyons), J. Carrol Naish (Costello), W. C. Fields (Professor Postlewhistle), Margaret Dumont (Madame Langahankie), Phil Silvers (Tailor), Chester Clute (Mr. Langahankie), Edgar Norton (Langahankie's Butler), Hall Johnson Choir (Themselves), Frank Orth (Secondhand Clothes Dealer), Christian Rub (Cello Player, Smith's Friend), Sig Arno (Piccolo Player), James Rennie (H. R. "Hank" Bronson), Harry Hayden ("Soupy" Davis), Morris Ankrum (Judge Tom Barnes), Donald Douglas ("Hen" Henderson), Mae Marsh (Molly, Mission Chief's Wife), Clarence Muse (Grandpa), George Reed (Christopher), Cordell Hickman (Little Nicodemus), Paul Renay ("Spud" Johnson), Barbara Lynn (Mary, Joe's Daughter), Adeline De Walt Reynolds (Elsa's Old Mother), Helene Reynolds (Actress), Rene Austin (Susan), Olive Ball (Shantytown Woman), Joseph E. Bernard (Wally, the Postman), Ted Billings (Man at City Mission), Buster Brodie (Call Boy), Don Brodie (Whistler at Mission), Ralph Brooks (Man at Reunion), Jack Chefe (Mr. Martinelli, Assistant Tailor), Rita Christiani (Young Woman in Embrace), Gino Corrado (Spectator at Concert), Frank Dae (Elderly Man), Frank Darien (Elsa's Old Father), Sayre Dearing (Man at Reunion), Maggie Dorsey (Woman), Bess Flowers (Concertgoer), Alberta Gary (Shantytown Woman), Charles H. Gray (Rod), Robert Greig (Lazar, Tall Clothier), William Halligan (Oliver Webb, Orman's Manager), Esther Howard (Woman Bumming Cigarette from Joe), Phillip Hurlic (Jeff), Frank Jaquet (Oboist), John Kelly (Burglar No. 2), Kenner G. Kemp (Gambling House Patron), Colin Kenny (Concertgoer), Ella Mae Lashley (Woman), Johnny Lee (Shantytown Carpenter), Connie Leon (Mary, Diane's Maid),

Pat McKee (Bartender), Harold Miller (Man at Reunion), Bert Moorhouse (Concertgoer), Forbes Murray (Dignified Man), Lonnie Nichols (Brad), Tom O'Grady (Concert Latecomer), Manuel Paris (Doorman at Gambling Casino), Alexander Pollard (Waiter), Cyril Ring (Assistant Tailor), Dewey Robinson (Charles Smith's Bullying Boss), Archie Savage (Shantytown Man), Ted Stanhope (Henderson's Chauffeur Returning Wallet), Bert Stevens (Assistant Tailor), Charles Tannen (Pilot), Curly Twiford (Bird Man), Laura Vaughn (Woman), Blue Washington (Shantytown Man), Charles Williams (Orman's Bespectacled Agent), Eric Wilton (Halloway's Butler), Will Wright (Old Concertgoer Last to Doff Tailcoat), Jester Hairston (bit).

The collective effort of a diverse group of 13 writers (including such superlative talents as Ben Hecht, Buster Keaton and Ferenc Molnar), *Tales of Manhattan*, featuring six separate stories, follows the adventures of a black tuxedo tailcoat as it passes from one owner to the next. As with *Sanders of the River*, Paul initially saw this film as an opportunity to address seriously an aspect of black culture, here the squalid living conditions of poor sharecroppers, but in the end was bitterly disappointed by the final product.

Upon completion of the film, the blatant stereotypes permeating the African American story were immediately criticized by both Edward G. Robinson and Paul, who had tried in vain to protest the screenplay during production. Although he had hoped the depiction of his character, Luke, and Esther (Ethel Waters) endeavoring to share their windfall with the rural community would create a positive black image, Paul realized the finished film made "the Negro childlike and innocent and is in the old plantation hallelujah shouter tradition."[2] Actor-songwriter Clarence Muse and NAACP Secretary Walter White approved of the film, but several civil rights groups protested at screenings. Paul first threatened to buy all prints in an attempt to halt distribution and then held a press conference to announce that he was retiring from films, with a promise to join others in picketing *Tales of Manhattan*.

Prior to releasing the film on September 24, 1942, 20th Century–Fox, citing an excessive running time, cut the entire story featuring W. C. Fields, Margaret Dumont and Phil Silvers. It has been suggested, however, that other prominent members of the cast objected to Fields' inordinately large salary, inducing the studio to eliminate the episode. (The scene languished in the Fox vaults until being partially restored for a 1996 video release.)

Other than *Show Boat*, *Tales of Manhattan* is the only Hollywood studio project putting Paul on the screen with A-list movie stars, including such noted liberals as Edward G. Robinson and Henry Fonda, both of whom later joined the Committee for the First Amendment to protest the unconstitutional activities of the House Committee on Un-American Activities (HUAC) in September 1947. The 120-minute version of the film (including the Fields sequence) democratically bills the stars "in the order of their appearance," with Paul, Ethel Waters and Eddie "Rochester" Anderson grabbing the seventh through ninth positions, behind Charles Boyer, Rita Hayworth, Ginger Rogers, Henry Fonda, Charles Laughton and Edward G. Robinson. The African Americans do land last on the "starring" list, but ahead of such fine actors as Thomas Mitchell, George Sanders and (Paul's *King Solomon's Mines* costar) Roland Young, who are relegated to the "with" designation.

The film opens at 5th Avenue and East 60th Street in Manhattan, where an expensive tuxedo is ceremoniously delivered to the apartment of famous stage actor Charles Orman (Charles Boyer) by a tailor who claims the garment has been "cursed." After his performance that evening, Orman meets with his lover, Ethel Halloway (Rita Hayworth), whose drunkard husband, John (Thomas Mitchell), "accidentally" shoots him with a .32-caliber hunting rifle.

While Orman is in the hospital, his butler, Luther (Eugene Pallette), passes the "spoiled

new suit" on to his pal and colleague, Edgar (Roland Young), who is running damage control for his employer, Harry Wilson (Cesar Romero), a notorious two-timer attempting to quell a hangover before his wedding to Diane (Ginger Rogers) that evening. Attempting to cover for the prospective bridegroom, George (Henry Fonda), his best man, claims the tailcoat *and* his buddy's fiancée.

The two butlers pawn the coat, which eventually is snapped up by a woman (Elsa Lanchester) whose husband, Charles Smith (Charles Laughton), is a struggling composer currently banging out boogie-woogie in a local barroom. At the nearby opera house, Smith walks in on a rehearsal conducted by the irate Arturo Bellini (Victor Francen), for whom he auditions his "Bacchanale Moderne." Hired to conduct his own composition, the robust Smith appears on stage, wearing the ill-fitting coat, which elicits roars of laughter from the audience as its seams rip away during the performance. Turning to the sea of hecklers, he tosses the coat onto the stage and sits down to weep, until the maestro, also removing his tailcoat, stands up in his opera box, requesting, "Continue, please." As the orchestra plays, all the men in the audience redeem themselves by doffing their coats. A stunning success, Smith donates his damaged garment, referring to it as a "rabbit's foot," to the Society to Aid the Friendless.

Avery L. "Larry" Browne (Edward G. Robinson), a homeless, alcohol-wracked, ex-attorney sleeping under newspapers in New York's Chinatown, is visited by Joe (James Gleason), a social worker, who delivers an invitation to a 25th reunion of the Class of 1917 at the Waldorf-Astoria, to be held that evening. After six years of "gutters, flophouses and handouts," Browne is decked out by the Aid Society in full formal attire, including the mended tailcoat, and handed enough change to buy "a couple drinks." He refuses drinks and dinner, lies about having been "in China," and then is offered a Wall Street position by "Soupy" Davis (Harry Hayden) before Williams (George Sanders), a former Chicago colleague and rival, inspires a mock "court" to discover a wallet pilfered from "Hen" Henderson (Donald Douglas). Revealing his true situation to the assemblage, Browne makes his exit, just as the wallet is discovered in Henderson's car. The next morning, Browne, loaded, returns to the mission to dump the "J. P. Morgan outfit," quickly followed by H. R. Bronson (James Rennie), Judge Tom Barnes (Morris Ankrum) and Davis, who has arrived to accompany him to the new job.

This poignant scene is succeeded by pure comic farce. The coat is sold to Santelli Bros. Secondhand Clothing across the street from the mission, where it is purchased for $15 by a boisterous, sarcastic customer (W. C. Fields) after he discovers a wallet in the inside pocket (which proves to be filled with slips of newspaper). The "hoodwinked" buyer turns out to be none other than Professor Postlewhistle, evening speaker at the Uptown Association for the Downfall of Alcohol, organized by Madame Langahankie (Margaret Dumont), whose husband (Chester Clute) sabotages the temperance affair by spiking the vat of coconut milk with gin from his fully stocked "secret oasis" of booze.

The drink-sodden conclusion of the "temperance" lecture is followed by the sixth and final story, as two burglars purloin the tailcoat from the basement of the Santelli Bros. store. One of the crooks (J. Carrol Naish) sticks up a gambling joint while wearing the coat but then ditches the garment after it catches fire during his airborne getaway. The smoldering coat, still stuffed with $43,000, lands in a sharecroppers' field, where a black couple, Luke and Esther, pick it up. Luke doesn't care "where it come from, or why," but Esther superstitiously assumes it fell, on the day before Christmas, from "Heaven ... Hallelujah! Praise the Lord!" Luke wants to buy land and farm machinery, but Esther, pointing out that he

never prays, says "it's sinful to have so much money." They seek out the Reverend Lazarus (Eddie "Rochester" Anderson), who fairly doles out the dough to the shantytown residents who pray properly for it.

Every possible cliché is loaded into the scene as the black folks dance, sing gospel songs, praise the Lord, and generally shuck and jive all over the place. Even Grandpa (Clarence Muse), the elderly town drunk, crawls from his cot to claim $25 for his "coffin ... with wheels on it, so I can roll right through the Pearly Gates." After all the "true believers" have claimed their individual requests, the residents collectively have $41,545.50 remaining for a new church, land and tools. Luke pays a visit to nearly forgotten, old Brother Christopher (George Reed), who admits that he prayed for "a scarecrow."

Luke, handing the tailcoat to Christopher, replies, "So that's what they mean when they says, 'The Lord moves in mysterious ways.'" As the old man places the garment out to frighten off the troublesome birds, Luke leads his fellows in the gospel song "Glory Day."

Tales of Manhattan is slickly directed in glossy, major-studio style by Julien Duvivier (a legend of French cinema [*Pepe le Moko*, 1937] who occasionally worked in Hollywood). Charles Boyer and Thomas Mitchell characteristically chew the scenery designed by 20th Century–Fox art directors Richard Day and Boris Leven in the first story, which eats up a

Tales of Manhattan (1942). This U.S.–release title lobby card segregates Robeson, Ethel Waters and Eddie "Rochester" Anderson to its bottom right corner, but they receive billing with the top stars, above "46 Featured Players," in this Hollywood omnibus film that proved a literal career killer for Robeson.

Tales of Manhattan (1942). In the film's closing, cliché-ridden African American episode, Esther (Ethel Waters), the Reverend Lazarus (Eddie "Rochester" Anderson) and Luke (Robeson) ponder the ultimate fate of a satchel stuffed with $43,000 [U.S.–release lobby card].

full fourth of the film's running time. During the second story, Henry Fonda infuses his welcome naturalism into the Hollywood hokum; and Charles Laughton contributes a brilliant, restrained turn opposite his real-life wife, Elsa Lanchester, in the genuinely moving third installment. In the fourth tale, Edward G. Robinson steals the film, bringing his irresistible, unassuming charm to a sympathetic character who speaks the truth to a pack of pretenders, graced by a perfectly cast George Sanders.

In the restored fifth segment (directed by comedy specialist Malcolm St. Clair), the physically debilitated W. C. Fields (at the tail end of his career) unleashes his broad, partly improvised shtick opposite Groucho Marx foil Margaret Dumont. Perhaps this sequence, a satire of drunkenness captained by a painfully alcohol-ravaged former star, was removed from the release print because it differs so markedly from the rest of the material (aside from being more pitiful than funny). Regardless of the reason for its 54-year disappearance, this episode is decidedly out of place, coming right after the Robinson redemption scene. (The "pre-restoration" version of the film makes more sense. With the Fields segment restored, the reappearance of the tailcoat at Santelli's store is inexplicable.)

Regardless of the racist nature of the climactic scene, Paul, the incomparable Ethel Waters, and the reliable, gravel-voiced Eddie Anderson do the best they can with hackneyed material in a highly stylized, studio-bound setting. Paul, perhaps incapable of playing a

truly clichéd character, is the least stereotypical of the three. (Waters and "Rochester" would go on to play husband and wife in the clichéd yet innovative all-black musical *Cabin in the Sky*, directed by Vincente Minnelli and featuring Lena Horne, Rex Ingram, Mantan Moreland, Willie Best, Butterfly McQueen and Louis Armstrong, at MGM the following year.)

Waters was performing at the Orpheum Theatre in Los Angeles when 20th Century–Fox first approached her about *Tales of Manhattan*, offering her $10,000 for 10 days' work and a chance to costar with Paul, whom she had befriended in New York nearly 17 years earlier. These two promises certainly were tempting, but she signed the contract only after learning about the "religious" content of the African American story. She later revealed that the episode originally was to run much longer:

> I had my best scene in a hut where an old woman of over eighty lies dying. When she asks me to sing her across the River Jordan, I stroke her head and softly sing "Nobody Knows the Trouble I've Seen." They had the Hall Johnson Choir furnishing a musical background. As the old woman passes on to her reward a lovely light shines down on her head from above, and it is as though this light is the ladder that her soul can ascend to reach her Maker and the Lord of us all.
>
> The scene was reverently and tenderly done, and all the studio executives raved about it. But when I went to the preview my heart broke. The entire scene had been cut out.[3]

Though Paul was disgusted with *Tales of Manhattan*, he did have one opportunity to inject the values he hoped would be represented in the sharecropping scene. Luke's speech

Tales of Manhattan (1942). Luke (Robeson), the Reverend Lazarus (Eddie "Rochester" Anderson) and Esther (Ethel Waters) begin to dole out the dough to those who "say their prayers." Regardless of the hackneyed material and highly stylized, studio-bound setting, these performers rise above it all.

about the benefit of the windfall is the highpoint of the sequence (with Paul, regardless of the overall style of the scene, rising to a level no other black actor of the period could attain; the viewer need only listen to the emphasis he places on certain words). Luke tells his brothers and sisters (who look upon him with reverence):

> We're going to buy the land, do you hear? The land, and it'll be our'n. And we're going to buy tools, with edges so sharp the earth will jump up to meet 'em. And we're going to work that ground, *side by side*, raisin' corn and cotton, and *what we gets, we shares*. There won't be *no rich* and *no more poor*. Yes, folks, a new day is dawnin'!

But the "new day" Paul was seeking would not be gained by his further appearances in Hollywood (or any other) feature films. Director William Greaves said:

> *Tales of Manhattan* was a *disaster*, because it really played very heavily on all the stereotypical manifestations of the black experience as it could. Robeson himself, when he saw the film, was outraged by Hollywood and its secret agendas with respect to people of color.[4]

At the time of the film's release, Ethel Waters, however, shared the positive opinion of the film expressed by her fellow musician-actor Clarence Muse and the NAACP's Walter White. In 1951 (two years after becoming the second African American to be nominated for an Academy Award, as Best Supporting Actress for her portrayal of "Granny" in Elia Kazan's *Pinky* [1949]), she wrote:

> [V]arious Negro organizations picketed the theaters.... Their placards protested picturing us colored people as wretched, dirty, and poorly clad.
> I didn't understand that. These same organizations were forever complaining that we Negroes in America are underprivileged. So why did they object to anyone showing us that way on the screen?
> I realize, of course, that many of these organizations are led by men and women of the highest ideals. They've done a great deal in the fight to win the Negro equality. But they are making a mistake, I think, when they protest showing colored people as they really are.
> There are thieves and murderers and wife-beaters among my people. There are also geniuses and saints and many Negroes who walk all their days down God's pathway. In other words, Negroes are human beings with exactly the same faults and virtues as members of the other races.[5]

More than 30 years after the controversy, Edward G. Robinson (whose career also suffered mightily from the HUAC blacklist), in his (posthumously published) 1973 autobiography, included only a single terse reference to *Tales of Manhattan*: "It was in five parts, and I appeared in only one of them. Was it good or bad? I don't know. I didn't much care."[6]

James Earl Jones commented:

> [Paul] abandoned all that lucrative work. Even though it was unsatisfactory, it certainly *paid well*. He abandoned being a millionaire. He abandoned being a superstar for what he thought he could commit to, in the cause of equal rights as conceived by socialism. But it was a choice he made. No one *forced* him.[7]

Paul Robeson, Jr., identified some specific offers his father received in the wake of *Tales of Manhattan*:

> For years Paul had refused virtually every major black male part in American film — from *Hallelujah* and *Green Pastures* to *Gone with the Wind* and *Uncle Tom's Cabin*. Currently he was being offered leading parts in *Porgy and Bess* and *Moby Dick*, and an excellent singing part in *The Life of Rimsky-Korsakov*. Despite the furor over *Tales of Manhattan*,

Tales of Manhattan (1942). The film's nine costars rise higher than the legendary New York City skyline on this U.S.–release one-sheet poster. Some of them (namely the six billed below Ginger Rogers) do the same with the content of the screenplay, cobbled together by 13 screenwriters and directed by French cinema legend Julien Duvivier.

there was little doubt that he could pioneer a new, greatly improved black male image in American film. Yet Paul chose an entirely different course.[8]

On December 8, 1942, a little more than two months after the release of *Tales of Manhattan*, an FBI agent in New York filed a 14-page "internal security" report, claiming that an informant had overheard a dinner conversation during which Paul told a companion, Roy Hudson, that he "was working on a Communist moving picture."[9] The agent continued with his second-hand "information":

> Robeson stated that one of the most important things was to get the picture out without adverse publicity. He said that the financial problem is one of the greatest, but that he, Robeson, was working on that phase at the present time. Hudson is said to have replied that the picture will be a powerful experiment as there has never been a movie like it before.... Robeson said that it was their intention to take the picture to Carnegie Hall and present it in conjunction with a concert. The concert would be the "blind." Hudson is said to have replied that it would have a direct appeal to the labor, as they would be able to witness a gallant struggle for their own rights, and further, even if the picture would not now be a success, it must come out as there has been so much delay, and promises.[10]

Later in the same report, the agent refers directly to *Native Land* and (incorrectly) identifies Paul as a "Communist" (a term he mentions six times in this single paragraph):

> The motion picture, "Native Land" ... is receiving copious reviews in the New York press. It advises that "Native Land" is obviously a Communist project. It is produced by the Frontier Films, which is a Communist instrumentality; it is directed by Paul Strand (Communist) and Leo Hurwitz who has many Communist connections. The commentary is written by David Wolff, is spoken by Paul Robeson and an avowed Communist, and the music is by Marc Blitzstein, Communist song writer.[11]

Eight months later, in an August 26, 1943, letter to J. Edgar Hoover, Washington Field Office Special Agent Guy Hottel reported, *fourth*-hand, the following hearsay "evidence" on which the FBI based its Red investigation of Paul:

> [R]ecently an unidentified woman related information ... concerning Paul Robeson.
> According to the unidentified woman, a colored man who has worked for the woman's husband a number of years told her husband of having been solicited by another Negro in Washington to join the Communist Party. The soliciting member is alleged to have said, by way of attempting to influence the other man, that Paul Robeson, the singer, is a leading figure in the Communist Party, and is at the present time actively attempting to influence the Negroes of America to Communism.[12]

Chapter 14

Deep River

In the end, his film career left a dubious legacy.... He ultimately realized that he was powerless to control the final product of the complicated, politically and culturally compromised film industry.

— Clement Alexander Price[1]

On October 19, 1943, Paul returned to Broadway in Margaret Webster's production of Shakespeare's *Othello* at the Sam S. Shubert Theatre, costarring with Uta Hagen and José Ferrer (then husband and wife). Hagen later recalled:

You saw that [he] was a phenomenally, potentially wonderful actor. His lack of skill did not seem to bother anybody, but I think there was a lack of skill. He was, of course, *brilliant*. He had wonderful speech. He had a magnificent voice. He had great intelligence. What he had [was] a presence, charisma, and a *human vibration* that was so overpowering. Suddenly a genuine black man in that role made the play have a meaning that it couldn't have had when someone was going around with coal on [his] face.[2]

Margaret Webster revealed:

I had seen Robeson play Othello in London quite a few years earlier, and I frankly hadn't thought that he was very good. But he said to me then that he himself didn't think that he was very good, but now he had studied and re-studied the role and he felt that he was ready to play it, and why couldn't we do it together? And I was enthusiastic about this idea ... but ... Paul and I between us couldn't persuade any ... New York management to take the risk of doing a play in which a black man (a) made love to, and (b) murdered a white woman. We finally got management and it wasn't then altogether an easy job to get actors to do it...

Paul brought qualities with him which I never have seen equaled before or since. The moment he stepped onto that stage, he was not only a black man, he was a *great* black man, a man of stature....[3]

The *Playbill* for the Shubert Theatre, which afforded Paul a biography that dwarfed those of his colleagues, typically stressed his "legitimate" stage roles to the detriment of his film career, exiled to a lone, concluding sentence: "Among the motion pictures in which Mr. Robeson has played are 'Emperor Jones,' 'Song of Freedom,' 'King Solomon's Mines,' 'Jericho' and 'Show Boat.'" The New York run of 296 performances (a standing record for any Shakespearean play on Broadway) was followed by a cross-country tour, during which the company refused to play to segregated audiences. Paul remembered the tension when they appeared in Cincinnati:

[J]ust on the border of the South —from Louisville, Kentucky, across the river, quite a few people came over. For about half of the performance, nobody quite knew what was going to happen. It was very tense. I was very careful how close I got to Desdemona, for example.[4]

Though Paul received offers from Hollywood producers to star in a feature-film adaptation of *Othello*, he declined, firmly believing that his only chance to do justice to the role

154

cinematically would have to occur in England. "I don't think I would be allowed to do the role properly in Hollywood," he said.[5]

Four months after the *Othello* tour ended in June 1945, Paul was awarded the prestigious Spingarn Medal by the NAACP for his "distinguished achievements in the theater and on the concert stage, as well as his active concern for the rights of the common man for every race, color, religion, and nationality." Only two other African American actors (Charles Gilpin and Richard B. Harrison) had previously received the honor.

During World War II, Paul's support for the Allied war effort (which tied in solidly with his antifascist views), including free concerts, touring with the USO, and campaigning to sell War Bonds, made him the most famous African American on the planet, and his previous public statements about socialism and the Soviet Union were temporarily forgotten. He

On October 19, 1943, Robeson returned to Broadway in Margaret Webster's production of Shakespeare's *Othello* at the Sam S. Shubert Theatre [original *Playbill*].

believed that the patriotic participation of blacks in joining the white establishment to defeat fascism would draw attention to racism in the United States. Paul Robeson, Jr., recalled:

> In the '40s, when everyone agreed that the Axis had to be defeated, he also said that, in fighting against fascism and their kind of racism, we had to, at the same time, fight against black oppression here.... As a matter of fact, I recall his calling the racists and the Ku Klux Klan and so on, in the U.S., as the cousins, if not the brothers, of Hitler's Nazis—and that was unusual then.... At the same time that the War Bond rallies were going on, and he was one of the champion fundraisers for those kinds of things, he was vocally and publicly very critical of racism in the United States, that it was absolutely necessary to eradicate it.[6]

While touring with the *Othello* company during the autumn of 1944, Paul had stumped for President Roosevelt's third reelection whenever an opportunity arose. On November 5, during a broadcast on radio station WHK, he said, "It is Roosevelt who rightly believes the

SAM S. SHUBERT THEATRE

CENTRAL THEATRES LEASING & CONSTRUCTION CO.

EMERGENCY NOTICE: In the event of an alert, remain in your seats. A competent staff has been trained for this emergency. Keep calm. You will receive information and instructions from the stage. F. H. La GUARDIA, Mayor

FIRE NOTICE: The exit indicated by a red light and sign nearest to the seat you occupy is the shortest route to the street. In the event of fire please do not run—WALK TO THAT EXIT.
Patrick Walsh, Fire Commissioner
and Chief of Department

It is urged for the comfort and safety of all, that theatre patrons refrain from lighting matches in this theatre.

THE · PLAYBILL · A · WEEKLY · PUBLICATION · OF · PLAYBILL · INCORPORATED

Week beginning Sunday, December 12, 1943 • Matinees Wednesday and Saturday

THE THEATRE GUILD

Administration: LAWRENCE LANGNER and THERESA HELBURN

presents

PAUL ROBESON

in

The Margaret Webster Production of

OTHELLO

by

William Shakespeare

with

JOSE FERRER UTA HAGEN
MARGARET WEBSTER JAMES MONKS

Production Designed and Lighted by
ROBERT EDMOND JONES

Music Composed by Tom Bennett

Associate Producer
JOHN HAGGOTT

Given the respect of his peers that had eluded him so often in the U.S. film industry, Robeson looms large in the billing for *Othello* [original *Playbill*].

rights of man [are] more important than the rights of private property."[7] Although he turned down requests to perform at the White House, due to FDR's decisions not to end segregation in Washington, D.C., or not to integrate the U.S. military, Paul was supportive of the president in general and joined the nation in mourning when FDR suddenly passed away on April 12, 1945. The *Othello* cast dedicated its evening performance in Chicago to the fallen leader, and, following the curtain calls, Paul delivered an eloquent tribute.

At various New York sessions during 1945–1947, Paul and Lawrence Brown recorded an impressive collection of traditional spirituals and gospel songs representative of their live concerts. Such standards as "Sometimes I Feel Like a Motherless Child," "Go Down, Moses," "Nobody Knows the Trouble I've Seen" and "Swing Low, Sweet Chariot," were supplemented by his *Emperor Jones* numbers "John Henry" and "Water Boy."

When Paul accepted the NAACP's Spingarn Medal, he had startled many in the audience by stating:

> If you are for the people, you are for them; if you are against them, you are for fascism. We people in America had better help our allies all over the world. Democracy can take many forms. We must be careful in selecting the proper way of progress, so that the wealth of the world can be used for the advancement of mankind.[8]

On January 5, 1946, while participating in the "Artist as Citizen" symposium at Henry Miller's Theatre in New York, he stressed that the American people could go "back to fascism, or on to socialism."[9]

Two months later, at Westminster College in Fulton, Missouri, former British Prime Minister Winston Churchill, at the invitation of President Harry Truman, gave his "Sinews of Peace" address, during which he used the term "iron curtain." Subsequently referred to as the "Iron Curtain Speech," Churchill's comments initially were criticized by many in the West; but, as pointed out by Paul Robeson, Jr., this view

> officially launched the Cold War with a thinly veiled call for an Anglo-Saxon alliance against the Soviet Union. Mutual recriminations between the United States and Russia escalated dramatically in the wake of his address, and burgeoning anti–Soviet public opinion presaged a domestic anticommunist crusade.[10]

Over the course of 1946, the lynching of 41 blacks prompted Paul to join Albert Einstein in co-chairing the American Crusade to End Lynching, an organization that sent a delegation of nine members to meet with President Truman at the White House on September 23. Following the death of FDR, Paul quickly had become wary of Truman's dismantling of the former administration's progressive policies, moving the country further to the right and transforming Roosevelt's wartime cooperation with the Soviet Union into one of hard-line confrontation.

Representing 1,500 delegates, Paul read the organization's prepared statement to the president, who made a noncommittal remark that he was "thinking about" their concerns but ultimately "said that it wasn't politically expedient to do anything about lynching."[11] When Paul stated that the administration's refusal to act might eventually elicit a stronger response from the Negro people, Truman stood up and accused him of making a threat. Paul, too, rose from his seat as two Secret Service agents moved forward, ready to act if necessary. Explaining that he didn't intend to offend the president, Paul added that his statement referred to the fact that blacks constituted 10 percent of the U.S. population. Truman sat down, adjourned the meeting, and the delegation departed. Reporters waiting on the White House grounds immediately surrounded Paul, asking the usual question, "Are you a Communist?"

"I describe myself as violently antifascist," he replied. A follow-up question about "Negroes turning the other cheek" was met with an uncharacteristically brutal response from Paul: "If a lyncher hit me on one cheek, I'd tear his head off before he hit me on the other one."[12]

The FBI quickly labeled the anti-lynching group a Communist front and even branded Einstein a Commie sympathizer. J. Edgar Hoover increased the Bureau's surveillance of Paul's every move and pressured his pals at the conservative Hearst newspapers to increase their propaganda assaults. While spending the holidays in New York, Paul enjoyed a chess game with his friend Ellsworth "Bumpy" Johnson, the very intelligent and well-read boss of the Harlem "Black Mafia," who mentioned the incident with Truman. Paul Jr. revealed:

> Bumpy felt Paul had crossed a line and should be concerned about his personal security. The U.S. government would never let a black man get away with something like that and stay in one piece. Paul tried to laugh off the idea but accepted Bumpy's offer of protection whenever he would need it.[13]

During 1946, the Civil Rights Section of the Justice Department, established by FDR seven years earlier, finally convicted a lyncher, Tom Crews, a Florida constable, though he was sentenced to only one year in prison for killing an African American farm worker. Truman himself had nearly joined the KKK in 1922, while serving as a county court judge in Missouri; but, as president, he did finally advocate making lynching a federal crime in 1947. The proposed legislation, however, was defeated by Southern Democrats in the Senate and House of Representatives. In July 1948, Truman, concerned that blacks wouldn't comply with a reinstitution of the draft to counter Soviet military might, issued Executive Order 9981, which set forth the president's new policy of "equality of treatment and opportunity for all persons in the armed services without regard to race, color, religion or national origin."

Paul performed at the Kiel Auditorium in St. Louis, Missouri, in a benefit for the People's Hospital on Friday, January 24, 1947. While in the city, he marched in a picket organized by the Civil Rights Congress to protest the segregation policy of the American Theater. On Friday evening, Walter Huston, who was starring in a play at the theater, met with members of the CRC to voice his support for their anti–Jim Crow demonstration. (Huston, father of the great liberal, renegade director John Huston, had portrayed Ambassador Joseph E. Davies in Warner Bros.' pro–Soviet wartime propaganda feature *Mission to Moscow* [1943] four years earlier.) An FBI agent reporting on the event to J. Edgar Hoover listed other organizations involved in the protest, including the Citizens Council for Democracy, which he identified as a "local Communist Party front," and the local branch of the National Negro Congress, branding it "completely controlled by the CP."[14]

On Saturday, March 15, 1947, Paul performed at the Philharmonic Auditorium in Los Angeles. The following Thursday, Red-baiting gossip columnist and HUAC collaborator Hedda Hopper roundly condemned him in her *Los Angeles Times* "Looking at Hollywood" column:

> When Paul Robeson sang the Communist "People's Battle Song" here and dedicated it to Gerhardt Eisler, some members of his audience walked out. Why one remained is beyond me. To sit idly listening to a man abusing the precious heritage of freedom given us by our Constitution in flaunting the preachings of our most dangerous enemy is inviting disaster. When such people as Robeson are attacked they scream "persecution" and "Fascism"—the obvious dodge that our Red brethren attempt when cornered by people whom they've goaded out of lethargy. Yet they believe it perfectly right that they be allowed to attack the

very foundations of our country — simply because one of our principles provides freedom of speech.[15]

A few months later, when a Truman-endorsed plan to send a "Freedom Train" on a nationwide tour was tainted by the American Heritage Foundation's refusal to create a non-segregated exhibit (ironically featuring the Declaration of Independence and other "documents of freedom"), the African American community chose poet Langston Hughes to express its outrage. After penning the poem "Freedom Train," Hughes elected his own representative to give it a voice; and, throughout the autumn of 1947, Paul recited this powerful poetical statement at his concerts and speaking engagements. He also made a three-minute recording of the poem, which has endured far longer than the actual Freedom Train. After only a few months of stopping at what Hughes accurately called "Jim Crow stations," the tour ran out of steam in January 1948.

In the meantime, the House Committee on Un-American Activities, announced with great fanfare in the national media, had begun its hearings in Washington, D.C., on October 20, 1947. That same day, the Censor Board of Memphis, Tennessee, banned the exhibition of the classic Hal Roach *Our Gang* comedies (originally produced from 1922 to 1944, and reissued as *The Little Rascals*) because the films show a "Negro" boy attending the same school with white children. (*Our Gang* had broken new ground by depicting its characters, regardless of gender or race, as relative equals. The inaugural African American actor in the series, Ernest "Sunshine Sammy" Morrison, was quite proud of being "at the age of six, the first black actor to sign a long-term Hollywood contract."[16] He was succeeded in the series by Allen "Farina" Hoskins, Matthew "Stymie" Beard and Billie "Buckwheat" Thomas.)

Following his retirement from commercial motion pictures, Paul contributed to a few politically oriented documentaries. During the 1948 presidential campaign, he publicly stumped for the Progressive Party candidate, Iowa-born Henry A. Wallace, Truman's former Secretary of Commerce (1945-1946) and Franklin Roosevelt's Secretary of Agriculture (1933–1940) and vice president during the historic third FDR term (1941–1945).

Paul narrated and appeared in *The People's Congressman*, a short campaign film for Vito Marcantonio of New York, a former Republican representative who had been reelected on the American Labor Party ticket (eventually serving six terms from 1939 to 1951). Born in New York City of Italian ancestry, Marcantonio, after graduating from NYU with a law degree, fought for the rights of various ethnic groups, including Italian-Americans, Puerto Ricans and African Americans. Like Paul, his support for labor and other left-wing causes earned him long-term surveillance as a "Communist sympathizer" by the FBI.

The conclusion of *The People's Congressman* includes footage of Paul and Marcantonio campaigning for Henry Wallace at Yankee Stadium on September 11, 1948. During his speech, Wallace vows, "I am committed to wipe out segregation to prevent the fear-makers from clogging the minds of the people with the Red issue," part of his platform that focused on civil rights, a lifting of the Israel Embargo, and repeal of the "Taft-Hartley Act." (Referred to as the "slave-labor bill" by union leaders, the Labor-Management Relations Act, which placed serious restrictions on the activities of workers [and required leaders to sign non–Communist affidavits], was vetoed by Truman in June 1947, but subsequently overridden by Congress.) The film features an excerpt from Paul and Lawrence Brown's "progressive version" of "The Battle Hymn of the Republic," which includes the transformation of the lyrics "Glory, Glory, Hallelujah!" to "Marching on with Henry Wallace!" Branded a "pinko," Wallace, winning only 2.4 percent of the popular vote, handily lost the nomination to Truman.

Following a successful U.S. and Caribbean tour during the autumn of 1948, Paul took a break to celebrate the holidays at his home in Connecticut, with plans to rejoin Lawrence Brown at more concert dates scheduled for January through April 1949. He soon was informed, however, that his upcoming performances had been canceled by local booking agents whom the FBI had threatened to brand "pro–Communist" if they objected to such intimidation. In turn, conservative journalists, led by Walter Winchell, continued to pillory Paul in newspaper columns across the nation.

As the United States government coerced the entertainment industry into blacklisting him, Paul, joined by Brown, returned to Europe for a series of concerts. During his absence, Essie delivered a lecture, "The Negro Contribution to Culture," at the Negro Actors Guild's 12th Annual Meeting at the Grand Street Boys Association in New York on March 27. Focusing on "the treatment of Negroes in films," she mentioned several current Hollywood productions featuring prominent black performers, including *Lost Boundaries* (William Greaves and Leigh Whipper), *Intruder in the Dust* (Juano Hernandez), *Home of the Brave* (James Edwards, in his second film) and *No Way Out* (Ossie Davis, Ruby Dee, and costarring Sidney Poitier in his first major screen role):

> This kind of program in Hollywood, and *South Pacific* for Broadway, certainly make things look up for the Negro actor, and certainly make things look up for the 15 million Negroes who have been so misrepresented on stage and screen for so many years.
> It does seem to be taking a long time for us Negroes to find our rightful place in our country. We know, of course, that we are not all Uncle Toms and Aunt Jemimas, no more than all Irishmen are policemen, all Chinese laundrymen, all Italians fruit vendors, and so on. Along with other Americans, we can look back into our history, and find much to be proud of, and can be reassured when we see what substantial contributions we have made to the culture of our country, and of the world.[17]

In Paris on April 20, Paul addressed the Congress of the World Partisans of Peace. His impromptu "make peace, not war" speech was outrageously misquoted by the Associated Press, whose fabricated report claimed that Paul had urged blacks to "denounce" the U.S. government, oppressors for whom they wouldn't fight in a war against the Soviet Union, a nation that promoted racial equality. While Paul was still in Paris that evening, this propaganda, supported by J. Edgar Hoover, sparked mass indignation and cries of treason across the States, pitting him even more squarely against the white establishment he enthusiastically had joined in the battle against fascism during World War II.

The next day, Paul, oblivious to the outrage increasing in his homeland, performed in Stockholm. During an unscheduled press conference, he was baited into giving an answer closely resembling the falsified Associated Press report. An accurate transcription of his original Paris remarks appeared in only two publications, *Daily Worker* and the weekly progressive newspaper *National Guardian*. Influenced by the barrage of misinformation claiming that Paul fancied himself a spokesman for all blacks in the United States, African American leaders, including Roy Wilkins, acting executive secretary of the NAACP, spoke out against "radical" views that apparently were not shared by a majority of their brethren. Many blacks, however, doubted the accuracy of the news reports. Adam Clayton Powell, Jr., took a level-headed view of the situation, and W. E. B. DuBois, who had attended the Paris conference, wholly supported Paul's view that "Negroes should never willingly fight in an unjust war."[18]

Following more dates in Sweden, Denmark, Norway and England, Paul, with Bruno Raikin replacing Lawrence Brown as his accompanist, set out on a tour of Eastern Europe

including performances in Prague and Warsaw. On June 4, he returned to Moscow, where he again was well received by concertgoers but had to perform without the Jewish Raikin, whose visa was denied. Paul began further to question his feelings toward the Soviets following a visit with his friend, Russian-born Jewish poet and war veteran Itzik Feffer, who was briefly released from his cell at Lubyanka prison and then forced to communicate using only written notes and hand gestures in a hotel room bugged by the State Police. (Feffer, who indicated that their mutual friend, Solomon Mikhoels, had been murdered on Stalin's order, eventually was executed, along with 14 other Jewish intellectuals, in 1952.)

On June 14, during a nationally broadcast concert at Moscow's Tchaikovsky Hall, Paul sang "Zog Nit Keynmol," the resistance anthem of the Warsaw Ghetto, in both Russian and Yiddish, as a tribute to Feffer and the late Mikhoels. However, at Feffer's prompting, he refrained from criticizing the Soviet Union in public, both to avoid worsening his friend's situation and creating additional support for the already powerful reactionary voices in the United States. Before flying back to New York two days later, Paul was offered asylum by a high-ranking Soviet official, who spoke of the danger, including his possible assassination, that might be looming in the U.S. Though he expressed gratitude for the proposal, he explained that he must return home to help his own people.

Prior to attending a Welcome Home rally at Rockland Palace in Harlem on June 19 (the same day that Paul Jr. was scheduled to marry his fiancée, Marilyn Greenburg), Paul met with Walter White, who was on leave from his position as executive secretary of the NAACP but acting on behalf of Secretary of State Dean Acheson. White repeated Acheson's "unofficially" conveyed offer from President Truman, who was willing to allow Paul to resume his full professional career free of government interference *if* he agreed in writing to avoid political statements and gatherings for one year. In no uncertain terms, White urged Paul to accept the private gag order or face possible assassination. Paul thanked him but gave no answer.

Following the marriage ceremony, the small wedding party braved an angry all-white mob shouting racial epithets at Paul Jr. and his Jewish bride before police escorted them to waiting taxis. Later that afternoon, 5,000 people, black and white, assembled at Rockland Palace. Before Paul spoke and sang five songs, he was preceded by several dignitaries, including W. E. B. DuBois, Vito Marcantonio and Charles P. Howard of the Des Moines, Iowa, NAACP. Tributes sent by Henry Wallace and socialist playwright and screenwriter Clifford Odets also were read to the crowd. Paul confirmed what he had said in Paris, clearly stated his intentions, and gave a "defiant public answer to the State Department's privately conveyed offer":

> To fulfill our responsibilities as Americans, we must unite, especially we Negro people. We must know our strength.... If we unite, we'll get our law against lynching, our rights to vote and to labor. Let us march on Washington, representing 14,000,000 strong. Let us push aside the sycophants who tell us to be quiet.... We do not want to die in vain any more on foreign battlefields for Wall Street and the greedy supporters of domestic fascism. If we must die, let it be in Mississippi or Georgia! Let it be wherever we are lynched and deprived of our rights as human beings![19]

On July 13, 1949, the House Committee on Un-American Activities convened the "Hearings Regarding Communist Infiltration of Minority Groups" in Washington, D.C. African American HUAC investigator Alvin Stokes made the preposterous assertions that Paul was "the voice of the Kremlin" and that the Communist Party intended to create a separate republic for blacks in the South. Blatantly lying under oath, CPUSA turncoat Man-

ning Johnson testified that Paul used the alias "John Thomas" as a member of the Party and had definite plans to become the "Black Stalin."

On July 18, the ultimate symbol of integration, Jackie Robinson, concerned about the future of his baseball career (which Paul had helped bring about), testified under pressure from both HUAC and the Brooklyn Dodgers. His appearance had been arranged by the Urban League, whose assistant executive secretary, Lester Granger, counseled the committee to direct its investigation toward the KKK if the government wished to prove it was doing anything to combat racism. Before Robinson went to Washington, Paul had sent him a letter, again repeating the actual remarks made in Paris. All the major newsreel companies sent cameramen to cover the event, but the star slugger disappointed the Red-baiters by merely referring to Paul's reported views on blacks and the Soviet Union as "silly." Furthermore, Robinson added that Paul "has a right to his personal views, and if he wants to sound silly when he expresses them in public, that is his business and not mine. He's still a famous ex-athlete and a great singer and actor." When the Minority Groups hearings ended, Paul, who wasn't called to testify, had gained stronger support from a majority of blacks, progressives and the leadership of the CPUSA.

During August and September 1949, a five-part interview with Paul appeared in the black newspaper *New York Age*, in which he clearly explained his views that were being distorted by the media:

> The whole Negro problem has its basis in the South — in the cotton belt where Negroes are in the majority. That is the only thing that explains me completely. The Negro upper class wants to know why I am out here struggling in behalf of the oppressed, exploited Negro of the South when I could isolate myself from them like they do and become wealthy by keeping quiet on such disturbing subjects.... We must come together as a people, and with our own unity we must try to find the right allies — those whose struggles over the past years have driven us together. Suppose that in the South, where the Negroes are in the majority in the agricultural belt, we had the vote like everyone else? What would happen? Wouldn't Negroes be in Congress, be governors, judges, mayors, sheriffs and so on? ... Negroes of the South must realize that they are the ones who built that which has been and still is being taken from them. Maybe they should think of someday gaining control through constitutional means of that which should have been theirs all along.[20]

On August 27, Paul was scheduled to perform during the fourth annual benefit concert for the Harlem chapter of the Civil Rights Congress at Lakeland Acres, north of Peekskill, New York. Before he arrived at the site, a riot, spurred by local press attacks and organized by chapters of the VFW and American Legion, broke out, led by a 200-strong, obscenity-shouting mob wielding baseball bats. Cars were searched for black riders, rocks were tossed into the crowd, the stage was torn apart, and a cross was set ablaze. Local law enforcement merely shot the breeze with the rioters, while FBI agents calmly stood by, noting their own versions of the event. Friends attempted to drive Paul and Lawrence Brown into the grounds but were hesitant to proceed when they saw gangs of men pulling over cars, shouting such insults as "Dirty Commies!" and "Niggers!" Paul finally agreed to leave after he saw the flaming cross on the hill.

When an effigy of Paul also was torched, accompanied by shouts of "Lynch Robeson!" a group of 40 men attempted to defend the remaining crowd against the 200 attackers, who were satisfied to burn nearly everything else in sight. Twelve of the defenders were injured before state police, having been called hours earlier, finally intervened.

The next day, 1,500 local residents organized the Westchester Committee for Law and

Order to sponsor a new concert, scheduled for September 4 on the grounds of the Hollow Brook Country Club. Henry Wallace, the ACLU and the New York NAACP backed the initiative against the conservatives and veterans groups who continued to spread propaganda and intimidate local Robeson supporters. Paul was particularly concerned with the safety of his audience at the rescheduled event. Longshoremen, members of the United Electrical Workers and other trade unions signed on to provide security against further reactionary demonstrations.

On August 30, 3,000 supporters arrived at Harlem's Golden Gate Ballroom to hear Paul address the "attempted assassination" and perform "No More Auction Block," "Scandalize My Name" and "Ol' Man River." During his remarks, he vowed that his people would now "take the offensive":

> We're going to have our concerts across this land, and we'll see that our women and children are not harmed again ... we'll protect ourselves.... That's all I'm saying — to the Klan, to the Legionnaires, to big business, even to the chief executive of these United States! ... Any, any time, that you want to call on me, I'm in there fighting for my people. Because you're with me; because we're all fighting together, for the freedom not only of the Negro people, but of an America which, years hence, our children can be proud of. We'll be proud we helped create an America where they could walk this earth with their shoulders back, full of the dignity of humankind.[21]

When Paul left the building, his car was escorted by a small fleet of Cadillacs provided by Bumpy Johnson. A crowd of several thousand people calmly and quietly marched down Lenox Avenue as startled members of the NYPD moved onto the sidewalks. All of the officers were treated with respect by the marchers, who had been ordered not to continue without a permit. One young white policeman, whose fear was apparent, was assured by an elderly woman that he would not be molested in any way, adding, "Just you-all make sure nothin' happens to Paul Robeson."[22]

Shortly after dawn on September 4, a security force of 4,000 union men, most of whom were World War II veterans, assembled on the Hollow Brook grounds. This time, every contingency was considered in a well-organized plan. All units communicated by walkie-talkie, and softball bats were stashed at key points. Though state policemen also arrived, they spent as much time harassing the union guards as they did patrolling the area. A group of guards wearing hardhats and armed with bats soon disarmed two snipers with high-powered rifles. The police ignored the situation and were asked to leave, placing all further security responsibilities with the union men.

Paul and Lawrence Brown, each in a separate car, arrived in a convoy, driving through a complement of guards who conducted another patrol of the area. Howard Fast, the master of ceremonies, and singer-songwriter Pete Seeger conferred with Paul on his decision to perform two sets of five songs, with no speeches in between. Informed about the snipers, Paul nonetheless walked onto the stage, with a group of 15 volunteers forming a "human barrier" around him. This time, a mob of 8,000 surrounded the entrance to the site, carrying banners of hate and shouting, "Go back to Russia, you white niggers" and "Niggers, Jews, commies— Hitler didn't finish the job, but we will!"

An enormous audience of 25,000, including about 7,000 blacks, had arrived by the time the concert began at 2 P.M. The remaining state police now forced the union guards back inside the concert area, leaving all further arrivals at the mercy of the protesters. Blacks who attempted to talk back to anyone hurling racial epithets were beaten by the police. The situation was tolerable once they managed to enter the site, which now was encircled by

2,500 union men. As a police helicopter whirred in the sky above, two pianists opened the show, followed by Pete Seeger. Paul's program, bracketed with "Go Down, Moses" and "Ol' Man River," was uninterrupted as everyone, including the police and protesters, listened to his powerful performance.

But this was only the calm before the storm. As the audience began to disperse from the concert area, all hell broke loose as the mob, egged on by the police, hurled large stones at the cars and buses. Any injured riders who asked for help were beaten and ordered to get back into their vehicles and exit the area. Paul was lying on the floor, with two guards on top of him, in the back seat of his car, as the convoy drove toward the gate. Police officers attempted to beat in the windshield with their nightsticks, but Paul's driver maneuvered between the other cars, protecting him from both the cops and the crazed lynch mob.

The remaining concertgoers attempted marching peacefully to their cars and buses, most of which had been damaged by the riot of rocks. White union members, forming protective barriers around their black brethren, were clubbed by the police but responded by singing labor songs. The road through the entrance was literally soaked with blood.

The battered buses arriving back in Harlem were teeming with injured black men, women and children. Paul stood outside the Hotel Theresa and cried. Bumpy Johnson, accompanied by a private army ready to be deployed to Peekskill should Paul give the order, was standing by. Informed that the union guards had successfully extricated the last of his patrons, Paul was grateful to tell Bumpy and his men to stand down.

Informed that 145 people had been seriously injured at Peekskill, New York, Republican Governor Thomas Dewey, who praised the police "for their excellent work," refused to meet with more than 300 of Paul's supporters, blaming the entire incident on "Communists" who were also mentioned in radio reports as "Robeson's followers." Eleanor Roosevelt, who deplored the violence, commented that, although she didn't agree with Paul's views, she wholly supported his right to freedom of speech. President Truman concurred with the former First Lady but said nothing more about the issue. During a subsequent Congressional debate, Representative John E. Rankin of Mississippi, a virulent segregationist, racist, anti–Semite and HUAC member who had uttered the word "nigger" in Adam Clayton Powell, Jr.'s, presence on the House floor, declared:

> The American people were not in sympathy with that gang of Communists who composed that traitorous gathering. When they now undertake to investigate and persecute those ex-servicemen who made that protest, when they begin to investigate them for trying to break up that Communist meeting, the American people are with the ex-servicemen and not with that Negro Communist and that bunch of Reds.

On October 9, 1949, the *New York Times* published an editorial supporting this heinous propaganda, praising the farcical investigation of the Westchester County grand jury and the Peekskill hate mob, who "were anti–Communist and not anti–Negro or anti–Semitic."[23]

More than 80 Robeson concerts were cancelled. No major venue in the United States would book him, for fear that the building would be burned to the ground. Stores no longer carried nor advertised his records. Angered by true accounts and photographs of the Peekskill incident published in the black press, a majority of African Americans held Paul in even higher esteem. Churches and halls in black communities were still open to him and, at every stop on his tour, including Cleveland, Chicago and Los Angeles, he was protected by Pullman porters, redcaps and skycaps. After performing at Hartford Avenue Baptist Church in Detroit, he said that "racism, not communism, loomed as humankind's greatest enemy,

and communists, who were both antiracist and anticolonialist, could not possibly be enemies of black people."[24]

On Sunday, March 19, 1950, Paul was scheduled to participate in a debate with Adam Clayton Powell, Jr., and Perry Howard about "the position of the Negro in American Political Life" on the NBC television program *Today with Mrs. Roosevelt*, hosted by the former First Lady. On March 13, the New York *Journal American* reported:

> Paul Robeson, pro–Communist Negro singer, has been taken off Mrs. Eleanor Roosevelt's television program next Sunday, it was announced today by Charles R. Denny, executive vice president of NBC. Robeson's removal followed hundreds of complaints from Negro leaders and spokesmen for veterans organizations.[25]

On the evening of Thursday, March 16, during a speech to 15,000 blacks on the South Side of Chicago, Paul addressed NBC's ban, promising, "I won't be silenced!"[26] In New York, the Harlem Trade Union Council organized a picket at the main entrance of Radio City Music Hall. An FBI agent in New York reported that a "confidential informant of known reliability ... advised that the Harlem Trade Union Council is a Communist Party front organization and that its officers are members of the Communist Party."[27] (Such anti–Robeson activities ensured that he never would appear on a television program in the United States.)

Following Truman's commitment of U.S. troops to support South Korea on June 27, the Cold War began to warm up considerably. In September, Congress, overriding a presidential veto, passed the McCarran Internal Security Act, requiring the registration of "Communist organizations" and the creation of the Subversive Activities Control Board, which had broad powers to investigate anyone who might be engaged in "un–American and subversive activities."

Paul had planned a trip to Europe that month, but J. Edgar Hoover, authorizing agents from the FBI's International Security Division to confiscate his passport, had enacted every measure to prevent him from leaving the country. Paul refused and, on August 4, the State Department, declaring that his travel abroad would be "contrary to the best interests of the United States," demanded that he surrender it. This decision, supported by Secretary of State John Foster Dulles, coupled with the general blacklisting of Paul by the American entertainment industry, literally made it impossible for him to continue with his career on stage, radio, and in films. Though the State Department denied that the issue of "Negro rights" had anything to do with the decision, Paul insisted that the issue was "indeed at the heart of the case," an "attitude [that] should outrage every decent American."[28] Paul wrote, "When will Americans learn, that if they would encourage liberty in other countries, they must practice it at home?"[29]

On January 9, 1951, Roger P. Ross, a public affairs officer working for the State Department in Accra, requested that a fabricated story, describing Paul's support of socialism and ideas about representing African Americans as "an illness of the mind and heart which is not easily recognized, and thus a deadly danger," be distributed throughout Africa. The proposal, personally approved by Secretary Dulles, resulted in the article "Paul Robeson — the Lost Shepherd," ghostwritten by "Robert Alan" and published in the November 1951 issue of *The Crisis*, the official magazine of the NAACP, whose leadership apparently had collaborated closely with the State Department. Claiming that Paul had been duped by communists, this work of patent propaganda also was distributed in pamphlet form to Africans across the continent.

On June 2, 1951, Paul performed at Otis Hall in Roxbury, Massachusetts. The FBI again had in attendance a "confidential informant of known reliability," who claimed that Paul stated, "The capitalists of this country are not scaring anybody" during a concert in which he also noted that "he and other progressive artists will form a theatre and film group in the very near future."[30]

The FBI also assigned agents to cover all preparations for Paul's appearance at the International Peace Arch, located on the border between the state of Washington and British Columbia, on May 18, 1952. This concert of protest against the State Department's travel ban (which included the INS barring Paul from Canada and Mexico) was organized by U.S. and Canadian labor unions. A flatbed truck parked at the Blaine, Washington, location provided a stage for Paul, who sang for a crowd of 40,000 (35,000 of whom had gathered on the Canadian side of the border).

On April 26, an agent in Seattle reported to Hoover:

Communist Party members and their associates ... are making plans for this appearance....
A Paul Robeson Concert Committee has been organized at Seattle and the known principal
members of this committee are reliably reported to be Communist Party members....
Reportedly a strong-arm "honor guard" is being organized to make sure that the Peace
Arch appearance will not be another "Peekskill."[31]

The success of the concert inspired Paul to return to the site for annual performances over the next four years.

Prior to retiring from the screen, Paul had attempted to use the cinema in the struggle for civil rights. A decade later, the technology was being utilized for the opposite purpose, by FBI agents making their own "Robeson films" as part of their Internal Security Photographic Surveillance operation. On May 19, the day after the Peace Arch concert, five rolls of 16mm film were shipped via registered mail from the Seattle office to Hoover in Washington. On June 5, an agent in the Director's Office mailed the processed film back to Seattle, where the footage was examined in an effort to identify individuals who might be tagged as Communists or fellow travelers.

On June 24, an agent in Pittsburgh shipped two 16mm rolls containing footage of "persons entering Turner Hall," where Paul had performed four days earlier, in a concert sponsored by the local chapter of the National Negro Labor Council. The agent reported to Hoover that the processed film should be returned to Pittsburgh so that a still photograph "of each individual and/or group of individuals" could be made for the scrutiny of "Pittsburgh Security Informants in an effort to determine [their] identity."[32]

Every move Paul made was documented by the Bureau. Denied access to concert halls, he was forced to sing in schools and African American churches, but prospective patrons, fearing violence and intimidated by FBI agents who logged their license plate numbers, stayed home. Most of the union halls now were closed to him. Federal government employees could be fired for owning a Robeson record or even expressing "intent" to attend a concert. Always standing on principle, Paul said:

I was actually prevented from appearing in my *own* land.... I have never been on American
television, for example. That is, I have been *blacklisted*, as have many of my colleagues in
America, for whatever reason.... I do not regret, in any sense, what I have done. Some of
my friends feel I could have done things in other ways. One has to do them as one sees
life.... I am very proud, in one sense, of any contribution I have been able to make in the
struggles of my people. If you want freedom, you have to suffer sometimes.[33]

When all of the record companies in the U.S. closed their doors to him, Paul and his son formed the independent Othello Recording Corporation to distribute new material. On December 8, 1952, a confidential teletype received by the FBI noted that the company, located at 53 West 125th Street in New York, was "producing an album, 'Robeson Sings,' to be issued during January Fifty Three."[34]

On December 21, Paul was one of seven international figures awarded the Stalin Peace Prize, but he was unable to travel to the Soviet Union to accept it. Formally established as the International Stalin Prize for Strengthening Peace Among Peoples in 1949, it was the Soviet equivalent of the Nobel Prize.

On June 21, 1953, Paul returned to Los Angeles to perform at the First Unitarian Church under the auspices of the Hollywood Arts, Sciences and Professions Council, the Southern California chapter of the National Council of Arts, Sciences and Professions. An FBI informant reported that Paul, accompanied by "an escort of bodyguards," sang to a gathering "in excess of 1,200," many of them members of the Council, "the most important Communist controlled organization in the Hollywood professional field." The agent submitting the report to Hoover, however, uncharacteristically noted that "membership in the ... Council ... does not connote membership in or sympathy with the Communist Party."[35]

To Stan all the best
Paul Robeson

PAUL ROBESON

Robeson gladly autographed 3 × 5-inch portraits for his devoted fans, many of whom risked landing on FBI "fellow traveler" lists by attending his performances in union halls, schools and the few African American churches who would welcome him.

On September 23, the FBI kept a close watch on Paul as he picked up the Stalin Peace Prize from Howard Fast and W. E. B. DuBois at the Hotel Theresa in Harlem. FBI agents tailed journalists who covered the event. In a confidential report to J. Edgar Hoover, an agent noted that the gold medal was accompanied by "100,000 rubles ... roughly equivalent to $25,000.00 in American currency. Their [*sic*] was no explanation ... as to the reason for

When the U.S. record companies closed their doors to him, Robeson formed the independent Othello Recording Corporation, located at 53 West 125th Street in New York, a locale frequently staked out by the FBI. The album *Robeson Sings*, personally autographed by Paul for all subscribers, was issued in January 1953. The songs include "Curly-Headed Baby," the musical centerpiece of *Big Fella* (1937).

the payment to Robeson."[36] (More than five decades after his father received the award, Paul Jr. recalled, "As popular as my father was during his tours of the Soviet Union, Stalin never attended one of the concerts."[37])

By the time Paul accepted the award, Stalin was dead and a power struggle was under way within the collective leadership of the Presidium of the Supreme Soviet. Nikita Khrushchev, who had been elected by the Central Committee as First Secretary, eventually rose to the top, reinstating the party rule that had been eroded by the dictatorship of Stalin. In due course, Khrushchev instituted a series of reforms, including a "de–Stalinization" process that destroyed the cult of personality forged by the former leader. Paul was pleased to see that Stalin's abuses of power were being dealt with in such sweeping fashion.

Regardless of the continuing heat in the United States, Paul hadn't completely abandoned the cinematic medium for promoting his sociopolitical beliefs. For the East German documentary film *Song of the Rivers* (1954), a chronicle of the third World Trade Union Congress (helmed by directors from the Netherlands [Joris Ivens and Joop Huisken], France [Robert Menegoz] and Brazil [Ruy Santos]), Paul sang a translation of Bertolt Brecht and Dmitry Shostakovich's German-language "Lied von den Flussen," which was used in the English and French versions of the film. Paul also provided a recording of "Hymn of the Workers," which was included in the prologue. Promoted in part by a poster designed by Pablo Picasso, this World Federation of Trade Unions production eventually was shown to more than 250 million people. Paul wrote:

> It was a song for peace and freedom, a song of brotherhood for working people of all lands — of course I would do it.... It was a stirring song of six mighty rivers — the Mississippi, the Ganges, the Nile, the Yangtse, the Volga, the Amazon — and of the people who toil in the fertile valleys; and there was beauty and passion in the German lyrics.[38]

Paul asked writer Lloyd Brown to provide the English lyrics. To avoid "sabotage done by recording engineers whose ears, keenly attuned to the snarls of McCarthy, were deaf to a singer of Peace," he invited Paul Jr. to record his performance at the parsonage home of his older brother, the Reverend Ben Robeson. Paul later noted:

> [The] documentary film ... was, said the critics, "a masterpiece," "a monumental work," "a hymn to Man, honoring labor and assailing colonialism. The reviewers described as "magnificent" the score...
>
> Masters of culture, champions of peace — what a wonderful filmmaking company I had become associated with! And there was a warm glow of appreciation for the invitation they had sent me, making it possible for a Negro American to join with Hollander and Russian and German and Frenchman and all the others in creative work for peace and liberation.
>
> A year later, when I had a chance to visit Canada, I was very happy to see, in a trade union hall, this film which had carried the song from a house in Harlem to audiences around the world. Millions in many lands have seen "Song of the Rivers" ... but people in the United States have been denied that opportunity.
>
> But we know that such films for peace shall one day be welcomed to our land again, and singers of peace shall be given passports to travel abroad.[39]

Paul's popularity in the U.K. remained undiminished, and he continued to collect handsome royalties from his British films and records. Likewise, the FBI's filming of his appearances at the Peace Arch and elsewhere didn't prevent him from connecting with his supporters in Canada. On August 6, 1954, *Daily People's World* ran the article "Paul Robeson's Voice Soars Across National Barriers":

> The artistry of Paul Robeson winged unimpeded across an international frontier with the appearance of the world-beloved singer and actor in his third annual concert in beautiful Peace Arch park on the U.S.–Canadian border.
>
> Although denied a passport to appear in their countries Robeson sang to friends from many lands as the audience was swelled by athletes and visitors from all parts of the British Commonwealth who are in Vancouver for the famous Empire Games.[40]

Paul's continuing fight to regain his passport attracted the support of many British trade unions and journalists. Permanently exiled from the United States through the collaborative efforts of J. Edgar Hoover and the INS, fellow cinematic visionary Charles Chaplin said:

To deny a great artist like Paul Robeson his right to give his art to the world is to destroy the very foundation upon which our culture and civilization is built. It negates every principle of democracy and freedom and follows a path of the worst type of tyranny.[41]

In Harlem, Paul's local supporters organized a tribute at the Renaissance Casino. The progressive artists who participated included jazz virtuosi Dizzy Gillespie, Thelonious Monk and Charlie Parker, singers Leon Bibb and Pete Seeger, and blacklisted actress Karen Morley, who had starred in *Our Daily Bread* (1934), director King Vidor's classic film about farmers who form a collective during the Great Depression.

On May 16, 1955, the *Daily Worker* published an article, "Robeson Offered Othello Role in Soviet Film: Again Applied to State Department for Passport":

Paul Robeson, noted singer and actor, re-applied this week for a passport in order to appear in a film version of the Shakespeare classic, "Othello," scheduled for production this summer in the Soviet Union.[42]

This announcement that Paul wished to make a feature-film "comeback" attracted the New York FBI, who, on July 6, reported to Hoover that "the offer had been made by Sergei Yutkevich, Director of the Moscow Film Studio."[43] Five days later, an agent in the New York office wrote to Hoover:

Robeson has an offer to play the role of "Othello" in England, but is unable to accept the offer because he is unable to travel. Robeson also has an offer to act in a filmed production of "Othello" in East Germany. Robeson also has other offers from Europe, which he cannot fulfil [*sic*] because of his passport restriction. Robeson's time these days, therefore, is spent in attempting to have his passport restriction lifted.[44]

These FBI reports prove that Paul wasn't against acting in another feature film, if he believed the material suited his political views. The fact that he again would have needed to travel to Europe to make such a film was obvious (if he hadn't been "under house arrest" in his own country). In order to have his passport reinstated, the State Department required him to sign a "non–Communist affidavit."

Paul typically stood firm on principle. "Of course I won't sign," he said. "I consider it to be an invasion of every Constitutional liberty I have."[45] His name recently had been included on a list of artists the Soviets wished to welcome via a cultural exchange program with the United States. Paul explained, "I have specifically requested a passport to permit me to accept an offer to make a film version of *Othello* in Moscow and can think of no travel abroad that would be more enjoyable than another trip to the Soviet Union."[46] (Sergei Yutkevich and Mosfilm eventually made the *Othello* film, starring Ukrainian actor and future director Sergei Bondarchuk in the title role, in 1956. The film was dubbed into English and released in the United States by Universal in 1960.)

The non–Communist affidavits became business as usual at all the Hollywood studios, with some actors (such as master comic Lou Costello at Universal) personally "asking" colleagues to sign the repressive document if they wanted to work in a film. An up-and-coming African American actor following in Paul's trailblazing footsteps, Sidney Poitier, was currently preparing for his role in director Richard Brooks' *The Blackboard Jungle* (1955). Before production began, Poitier was called to the front office at MGM, where a studio lawyer accused him of associating with "questionable characters," namely "Paul Robeson [and] Canada Lee":

These, of course, were some of the most stand-up people in those days for things racial, and I was proud to be associated with them.

I said, "So what is it that you want from me?"

He said, "Well, we need you to sign a loyalty oath."

And I said, "What am I supposed to do by signing the oath? I must swear what?" It drove me wild that these men could see red but couldn't see black. That was galling enough. But what also appalled me was that I was being accused of being sympathetic toward, respectful of, even admiring of Paul Robeson and Canada Lee — men I *did* respect tremendously! How could I *not* admire men of such courage and integrity? Robeson had come to my house and played with my children, which filled me with pride. I got to know him well enough that he became concerned about me, urging me to be careful in my association with him.[47]

Poitier procrastinated long enough to inform Richard Brooks, who said of the lawyer, "You know what? Fuck him." Though the actor never learned the truth of the matter, he went to work on the film and "never heard from that guy again."[48]

But Poitier, now being subjected to FBI surveillance, again faced the "loyalty oath" while preparing for the October 21, 1955, *Philco Playhouse* episode "A Man Is Ten Feet Tall," a live television play produced by David Susskind:

We were about to go into rehearsal, no contracts yet, when I got a call from an NBC guy who said, "Could you come in?" So I went to see him, and again he gave me this form to sign. It was a loyalty oath, and once again it made a point of asking me to disassociate myself from this man I so greatly admired, Paul Robeson.... I told him that the man he was talking about was a man I respected a great deal, and yes I knew him, and yes I liked him. I liked the fact that he was a stand-up guy. He was a good person to me, I said, and I could not and would not, under any circumstances, be a party to anything that denigrated him.[49]

Susskind, like Brooks, just wanted to get to work. "Listen, I think these guys are nuts," he told Poitier. "Let's just go into rehearsal and see."[50] Again, no one called back to harass the actor, who wrote, "[W]hatever list I was on that prompted these encounters with studio and network attorneys didn't in the end have any discernible effect on my career."[51] (A critical success, "A Man Is Ten Feet Tall" outraged viewers who thought Hilda Simms, the light-skinned African American actress who played Poitier's wife, was white. The controversy inspired director Martin Ritt to make a big-screen adaptation, *Edge of the City* [1957], costarring Poitier and John Cassavetes. In this version, Ruby Dee plays Poitier's wife.)

When the Reverend Martin Luther King, Jr., helped organize the Montgomery Bus Boycott in Alabama following the arrest of Rosa Parks on December 1, 1955, he ushered in a new era for civil rights. Aware that any direct participation on his part would certainly fuel reactionary accusations that the movement was "subversive" and "Communist," Paul wisely kept his distance.

On April 17, 1956, an agent in the FBI's New York office prepared a 76-page Confidential Internal Security report titled "Paul Le Roy Robeson" that included "information" gathered over the past 15 years. (Prior to this report, which includes the identifier "Changed," the Bureau incorrectly referred to him as "Paul *Leo* Robeson.") The Table of Contents alone includes a listing of 35 educational, political, human rights and charity groups branded "Communist Party Front Organizations." The agent, relying primarily on the 1954-55 edition of *Who's Who in America* for material on Paul's concert and acting careers, compiled such blatantly erroneous statements as "in the 1940s, Robeson played many movie and radio roles and appeared in a number of Broadway plays."[52]

Prior to attending the Paris Peace Conference in 1949, Paul had met with the Coordinating Committee of Colonial Peoples and Dr. Yusef M. Dadoo, president of the South

African Indian Congress. On June 12, 1956, HUAC questioned Paul about these relationships and the remarks he subsequently made in Paris. During his testimony, Paul mentioned that he had been asked to represent "2,000 students from various parts of the colonial world [who] did not want war":

> I did say, in passing, that it was unthinkable to me that any people would take up arms in the name of an Eastland to go against anybody, and, gentlemen, I still say that. I thought it was healthy for Americans to consider whether or not Negroes should fight for people who kick them around.
>
> What should happen, would be that this U.S. Government should go down to Mississippi and protect my people. This is what should happen.[53]

When HUAC asked Paul why he did not remain in the U.S.S.R., he replied:

> Because my father was a slave and my people died to build this country, and I am going to stay right here and have a part of it, just like you. And no fascist-minded people will drive me from it. Is that clear?[54]

Paul's HUAC testimony, which involved answering 150 questions, was addressed in newspapers across the nation during June 1956. In Virginia, the *Charlottesville-Albemarle Tribune* published the editorial "The House Un-American Activities Fiasco":

> Paul Robeson is a great artist and a deeply sympathetic human being.... To deny him the right to travel, to sing and to speak as he pleases; to put him in the pillory of a Congressional Committee and let lesser men bait him is more hurtful of American prestige abroad than any intemperate statement he ever made.[55]

In 1957, Paul mentioned another African American singer-actor who helped to make strides (although less overtly) for blacks in the cinema:

> Recently when Louis Armstrong denounced mistreatment of Negroes, and in stronger words than I have chosen, and when the response from other Negroes (including Jackie Robinson, as I was pleased to see) was a fervent Amen!—well, it looked like the "Old Ark's a-movering" for real![56]

Paul also mentioned Armstrong's recent response to racial discrimination in Arkansas, which had quashed the beloved "Satchmo's" proposed touring work for the State Department:

> In the heartfelt outburst that the events in Little Rock evoked from him, Louis Armstrong, the great musician who was scheduled to go to the Soviet Union, asked: "If the people over there ask me what is wrong with my country, what am I supposed to say?"
>
> Well, I would reply: "Speak the truth that is in your heart, Brother Armstrong, the same as you would here on the streets of Harlem." And all of us Negroes should tell him: "If they victimize you for doing that, we will come to your defense. We will raise such a storm that no narrow-minded and prejudiced bureaucrat in Washington will dare to take away your passport!"[57]

On May 17, 1957, Martin Luther King spoke to a crowd of 30,000 during the Prayer Pilgrimage held at the Lincoln Memorial in Washington, D.C. Far in the background, Paul, accompanied by Essie, sat under a large tree, where a broad cross-section of people came to express their gratitude for his civil rights efforts. Paul Jr. who also was there, wrote, "At times we were close to tears. It seemed of small consequence to Paul that the proceedings taking place on the platform ignored his existence."[58]

Nine days later, Paul sang his first "concert by telephone" to an audience of 1,000 Lon-

doners who had gathered at St. Pancras Town Hall. The performance coincided with a conference held by Britain's National Paul Robeson Committee comprised of scholars, writers, actors, lawyers, trade union leaders, and 16 Members of Parliament. (According to Paul, the existence of the committee was "completely suppressed" by the esteemed *New York Times*.[59]) Paul also was pleased when the British Actors' Equity Association passed a resolution, supported by a letter signed by the 27 members of the Cooperative Committee of Parliament, urging the U.S. government to allow him to return to England. The *Manchester Guardian* reported:

> [S]ince he was blacklisted in his own country, Mr. Robeson was barred from practicing his profession. The signatories believe that there was "never a more vital time for free countries to uphold their professions with regard to freedom of travel, as solemnly undertaken in the U.N. Declaration of Human Rights." The letter concludes: "Is this not doubly important in the case of so outstanding an artist as Paul Robeson, who properly belongs to all humanity?"[60]

On October 5, 1957, Paul gave another performance via telephone, this time for the South Wales Miners' Federation Eisteddfod at Porthcrawl, where an audience of 5,000 had gathered to hear "All Through the Night," "Didn't My Lord Deliver Daniel?" and "All Men Are Brothers," as well as an introduction delivered by SWMF President Will Paynter, a Communist Party member who had fought with the International Brigade during the Spanish Civil War.

In mid–November, Paul received a letter from Glen Byam Shaw, general manager of the Shakespeare Memorial Theatre, who invited him to appear as Gower in *Pericles* during the upcoming season at Stratford-upon-Avon. Paul wrote:

> Such an invitation is truly a great honor, but will the State Department permit me to go? Certainly I shall make still another request for a passport, as I have done in response to the many invitations that have come from countries other than Britain—for concert appearances on the Continent and elsewhere, for a role in a Soviet film production, and other similar offers.[61]

Prior to performing in Oakland, California, on February 9, 1958, Paul was interviewed on Pacifica Radio station KPFA. Referring to his singing and acting careers, he said:

> Because of my political views, which I certainly did not *expect* in a democracy ... I've been prevented from exercising my craft. However, I've kept singing all through the years ... I just made a recording the other day for Vanguard, which they felt was superior to any records I have ever made. My voice is still in fine shape ... and, as far as *Othello*, I've worked on it. I've just been invited to play it at Stratford-on-Avon ... and I would certainly do [it] at some point in London, and I feel I would give a better performance.... I would say that my interest in my art has deepened, just to no end, in the last years.... I have never separated my work as an artist from my work as a human being: I've always put it, even more strongly, that, to me, my art is always a *weapon*. It's got to be good art. *Othello* was a weapon in racial relations ... I've never been able to divorce one thing from the other.[62]

Indeed, the 1958 Vanguard sessions produced some of Paul's finest recorded performances, including a definitive version of "Shenandoah" and several songs featured in his films, including "Deep River," "Water Boy" and "All Through the Night."

On April 1, 1958, an FBI agent in New York mailed a report to J. Edgar Hoover, noting:

> Informant advised that on 3/30/58 Eslanda Robeson, subject's wife, commented on a resolution passed by Actors Equity the previous Friday (3/21/58), which endorsed a resolu-

tion of the British Actors Equity that Paul Robeson be granted a tentative passport. Eslanda Robeson expressed surprise at this action because since actor, Ralph Bellamy, had assumed the leadership of Actors Equity, all "of our people" have been out and a reactionary group had taken over.

Eslanda stated that Ossie Davis had introduced the resolution and despite the fact that the Equity President, Bellamy, spoke against it, the resolution was carried by approximately 110 votes to 75. Eslanda continued that Ossie Davis refers to this effort as his birthday contribution to Paul Robeson, Sr.[63]

The Bureau immediately put together a report on Ossie Davis:

> The "Daily Worker," issue of January 21, 1953, page 7, column 3, contained an article entitled, "U.S. Writers Urge Clemency," which reflected that one Ossie Davis was among writers urging clemency for Ethel and Julius Rosenberg ... [who] were legally executed at Sing Sing Prison, Ossining, New York, on June 19, 1953.[64]

(The controversial electric-chair executions of the Rosenbergs—Julius [whose guilt later was confirmed by co-defendant Mortin Sobell, who served nearly 18 years in prison] and Ethel [who apparently knew about her husband's activities but didn't participate; and whose slow death was particularly grisly]—were decried by an international cross-section of notable people with various political affiliations: Nelson Algren, Bertolt Brecht, Jean Cocteau, Albert Einstein, Dashiell Hammett, Fritz Lang, Diego Rivera, Pablo Picasso, Jean-Paul Sartre and Pope Pius XII. President Dwight D. Eisenhower refused all appeals.)

Paul said:

> At Geneva, the President of the United States made it clear that *nobody* wants to go to war with the Soviet Union. No Americans want to fight them, and I presume certainly the Negro peoples of the United States don't want any war with them, either. *Nobody* does, because we want *peace* and friendship in the world. And it's rather absurd that the Soviet farmers can be here in the United States, that Baptist preachers can be in Moscow ... but I'm not allowed to travel because of my friendship—open, spoken friendship, *that's right*—for the Soviet people and for the peoples of *all the world*. And I want to, very soon, I hope, pursue my career as a singer and as an actor. I still have a pretty good voice rolling around, they tell me, yet. And I want to play Othello.[65]

In a recent interview with the *San Francisco Chronicle*, Paul had said:

> I am sorry now that I quit the concert stage because of politics. It happened six years ago in St. Louis when I was singing in a non-segregated hall across the street from a segregated theater that I had picketed with the NAACP the same afternoon. I told the audience I would stop singing until these two things were reconciled. They are not yet, but I see now that I should have gone on with my work.[66]

(If Paul experienced a similar regret for walking away from the cinema more than 15 years earlier, he didn't voice it in public.)

During April 1958, 27 countries across the globe held celebrations for Paul's 60th birthday. In India, preparations for a government-sponsored, nationwide salute to a man whom Prime Minister Jawaharlal Nehru praised as having "represented and suffered for a cause which should be dear to all of us—the cause of human dignity" caused quite a stir at the State Department. Secretary Dulles first threatened the Indian ambassador with a possible "damaging effect on Indo-American relations" and then ordered all U.S. diplomatic personnel stationed in India to boycott the events.[67]

In East Germany, the release of the concert film *Bridge Over the Ocean*, featuring Paul and composer Earl Robinson, marked his sexagenarian milestone. In the film, Paul sings

two songs, "Ol' Man River" (featuring his own revised lyrics) and "Four Rivers," a Popular Front number referring to the Thames, Mississippi, Yangtze and Don. Concert venues in the U.S. began to open back up to him; and, on the evenings of May 9 and 23, the seats at Carnegie Hall were filled by music lovers eager to hear his powerful voice on such classics as "Balm in Gilead," "Jacob's Ladder" and "Ol' Man River," for which he further altered the lyrics to reflect his current political concerns.

As the result of a recent legal precedent, the Supreme Court overturned State Department regulations affecting "suspected communists and others of doubtful loyalty," and, on June 25, 1958, passport number 1145187 was issued in the name of Paul Robeson "for travel to Europe for the purpose of singing and acting." Aside from a brief visit to Canada, he had been denied the right to leave the United States for eight years.[68] He now had misgivings about leaving the U.S. just when the Civil Rights Movement was gaining steam, but he set out on an extensive overseas tour just two weeks later.

After being denied his basic rights by the U.S. government, Paul once again enjoyed British hospitality, including tea and lunch dates at both Houses of Parliament and with bureaucrats from China, Czechoslovakia, Ghana, Hungary, India, Nigeria, Poland, Romania and the U.S.S.R. Prevented from appearing on American television, he made three half-hour British "telly" appearances, each devoted to a different musical genre: folk, spirituals and popular songs, respectively. He also attended the Welsh national Eisteddfod in Ebbw Vale, South Wales, where he enjoyed listening to the choirs and performing for several thousand miners and their families.

Paul went far beyond Oscar Wilde's aphorism, "Life imitates art far more than art imitates life." He literally *brought art to life* as he elevated a character from his cinematic realm into the real world. *The Proud Valley*'s "David Goliath" had come home — as *Paul Robeson*.

Back in London, Paul sang to a packed house of 7,500 at the Albert Hall, a performance that garnered tremendous reviews in the major newspapers. During an interview with Therese Denny, an Australian journalist, he was asked if he regretted the loss of liberty he experienced due to his steadfast political beliefs. "I can't even use the term 'regret,'" he replied. "I'm very proud of any contribution I've been able to make to the struggles of my people. If you want freedom, you have to suffer sometime." He also explained his intention to separate his career as a concert vocalist from his political activities as a private citizen: "I come back as an artist, as one who loves people."[69] Many of those people stopped him on the street to wish him well, and he was thrilled to interact with gracious Londoners who turned out to buy a copy of *Here I Stand* during his signing at Selfridges department store.

Crowds in the U.S.S.R. were so enormous that police and army escorts were required to clear a path for Paul and Essie to reach hotels and concert venues. During an interview on Soviet television, Paul spoke favorably of the United States with respect to the current strides being made by the Civil Rights Movement. During his autumn Soviet tour, he was filmed for a forthcoming documentary by Russian director Vasili Katanyan. In East Germany, the newspaper *Neues Deutschland* reported that Paul "expected to complete two films in Russia, one of which would deal with his life story."[70]

On September 3, 1958, *Variety* concurred:

> Paul Robeson plans to make a film comeback via Russian pix. So the actor-singer told an audience at the Asian-African Film Festival in Tashkent, Russia, at which he was guest of honor.
> A Soviet broadcast, beamed in English to India and Pakistan, and picked up by U.S.

Government monitors, described in great detail the Robeson stint at opening of the Com-mie-inspired film fete.

The Singer, who has frequently tangled with Congressional investigators and immigra-tion authorities because of his alleged Commie leanings, compared Western films unfavor-ably with those of Eastern producers, The West, he said, concentrates on detective stories, while pix made in Asia and Africa "truthfully reflect people's lives," and educate them in the spirit of humanism.

Pravda, commenting on the festival, stated editorially that it was a graphic illustration of the "solidarity of film workers of various countries with differing social systems."[71]

Paul and Essie visited the summer home of Khrushchev, where they were invited to dine with the Premier, his wife, Nina, and party leaders from East Germany, Hungary, Italy, Poland and Romania. Speaking in Russian, Paul and the Premier discussed the struggle for black freedom. In the United States, photos of the affair were published in mainstream, white-owned newspapers as "proof" that Paul was a "Communist dupe."

Back in Britain on September 21, Paul, beginning a 22-date concert tour of England, Scotland, Ireland and Wales with Lawrence Brown and Bruno Raikin, told an audience in Blackpool:

I find the British people very warm and I have lived here before. London will be my cen-ter, as Hollywood is the center for some British film stars. I don't want any overtones of suggestion that I am deserting the country of my birth. If I have a concert in New York, I will go there and return to London.[72]

After completing his third successful television show, Paul, who learned that future appearances would be taped, relieving him of having "the terror-stricken feeling of being bad before millions," was asked to host his own small-screen series.[73] In Britain, he con-tinued to be a pioneer. On October 12, during a performance at St. Paul's Cathedral in Lon-don, he relished the singular honor of being the first layperson to read scripture from the sanctified pulpit. He began with the familiar passage from Micah 4:3 in the King James Bible: "[A]nd they shall beat their swords into plowshares, and their spears into pruning hooks. Nation shall not lift up a sword against nation, neither shall they learn war any more."

Prior to flying back to Moscow at the end of December, Paul, accompanied by Lawrence Brown, performed holiday songs on the 30-minute Christmas program broadcast by the London BBC. While planning a trip to accept an invitation from the Paul Robeson All-India Birthday Committee, Paul and Essie both fell seriously ill. Essie, who had suffered from breast cancer, was hospitalized and ordered to take radiation treatments for the next seven weeks. Paul was nearly leveled by dizzy spells brought on by a combination of flu and a bronchial infection.

Arrangements were made for Paul to undergo a month-long program of diet, exercise and rest at the Barvikha Sanitorium, a health resort for Soviet government officials. After wrangling with Essie, he wired Glen Byam Shaw that he would accept a less taxing rehearsal schedule for *Othello*, which was to open in Stratford-upon-Avon on April 7, 1959. While becoming physically and mentally fit, he developed a new approach to the Shakespearean role that would reflect his increasing age.

Fresh from his rehabilitation, Paul spoke at a tribute to the late Jewish writer Sholem Aleichem (born Sholem Naumovich Rabinovich in Pereyaslav, Russia), whose Yiddish sto-ries were enjoyed by his young grandchildren, David and Susan. He also performed three Yiddish songs and the anthem of the Warsaw Ghetto Uprising.

On March 9, Paul bid farewell to Essie, who was still undergoing treatments in Moscow, and flew to London to rehearse *Othello* with Sam Wanamaker, Mary Ure and 27-year-old director Tony Richardson, who intended to stage a furiously physical version of the play. All 13 performances sold out, and the critics acclaimed Paul, some calling him the best Othello they'd ever seen, but faulted the inexperienced supporting cast and director. Words of praise arrived from Shakespearean heavyweights John Gielgud and Laurence Olivier (who, five years later, would bulk up, black up and develop a deeper vocal range for the 1964–1966 staging of *Othello* at the National Theatre and the 1965 film version directed by Stuart Burge). After the opening engagement (which encompassed Paul's 61st birthday), the play was scheduled for two or three weekly performances through November.

At one point during the seven-month run, Paul, while lunching with his son, spied Olivier reading at a table across the restaurant. Wishing for Paul Jr. to meet the man he called "the greatest living actor in the English-speaking theater," he provided an introduction, but Olivier neglected to shake hands with the young man, merely offering a cursory greeting to Paul. Paul Jr. recalled his father's explanation:

> I wasn't surprised by that. Just wanted to check him out. He's one of the greatest actors of all time and I couldn't come near to matching him, but he couldn't stand the fact that I'm dominating this season with *Othello*.[74]

In the United States, J. Edgar Hoover, in collaboration with CIA Director Allen Dulles (the younger brother of Secretary of State John Foster Dulles, who had recently died) and a "confidential source" at British Intelligence, maintained his relentless, unconstitutional stakeout and bugging operations, including the examination of Paul's mail by an informant in the Inspector's Office at the New York City Post Office. For the time being, Paul intended to remain in Britain, agreeing with his son that, although "the civil rights movement was rapidly expanding in the South ... illegal persecution of dissent would continue as long as Hoover remained FBI director, regardless of who was president."[75] Tentatively he planned to return home after the 1960 presidential election.

On August 3, 1959, during a break from *Othello*, Paul performed at the World Youth Fes-

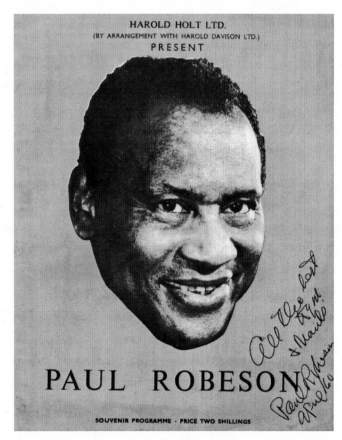

In April 1960, Robeson signed this souvenir program for two admirers at one of his London concerts.

tival in Vienna, where he also spoke about the connection between the struggle for civil rights in the United States and the antiapartheid movement in South Africa. During his visit to Austria, a pro–U.S. nation, he was watched by informants for the CIA and the State Department, whose official policy was to create chaos during the festival.

Two weeks later, while traveling to Romania, he spent a few hours in Budapest waiting for a connection. Though his passport was stamped "Not Valid for Hungary," he visited schoolchildren and performed a few songs, then (throwing a verbal punch at the State Department) told a reporter he would return the following year for a concert tour, something he also planned to undertake in China, another off-limits nation.

Playing to packed houses at Stratford for seven months began to take its toll on Paul. He wanted to move back to the United States eventually, mainly to reestablish his personal connections with friends and colleagues, but first he wanted to take trips to several lands, including China, Africa and India, that he hadn't been able to visit during his passport exile. Essie objected to this plan, fearing that his health would suffer further, with only potential assassination awaiting him at home.

In mid–September, during Khrushchev's historic visit to the United States, the Premier was rudely interrupted during a dinner speech at the Waldorf-Astoria. Asked why U.S. radio broadcasts to Russia were jammed, he responded, "Paul Robeson, singer and actor, was denied the right to go abroad. Why is that voice jammed?"[76]

Khrushchev's visit briefly eased the tense Cold War atmosphere. The new, more moderate Secretary of State, Christian Herter, was carrying out President Eisenhower's policy of "cautious negotiation" with the Soviets, but met hardcore resistance from the CIA's right-wing war hawk, Allen Dulles, who was authorizing covert operations against several leftist governments, including U-2 spy plane missions over the U.S.S.R. and hits against Castro in Cuba and Patrice Lumumba in the Congo. Eisenhower's refusal to apologize to Khrushchev for the disastrous U-2 incident involving captured U.S. pilot Gary Powers led to the Premier's walkout at their May 1960 summit in Paris. Believing that "cautious negotiation" really meant an "aggressive" foreign policy including a secret recon-

Robeson's Labour advocates at the British *Daily Worker* provided "peaceful and socially advanced" support for his 1960 concert appearances [souvenir program].

naissance war against his country, Khrushchev followed suit, ratcheting up the Cold War to the point of constructing the Berlin Wall and placing nuclear missiles in Cuba.

Although his health was failing, Paul continued to make further travel plans, including a two-month concert tour of Australia and New Zealand, where he and Essie intended to spend time with the indigenous inhabitants. During a busy schedule of 21 concerts beginning in mid–October, he found time to sing on a children's radio show and appear on the television program *Spotlight*. An interview with the German newspaper *Neue Zeit* also revealed that he hadn't given up on reviving some aspect of his film career:

> In Australia and New Zealand the people know me from Gramophone records and films which are twenty to thirty years old. Now they want to see and hear me.... I intend to return to Australia. I shall make films and give concerts. The proceeds shall benefit the aboriginal population languishing in poverty. I already did that in Africa, and now I want to repeat it in Australia.[77]

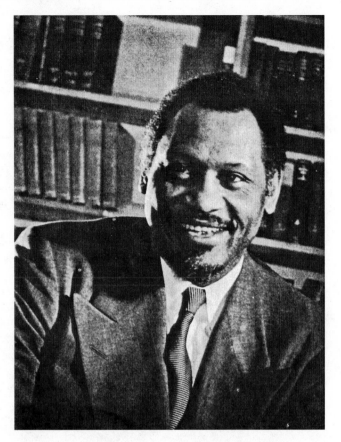

Robeson, his passport restored after eight years of political imprisonment in his own country, was back in Britain to perform for anxious concertgoers in 1960-61. Though he expressed an interest in reviving his film career, complicated circumstances (political, personal and physical) over the ensuing 15 years prevented any such developments. When this photo was taken, his signature smile was still there.

When the firing-squad murder of the anticolonialist Patrice Lumumba, in which the CIA and the Belgian government had conspired, was carried out on January 17, 1961, Paul became more edgy about his own security in London. Two weeks later, he again mentioned returning to the United States following his upcoming trip to Moscow, where he planned to make further travel arrangements for stops in Africa and Cuba on the way home. In early March, he received a call from Fidel Castro, who intended to invite him to Havana, but he didn't go to the phone, fearing it might be bugged. Paul Jr. revealed, "He was right. The same CIA personnel planning the Bay of Pigs invasion of Cuba were tracking his possible visit there."[78]

On March 20, Paul left for Moscow, where he was met by members of the Presidium, an interpreter, and an aide. For six days, he attended events all over the city, meeting with students, government newspaper staff, and factory workers; but, on the morning of March 27, he was discovered in an incoherent state by his interpreter on the floor of the bathroom

in his Sovietskaya Hotel suite, having cut both wrists. More than a week passed, and Paul, wracked with increasing anxiety and paranoia, refused to see anyone, including Essie.

On April 7, having arrived the previous day, Paul Jr. discussed the incident with Paul's aide and a Supreme Soviet vice president. Apparently Paul had intended to retire early on the evening of March 26; but, instead, a wild party in his room was reported to the hotel management, who had no knowledge of anyone who attended the affair. This seemed outlandish to Paul Jr., who was granted a meeting with members of the Communist Party's Central Committee. The next day, Paul spoke with him but still wouldn't allow Essie to enter the hospital room.

On April 9, Paul turned 63, and the staff threw a small party attended by Paul Jr. and Essie. When Paul seemed pleased, the chief physician read a birthday greeting sent from the Presidium. Paul Jr. returned to visit each day, but Paul, suspicious of everyone else, still allowed no other visitors.

During a reception for pioneer Soviet cosmonaut Yuri Gagarin at the Kremlin on April 12, Essie and Paul Jr. were comforted by the sincere concern of Khrushchev and his wife for Paul's recovery. At the hospital, three doctors, including Soviet chief psychiatrist A. V. Snezh-nevsky, concurred that Paul, suffering from psychosis, depression and a mild heart condition, should retire from performing and spend two months at Barvikha before moving back to the United States, where he would be among his own people in a more familiar environment.

Following his meeting with a Khrushchev loyalist and a security agent from the Central Committee, Paul Jr., already suspecting a plot against his father, drew the following conclusions:

> The party in his suite was arranged and imposed on him by a Western intelligence agent in the Soviet government; he was drugged and driven to suicidal paranoia. The incident was then covered up by the KGB to save him and the Soviet Union huge embarrassment. Paul had been immobilized just twenty-two days before the CIA's invasion of Cuba. The CIA knew he intended to visit Cuba from Moscow and it would seem likely that they would not want him there as they prepared for the invasion. All of this contributed to my belief that he had been subjected to a CIA "hit."[79]

Under the CIA mind-control program known as MKULTRA, a hallucinogenic drug (later known as LSD) had been developed as one part of a three-stage program, directed against foreign and domestic "enemies," that also involved the Personality Assessment System, which used psychological warfare to create mental instability, and "mind depatterning," or confining the subject to a psychiatric hospital where he was lobotomized through a combination of drugs and intensive "shock" treatments. The CIA's Richard Helms (who later, as the agency's director, ordered all project records destroyed) had approved the implementation of MKULTRA in overseas operations. In London, the MKULTRA Subproject 111 was overseen by Hans Jurgen Eysenck, director of the psychology department at Maudsley Hospital.

A few days after the disastrous Bay of Pigs invasion on April 17, Paul Jr. began developing paranoid delusions after drinking a cup of tea at a hotel banquet. He trashed his room, ran out into the streets and meandered around, continuing to hallucinate, before returning to the hotel, where he was placed in a straitjacket and rushed to "a KGB psychiatric hospital for intelligence personnel, police detectives, and foreign Communist Party leaders."[80] Following a three-week stay, he was allowed to leave if he agreed to deny that the incident had ever occurred. At the sanitarium in Barvikha, he discussed plans for the future with Paul, who indicated that they would return to London before moving back to the United States.

Paul was discharged on June 10 but, suffering a relapse in late July, was hospitalized

in Moscow and then taken back to Barvikha, where he was pronounced well enough to leave in early September. During this period, J. Edgar Hoover communicated with the FBI's legal attaché in London with regard to Paul Jr., Essie and Paul, whose "health status" was of particular concern. On July 21, 1961, Hoover received a memorandum from "Legat, London," on which he added the following hand-printed information: "INFO RE ROBESON'S HEALTH STATUS PREVIOUSLY FURNISHED STATE, CIA, AG [Attorney General] & WHITE HOUSE UNDER 'TOP SECRET' CLASSIFICATION."[81]

On September 5, Paul and Essie flew to London, where his anxiety again returned with a vengeance. Advised by the highly recommended Dr. Philip Lebon, Paul was admitted to Priory Hospital. Essie approved the selection of Dr. Brian Ackner, a consultant for the Maudsley Institute of Psychiatry who worked with patients suffering from chronic depression. Neither doctor bothered to obtain any of Paul's medical records but merely treated him based on comments made by Essie and their friend Helen Rosen, who (incorrectly) believed he was a chronic depressive.

Dr. O'Connor, the admitting psychiatrist, recommended electroconvulsive therapy (ECT) and the tranquilizer Largactil (known as Thorazine in the U.S.) after determining that Paul was suffering from a "chronic depressive state with severe delusional background with marked apprehension." He also wrote "Suicidal" on the chart.

Acting under the authority of Essie, who signed the consent forms, the staff gave Paul high doses of a variety of drugs and a lengthy series of 54 ECT treatments over the course of 23 months. Initially he was not allowed to see Paul Jr. or his close friends, including Lawrence Brown. Occasionally he was able to go into the city on holidays and weekends, when he was prescribed Paraldehyde, a powerful central nervous system depressive used in the treatment of patients with bipolar disorder (which was never diagnosed in his case). Sometimes he felt well enough to attend concerts, and he enjoyed meeting with Ella Fitzgerald, Sarah Vaughan and Miles Davis after their performances. At one point, he was reunited with his *Song of Freedom* and *Big Fella* costar Elisabeth Welch.

During these temporary reprieves from confinement, Paul was constantly under the surveillance of the Secret Intelligence Service (SIS or MI-6) branch of British Intelligence. On July 10, 1962, Essie applied for a new passport, the issuance of which was contingent on her signing a non–Communist affidavit. She willingly did so, stating, "categorically and without any reservations whatsoever, that I am not now, and have never been in all my life, a member of the Communist Party, United States of America, or in any other country. Never!"[82]

When Paul refused to follow suit, Essie contacted CPUSA leader Benjamin Davis and attorney John Abt, who informed him that new regulations guaranteed travel rights to declared members of the party. Arguably, the "pre-depressive" Paul still would have refused; but, on July 25, 1962, undoubtedly affected by the constant onslaught of shock treatments, plus an alarming and conflicting combination of both antidepressant and depressant drugs, he signed a sworn (but fairly tame) affidavit:

> I, Paul Robeson, am not now a member of the Communist Party, U.S.A., and have not been a member thereof at any time during the twelve months preceding May 25, 1962, the date of application for a passport.[83]

While some Robeson scholars have agreed with the depression diagnosis, suggesting that a bipolar disorder accounted for his actions, Paul Jr. maintained that such an explanation is a complete "myth" unsupported by any medical evidence, including the records from Priory, which he finally obtained in 1998.[84] He explained further:

I found this combined treatment especially troubling, because it resembled the "mind depatterning" treatment funded by the MKULTRA Project, which consisted of "intensive electroshocks, usually combined with prolonged, drug-induced sleep." The similarity is noteworthy because by early 1962 Richard Helms ... was in direct communication with Hoover concerning Paul's health.[85]

On January 23, 1963, an FBI agent in New York reported to Hoover that "the NY file on Paul Robeson is being placed in a closed status. Consideration will be given to reinstating him on the key figure list if and when he resumes activity on behalf of the CP.... Eslanda Robeson's file is currently maintained in a closed status."[86] However, it was business as usual for the FBI, whose Counterintelligence agents continued to monitor all the activities of Paul and Essie, who both remained on the Bureau's "Security Index."[87] A smear campaign, "the crudity of [which] pointed to Hoover's FBI," also was waged in the scandal tabloid *National Insider*, when a two-part, fabricated article written by "Paul Robeson" claimed that he had been a Communist *and* a Fascist![88]

Paul, thoroughly debilitated from the shock treatments and dangerous assortment of drugs, was unable to travel. However, concerned friends, intending to move him to a sanitarium where he could receive treatment favored by Soviet psychiatrists (a social-environmental approach in which ECT was considered "malpractice"), made arrangements to have him flown to the Buch Clinic in East Berlin on August 25, 1963.

The British press, responding to an initiative from the U.S. Information Agency supported by the State Department, made plans to interview Paul about "his" statements published in *The National Insider* before his departure. Thanks to a clever "covert" operation carried out with military precision, Paul's friends and the director of Polish Airways sneaked him past journalists and onto the plane. However, a reporter for the London *Sunday Telegraph* who was on board queried Paul, whose responses about his actual political convictions, proposed treatment in East Berlin, and Dr. King's historic March on Washington were published accurately in the next day's newspaper.

The story scored a rare public-relations success for Paul. On August 28, an operative in London, referring to the "general press disclaimers" generated by the *Sunday Telegraph*, advised CIA Director John A. McCone that it would be "best if whole matter [is] allowed to die a natural death." Two days later, McCone replied, "Headquarters taking no action."[89]

The staff at the Buch Clinic included clinical psychologist Dr. Alfred Katzenstein, whose U.S. Army service during World War II had involved treating death-camp survivors. Not surprisingly, Paul, diagnosed with an enlarged liver, was taken off all the drugs he had been given at the Priory. Concerned that some brain damage may have resulted from the long-term use of ECT, the staff ran a battery of tests, concluding that, while there was no evidence of physical deterioration, he was suffering from considerable anxiety and a lack of self-confidence.

The electrically induced lobotomy and heavy sedation waged by the Priory were replaced by intensive psychotherapy, a program of healthy social interaction, and infrequent use of the mild tranquilizer Librium. Essie, having been told in England that she was cancer-free, was examined by Buch doctors who informed her that the disease, which had metastasized, probably would not be alleviated by surgery. She was resigned not to tell Paul.

The assassination of President Kennedy on November 22, 1963, briefly worried Paul about the prospects of returning to the United States, but he was encouraged by the civil-rights support being gained by Dr. King and his associates. Fully intending to retire, Paul, accompanied by Essie and aided by the friends who had "smuggled" him past the English

reporters, left East Berlin on December 17, 1963, scheduled to stop over in London on his way back to the U.S.

J. Edgar Hoover, who had been advised about the travel plans, was immediately informed of their arrival at New York's Idlewild Airport when their BOAC flight landed at 3:40 P.M. on December 22. (The facility soon would be renamed John F. Kennedy International Airport.) Essie attempted to deflect some of the journalists, one of whom asked Paul if he was going to participate in the Civil Rights Movement. He replied concisely, "I've been a part of it all my life."[90] Nonetheless, the mainstream press inaccurately reported that he had been "behind the Iron Curtain" since leaving the U.S. in 1958, and now was returning belatedly to join the fight for civil rights.

Concerned that his father would be depressed if constantly watched over by his assertive mother, who behaved as if the traumatic Priory ordeal hadn't occurred, Paul Jr., encouraging a focus on her United Nations work, made daily visits to their home at 16 Jumel Terrace in Harlem. Eventually Paul resumed an interest in music and socializing with close friends. In Philadelphia, he enjoyed spending time with his sister, Marian Forsythe, and even began singing again, accompanied by her neighbor, retired music teacher Charlotte Bell. Eventually he moved in with Marian but made sporadic visits to the Harlem home. On one occasion, he and Essie spent some time with Josephine Baker, who was performing at Henry Miller's Theatre.

On August 22, 1964, Benjamin Davis (whom Paul recently had visited at Beth Israel Hospital, providing comfort with reminiscences and favorite songs) passed away from lung cancer. A committed U.S. Communist and civil rights activist, Davis had represented Harlem on the New York City Council prior to the Red Scare. In 1951, he was jailed for violating the Smith Act, an anti-insurrection law that was broadly interpreted to subjugate the left after World War II. (The Supreme Court declared the act unconstitutional in 1957.) Four days later, Paul, making his first public appearance since coming home, delivered the eulogy at Davis's funeral in New York.

On August 28, Paul sent a press release to several black newspapers, articulating his admiration for "the many thousands of Negro freedom fighters and their white associates who are waging the battle for civil rights throughout the country and especially in the South."[91] He also expressed his sorrow over the recent losses of Davis, W. E. B. DuBois, and his beloved brother, the Reverend Ben Robeson (who died on December 1, 1963; Paul, still in London, wasn't informed until his health improved). Six weeks after submitting his political statement to the press, Paul was troubled by the October 14 coup in the Soviet Union, in which the reformist Khrushchev was ousted by Leonid Ilyich Brezhnev, a conservative nationalist, but he didn't discuss the matter in public.

On January 19, 1965, when Paul appeared at Harlem's Church of the Master to speak at the funeral of Lorraine Hansberry, playwright of the groundbreaking *A Raisin in the Sun* who had succumbed to cancer at age 34, he received a request, via Paul Jr., that someone in the audience wished to meet with him. Risking his life to attend the service, Malcolm X wanted to discuss some ideas with Paul, who, under the protests of Essie, invited the former Nation of Islam disciple to visit him at Jumel Terrace. Unfortunately, Malcolm was brutally assassinated, by the very people for whom he'd struggled, just a few blocks away, while speaking at the Audubon Ballroom on February 21.

In March, a new article on W. E. B. DuBois written by Paul was published in the quarterly black journal *Freedomways*. On April 22, the editors held a special 67th-birthday Salute to Paul Robeson at Manhattan's Hotel Americana. Though the Civil Rights Movement had

made some impact on the Lyndon Johnson administration, there remained a strong, anti-leftist Cold War atmosphere that kept members of the liberal establishment, including Roy Wilkins of the NAACP, from sponsoring the event. Many individuals, black and white, did offer support, however: comedian Dick Gregory, actress Viveca Lindfors, Morehouse College president Benjamin E. Mays, chemist and peace activist Dr. Linus Pauling, historian Sterling Stuckey, and AME Zion Bishop W. J. Walls. Ossie Davis emceed the event attended by James Baldwin, Roscoe Lee Browne, Howard Da Silva, Dizzy Gillespie, Diana Sands and Pete Seeger. During his speech, Baldwin told the gathering, "At a time when there seemed to be no hope at all, Paul Robeson spoke out for all of us." Student Nonviolent Coordinating Committee chairman John Lewis said:

> The assassins of Freedom have been trying for years to erase the personality of one whose broad shoulders were squared to confront them.... For two generations of Americans, Paul Robeson represented the entire Negro people of this country. In many ways we of the SNCC are Paul Robeson's spiritual children. We too have been accused of being radicals, and of "Communist influence," and for the same reasons as Robeson.

Paul spoke for 25 minutes, improvising somewhat on his prepared text, during which he stressed the importance of music in the struggle for black freedom, from slavery through the present. The one spiritual he mentioned was the superlative "Go Down, Moses." Though he briefly considered the unlikely possibility of resuming a professional career, he returned to the beneficial peace of Marian's Philadelphia home a few days later.

In May 1965, Paul returned to Los Angeles, where he had arrived to make *Show Boat* nearly 30 years earlier. He and Essie stayed with friends in Watts, where they felt secure. A church dinner was held in their honor, and Paul, again in fine voice, responded by singing a cappella versions of "Eriskay Love Lilt" and "Jacob's Ladder." On May 16, they toured the black community, ate breakfast, attended a meeting at Mt. Sinai Church, where Paul sang briefly, and were guests at a private home hosting a group of professionals, one of whom requested six bars of "Go Down, Moses." Paul gladly performed an entire, moving version of the spiritual. Two days later, he spoke and, accompanied by Waldemar Hille, sang "Eriskay Love Lilt," "Peat Bog Soldiers" and his *Emperor Jones* signature number, "Water Boy," at Larchmont Hall while meeting with journalists from the *Peoples World* newspaper. Paul Jr. wrote:

> He thrived on the appearances, and his audiences loved him. He embodied a unique symbol—a great black warrior who had challenged the foundations of the Jim Crow system and survived. Here he stood, wounded, but unbowed and still defiant.[92]

Prior to leaving Los Angeles for San Francisco, Paul appeared confident during an interview with the *Los Angeles Times*:

> Robeson said he believes the Negro will become "a full American in every sense of the word. These are much more than exciting times—they're definitive. Whatever the difficulties, I'm optimistic the human race will find a way out. It's the great responsibility of us Americans to understand the need of other peoples."[93]

In San Francisco, Paul was uncomfortable staying in a white section of Marin County. Following 10 days of events, he became depressed, which was complicated by the deteriorating health of Essie, whose back pain was incapacitating. Too ill to attend the Salute to Paul Robeson at the Jack Tar Hotel on June 4, they booked a flight back to New York.

At Jumel Terrace, Paul's condition worsened, and he didn't want his son to leave him alone with Essie. On June 10, Paul Jr. arrived to discover his father holding a razor blade

to his neck, but he managed calmly to disarm him. Dr. Nathan Kline then admitted Paul to Gracie Square Hospital, where he remained for the next three weeks, being treated as a chronic depressive with suicidal tendencies. He then attended weekly counseling sessions with Dr. Ari Kiev. According to Paul Jr.:

> Kiev asked him about his career, expressing interest in his feeling of continuity with the civil rights movement and his current tentative involvement with his music. He replied alertly and accurately, sharing his trepidation about not being able to live up to the public's expectations. My father was melancholy during these conversations when reminded of his career.[94]

Engaged in his usual investigative activities, Paul Jr. discovered that Dr. Kiev had worked for five institutions, *all* connected to the CIA's MKULTRA Program: Maudsley Institute of Psychiatry, Harvard University, Cornell Medical College, Johns Hopkins Hospital and Wilford Hall Hospital.

On August 7, Paul was readmitted to Gracie Square Hospital, where he again was overmedicated, now with the antidepressants Niamid and Elavil, the antipsychotic Phenergan, and the sedative Chloral hydrate (famously used illegally as a "Mickey Finn"). Valium and Benadryl were added to the mix by Kiev, who then tossed in Thorazine, which becomes toxic in combination with Valium.

Realizing that his father would probably be killed by the onslaught of drugs, Paul Jr., aided by Sam Rosen, brought in Dr. Richard Nachtigall, who took Paul off all the medications and administered intravenous antibiotics. Kiev's Priory–like treatment had created a combination of maladies (dehydration, drug sensitivity, kidney trauma, meningitis, phenothiazine-induced rigidity, and pneumonia) that would have proved lethal.

Kline briefly inquired about Paul's condition, but Kiev did not return. Nachtigall transferred Paul to University Hospital, where he was diagnosed with "toxic metabolic encephalopathy probably secondary to combined drug therapy." He also had developed "elements of an organic mental syndrome" as a result of Kline and Kiev's barrage of drugs.[95] Following a brief release from the hospital, a head injury resulting from an unsupervised walking accident brought him back for another 18-day recuperation. Upon his release, Paul Jr. drove him to the security and comfort of Marian's Philadelphia home.

Essie passed away at Beth Israel Hospital in the wee hours of the morning on December 13, 1965, two days before her 70th birthday. She had been preparing to celebrate the occasion in her hospital room but, ironically, her remains were cremated at Ferncliffe Cemetery in Hartsdale, Westchester County, on that day. Paul remained with Marian in Philadelphia, rather than attending the private funeral. On January 10, 1966, J. Edgar Hoover was informed that the Secret Service had been notified of the death of "the subject," whose name also had been removed from the Security Index.[96]

In February, Paul Jr. and his family moved into the Jumel Terrace house, where Paul also lived part-time. The following month, at the SNCC annual dinner, Paul was lauded for his contributions to civil rights by chairman James Forman and credited for "inspiring" the movement by John Lewis.

Marilyn Robeson located a new residence, an apartment with a two-room suite for Paul, on the Upper West Side of Manhattan; but, after living there a short time, a depressive relapse resulted in Marian suggesting that he move in with her permanently. Paul Jr. and Marilyn, while preparing to sell the Jumel Terrace house, discovered Essie's "archives" on the ground floor, a historian's dream of more than 50,000 items including correspondence, documents, photographs, recordings and films.

Aside from a few public appearances, Paul lived very quietly. He continued to express his admiration for Dr. King's courage, organizational abilities and leadership, particularly his ability to respond to the needs of blacks in general. The, shocking, tragic assassination in Memphis on April 4, 1968, saddened Paul deeply, a feeling mildly alleviated by the kind greetings and tributes engendered by his 70th birthday just five days later. Celebrations were held across the globe: in London, where a group of actors including Michael Redgrave, Peter O'Toole and Dame Peggy Ashcroft gathered to read poetical tributes; East Germany; Moscow; and the United States, where the black commission of the CPUSA announced, "The white power structure has generated a conspiracy of silence around Paul Robeson. It wants to blot out all knowledge of this pioneering Black American warrior."[97]

Paul's final years were spent in Philadelphia, where the FBI continued its surveillance activities. In 1969 he had a pacemaker installed to improve his blood circulation and was pleased to be able to visit with his closest friends on a regular basis. When Paul Jr. asked him why he didn't want to see other "old friends and admirers," he made it clear that his current, reduced state would prove unacceptable:

He wanted to be remembered from the time when he performed and spoke publicly—"moved, sang, acted." He knew he had paved the way for those that came after him and needed no credit for it, so he had no desire to appear in person at events honoring him.[98]

In 1972, *Ebony* magazine featured an article in which a panel of leading African American historians voted Paul one of the "Ten Greats of Black History," referring to him as

one of the most multifaceted geniuses of recorded history for nearly a half-century ... the finest ideologist of black nationalism since Sidney of the 1840s ... [and] one of the century's most perceptive commentators on the cultures of the East, West and Africa. No black man has ever given more to his people than Robeson.[99]

His prodigious talents as an athlete, singer, and stage and film actor were undoubtedly considered essential components of his "multifaceted genius." His acting abilities were publicly recognized when, in November, he became a charter inductee in the National Theater Hall of Fame, in which he joined such performers as Fred Astaire, John and Ethel Barrymore, W. C. Fields, Helen Hayes, and one of his heroes, Bert Williams, the only other African American in the group.

On April 15, 1973, 3,000 people gathered to celebrate Paul's 75th birthday at Carnegie Hall, but he was too ill to attend. The audience included many film actors who were part of his cinematic legacy: Harry Belafonte (who also produced the event), Roscoe Lee Browne, Ossie Davis, Ruby Dee, James Earl Jones and Sidney Poitier. Also attending were Coretta Scott King, Angela Davis, Dizzy Gillespie, Odetta, Leon Bibb, Zero Mostel, Pete Seeger, and consummate film actor Robert Ryan (who, though ill with lung cancer, never desisted from his lifelong commitment to civil rights and other progressive causes).

Birthday wishes were sent by Arthur Ashe, Leonard Bernstein, Soviet ambassador Anatoly Dobrynin, Indian Prime Minister Indira Gandhi, Jamaican Prime Minister Michael Manley, the presidents of Guyana, Tanzania and Zambia, and the African National Congress. Paul's own recorded message opened with the comment, "Though I have not been able to be active for several years, I want you to know that I am the same Paul, dedicated as ever to the worldwide cause of humanity for freedom, peace, and brotherhood."

Proceeds from the Carnegie Hall event were used to establish the Paul Robeson Archives. Other tributes, received during the autumn of 1974, included the Congressional

Black Caucus Special Award of Merit and a documentary film produced by Tony Batten for the PBS program *Interface*.

In mid–January 1976, Paul, while walking down from his bedroom to dine with Marian, Marilyn and Paul Jr., stopped on the stairs to paraphrase, with that big Robeson smile, a line from "Deep River": "I'm going home. I'm going home over Jordan." Later that evening, he had a mild stroke, which was followed by a series of similar attacks after being admitted to University Hospital. On Friday, January 23, Paul Jr., while waiting at New York's Penn Station for the train to Philadelphia, learned of his father's death from a radio report.

After lying in state at Benta's Funeral Home in Harlem for two days, Paul was eulogized by Bishop James C. Hoggard during the funeral officiated by the Reverend George W. McMurray at Mother AME Zion Church, the spiritual home of his late brother Ben. Paul's memory was honored by 2,500 mourners, including Harry Belafonte, Eubie Blake, Uta Hagen, and Malcolm X's widow, Betty Shabazz. As the casket was borne from the church by 12 pallbearers headed by Belafonte, they were accompanied by a recording of Paul singing, most appropriately, "Deep River." Paul's cremated remains were interred beside Essie's at Ferncliff. His modest marker bears the epitaph:

> "THE ARTIST MUST TO ELECT TO FIGHT
> FOR FREEDOM OR SLAVERY. I
> HAVE MADE MY CHOICE. I HAD
> NO ALTERNATIVE."

Five days after the funeral, the U.S. House of Representatives held a tribute to Paul, who also was memorialized at Rutgers University, Columbia University, Actors Equity in Los Angeles, Shiloh Baptist Church in Washington, D.C., and the World Peace Council in Athens. A benefit held at Carnegie Hall on October 8, 1976, raised additional funds for the Paul Robeson Archives.

Though Paul received scant attention from the visual media in the United States, his professional and personal activities had been covered by European newsreel, documentary and amateur filmmakers. Charles Musser wrote, "Robeson's work in nonfiction film was part of a larger effort to establish his persona outside of a fictional, often stereotypical context."[100] Fifteen years after he retired from mainstream feature films, Paul had assessed the situation for his fellow African Americans:

> Progress has been made and today there are greater opportunities for Negro performers. But it is still a hard struggle to win an equal place for them in the theatre, films, radio and television; and I am very happy and proud to see that so many of our brilliant young actors, singers and dancers are fighting for decent scripts, for roles that are worthy of their artistic talents. Years ago when I refused to sing before a segregated audience the story was headline news, and today I am happy to note that many others also have taken that stand, and that nowadays it is considered news—and bad news, by our people—whenever a prominent Negro artist agrees to perform under Jim Crow arrangements. We have every right to take great pride in the new and rising generation of our artists and we ought to support them in their struggle for equal opportunity. Their notable effort to represent faithfully our people in the arts makes such support a duty for us all.[101]

Robeson biographer Martin Duberman said, "He was one of the giants of the [20th] century. Multitalented, multidimensional, willing to jeopardize his own privileges and career in order to help those less fortunate. He was a giant."[102] New York University professor Deborah Willis pointed out, "Robeson represents a puzzle—his brooding persona neither wholly refutes nor resists the racist implications of his era."[103]

Ruby Dee said:

I think it's important to keep the story of Paul Robeson alive, because he exemplified so much of what I believe the world is *still looking for.*

How do we get along with each other? How do we stop wars? How do we universalize love? And I think that Robeson said that loudest of all.[104]

James Earl Jones concluded:

The tragedy in the life of Paul Robeson is not the tragedy of the man but the tragedy of the country. That tragedy still exists in this country. He only pointed it out. He only *heightened* it. He only let us know that *it exists*—that great tragedy, that great *abuse of humanity.* It was called slavery. It still goes on, in some form or another. He was only trying to end it, that's all.[105]

Paul Robeson, Jr., posed the question:

Was he technically a great film actor? No—didn't try to be, didn't care about that. He was interested in the impact on an audience. His vision of what he did in film —overall, he was proud of the record. He felt he had projected a black male image of power and dignity and cultural integrity never equaled before or after, in American and Western film.[106]

Is Paul Robeson's cinematic legacy a "dubious" one? Given the tenor of his times, could any other African American performer have done more than he? Considering that no one else *did do more*, the answer has to be a resounding "No" to both questions. Paul certainly attempted to achieve greater things in his films, but the "compromised" results that sometimes frustrated him were predominantly the product of industry and society, and cannot be laid squarely at his own door. An essential aspect of this historic endeavor was his consistently *positive* attitude that disallowed criticism of his fellow black performers, who (though talented and well-intended) primarily tagged along with the status quo. Sidney Poitier wrote:

On very rare occasions there comes a Gandhi, and occasionally there comes a Martin Luther King, Jr., and occasionally there comes a guy like Paul Robeson or Nelson Mandela. When these people come along, their anger, their rage, their resentment, their frustration—these feelings ultimately mature by will of their own discipline into a positive energy that can be used to fuel their positive, healthy excursions in life.[107]

Paul Robeson was able to create a spectrum of emotions, ranging from joy to sadness, in his music. In his films, though limited by scripted dialogue and prevailing conventions, he had an opportunity to express intense feelings, including those mentioned by Sidney Poitier (anger, rage, resentment and frustration) undoubtedly fueled by a racist culture that classified him as inferior, seditious and, yes, *dangerous.* Even when saddled with comprised and clichéd material, Paul drew upon his natural talent as an actor and his innate convictions to better the lot of his fellows to create the most positive and progressive image possible. In the cinema, he was the first black man to drop the ball and chain in favor of raising the bar.

Like those three other eminent champions of human rights mentioned by Poitier, Paul Robeson was a *peaceful* revolutionary. A close examination of his pioneering, courageous, pre–Civil Rights screen roles proves that he accomplished (obviously in Britain, but also *stealthily* in the blatantly bigoted environment of Hollywood) more than any other individual could have hoped. Deep River, indeed.

Appendix A

Non–Feature Film Performances

Paul Robeson appears in, narrates, or sings on the soundtrack of the following documentary, political campaign and amateur short films.

Camille: The Fate of a Coquette (1926)

Credits: Director: Ralph Barton; Based on the novel and play *La dame aux Camellias* [*The Lady of the Camellias*] by Alexandre Dumas (fils); Running Time: 33 minutes.

Cast: Paul Robeson (Alexandre Dumas [fils]), Sinclair Lewis (Allegorical Figures), Anita Loos (Camille), George Jean Nathan (Arthur), Donald Freeman (Gustave), Pauline Starke (Nan), Theodore Dreiser (Gas-House Gleasen), Sherwood Anderson (Mr. X), Clarence Darrow (August Peters), Lois Moran (Alice Brown), Edouard Bourdet (The Earl of Idaho), Jacques Copeau (Radavinni), Georges Lepape (The Weasel), Denise Bourdet (Olga Petroff), Bernard Boulet de Monuel (Dou-Dou-Dou), Sacha Guitry (Mancha y Zaragosa), Yvonne Printemps (Angele Hemingway), Alfred Knopf (Abd-el-Hamann), Serge Koussevitzky (Grand Duke Michael), Wally Toscanini (Madge), H. L. Mencken (Andrew Volstead), Joseph Hergesheimer (Spirit of Valentino), Aileen Pringle (Estelle), Marie-Blanche de Polignac (Les Pacheux), Julia Hoyt (Kitty), Charles Chaplin (Mike), Ethel Barrymore (Olympe), John Emerson (Count de Varville), Sem (Archbishop of Canterbury), Paul Morand (Lars Nelson), Patsy Ruth Miller (Sadie), Morris Gest (Butter-and-Egg Man), Lily Darvas (Queenie), Rex Ingram (Charles Stewart Parnell), Paul Claudel (Jean Bart), W. Somerset Maugham (Monsieur Duval), Roland Young (Lord Kyne), Sultan of Morocco (Himself), Frank Keenan (Prince von Lindenstein), Ferenc Molnar (Drnskaqrsk), Max Reinhardt (Siegfried), Charles G. Shaw (Armand Duval), T. R. Smith (Doctor), Zena Naylor (Nurse), Mary Hutchins (Nanine), Richard Barthelmess (Gaston), Chauncey Olcott (Pierre), Nikita Balieff (Ivon), Dorothy Gish (Grace), James Rennie (Philippe), Carmel Myers (Agatha), Fanny Ward (The Virgin Mary).

My Song Goes Forth (1937)

Credits: Producer: Joseph Best; Released April 1937 and (as *Africa Sings*) in 1938; Running Time: 50 minutes.

Cast: Paul Robeson (Himself).

Canciones de Madrid (1938)

Credits: Director: Juan Manuel Plaza; Produced by Estado Mayor Comisariado del Ejercito del Centro; Filmed in Madrid, Spain; Released by Film Popular; Running Time: 10 minutes.

Cast: Paul Robeson (Himself).

The People's Congressman (1948)

Credits: Produced by the American Labor Party.

Cast: Paul Robeson (Himself/Narrator), Vito Marcantonio (Himself), Henry A. Wallace (Himself).

Das Lied der Ströme [Song of the Rivers] (1954)

Credits: Directors: Joop Huisken, Joris Ivens, Robert Menegoz; Screenplay: Joris Ivens, Vladimir Pozner; Editor: Ella Ensink; Musical Score and Songs: Bertolt Brecht, Dmitry Shostakovich, Lloyd Brown; Director, Screenplay, Director of Photography and Editor (Brazilian Segment): Ruy Santos; Sound (Brazilian Segment): Jaime Pinheiro; Produced for the World Federation of Trade Unions by Deutsche Film (DEFA); Running Time: 100 minutes.

Cast: Alex McCrindle (Narrator), Paul Robeson (Voice), Sergio Vasconcelos (Narrator, Brazilian Segment), Walter Ulbricht (Himself),

John Foster Dulles (Himself, archival footage), Mao Zedong (Himself, archival footage).

Bridge Over the Ocean (1958)

Credits: Released in East Germany.
Cast: Paul Robeson (Himself), Earl Robinson (Himself).

Concert Film [title unknown] (1958)
Credits: Director: Vasili Katanyan; Produced in the U.S.S.R.
Cast: Paul Robeson (Himself).

Stage Performances

Paul Robeson appeared in the following stage plays, musicals and revues in the United States, Great Britain and Germany.

Simon the Cyrenian
(Summer 1920)

Credits: Producer: Dora Cole Norman; Playwright: Ridgely Torrence; Venue: Harlem YMCA, New York.

Cast: Paul Robeson (Simon the Cyrenian), Amateur Players.

Taboo (April 1922)

Credits: Director: Augustin Duncan; Producer: Dora Cole Norman; Playwright: Mary Hoyt Wiborg; Venue: Sam H. Harris Theatre, New York.

Cast: Paul Robeson, Margaret Wycherly.

Shuffle Along (Summer 1922)

Credits: Writers: Flournoy Miller, Aubrey Lyles; Music and Lyrics: Eubie Blake, Noble Sissle; Venue: 63rd Street Music Hall, New York.

Cast: Florence Mills (Ruth Little), Lottie Gee (Jesse Williams), Adelaide Hall (Jazz Jasmine), Roger Matthews (Harry Walton), Noble Sissle (Tom Sharper), Harold Browning (One of the Four Harmony Kings), Paul Robeson (One of the Four Harmony Kings).

Voodoo [a.k.a. *Taboo*]
(July–August 1922)

Credits: Playwright: Mary Hoyt Wiborg; Tour: England and Scotland.

Cast: Paul Robeson, Mrs. Patrick Campbell.

The Plantation Revue (1922)

Credits: Director and Producer: Lew Leslie; Music: J. Russell Robinson; Lyrics: Roy Turk; Venue: Plantation Nightclub, Harlem, New York.

Cast: Florence Mills (Headliner), Will Vodery and His Celebrated Plantation Orchestra, Paul Robeson (Member of Chorus).

Roseanne (March–April 1924)

Credits: Playwright: Nan Bagby Stephens; Venues: Lafayette Theater, Harlem, New York; Dunbar Theater, Philadelphia.

Cast: Rose McClendon (Roseanne), Paul Robeson (Preacher), Charles Gilpin, Lafayette Players.

The Emperor Jones
(May–June 1924)

Credits: Playwright: Eugene O'Neill; Venue: Greenwich Village Theatre, New York.

Cast: Paul Robeson (Brutus Jones), Provincetown Players.

All God's Chillun Got Wings
(May–October 1924)

Credits: Directors: James Light, Kenneth McGowan, Robert Edmond Jones, Eugene O'Neill; Producer: Marguerite Abbott Barker; Playwright: Eugene O'Neill; Scenic Designer and Technical Director: Cleon Throckmorton; General Manager: M. Eleanor Fitzgerald; General Stage Manager: Harold McGee; Venue: Greenwich Village Theatre, New York.

Cast: Paul Robeson (Jim Harris), Mary Blair [or] Dorothy Peterson (Ella Downey), Dora Cole (Hattie Harris), Lillian Greene (Mrs. Harris), John Taylor (Shorty), James Martin (Mickey), Frank Wilson (Joe), James Meighan (Organ Grinder), William Davis (Jim Harris, Scene I), Virginia Wilson (Ella Downey, Scene I), James Ward (Mickey, Scene I), Malvin Myrck (Joe, Scene I).

The Emperor Jones
(January 1925)

Credits: Producer: Harry Weinberger; Playwright: Eugene O'Neill; Venue: 52nd Street Theatre, New York.

Cast: Paul Robeson (Brutus Jones).

The Emperor Jones
(September 10–October 17, 1925)

Credits: Producer: Sir Alfred Butt; Playwright: Eugene O'Neill; Venue: Ambassadors' Theatre, London.

Cast: Paul Robeson (Brutus Jones).

Black Boy
(October–November 1926)

Credits: Director: David Burton; Producer: Horace Liveright; Playwrights: Jim Tully, Frank Mitchell Dazey; Venue: Comedy Theatre, New York.

Cast: Paul Robeson (Black Boy), Fredi Washington.

Porgy (March 1928)

Credits: Director: Rouben Mamoulian; Playwrights: Dorothy Heyward, DuBose Heyward; Venue: Guild Theatre, New York.

Cast: Frank Wilson (Porgy), Paul Robeson (Crown), Evelyn Ellis (Crown's Bess), Rose McClendon (Serena), Leigh Whipper (The Crab Man), Marie Young (Clara), Percy Wervayne (Sporting Life), Lloyd Gray (Robbins), Ella Madison (Annie), Hayes Pryor (Peter), Dorothy Paul (Lily), Richard Huey (Mingo), Wesley Hill (Jake), Georgette Harvey (Maria), Peter Clark (Jim).

Show Boat
(May 1928–February 1929)

Credits: Producer: Sir Alfred Butt; Book and Lyrics: Oscar Hammerstein II; Music: Jerome Kern; Based on the novel by Edna Ferber; Venue: Theatre Royal, Drury Lane, London.

Cast: Paul Robeson (Joe).

The Emperor Jones (March 1930)

Credits: Playwright: Eugene O'Neill; Location: Berlin.

Cast: Paul Robeson (Brutus Jones).

Othello (May–July 1930)

Credits: Producer: Maurice Browne; Playwright: William Shakespeare; Venue: Savoy Theatre, London; Tour: English provinces.

Cast: Paul Robeson (Othello), Peggy Ashcroft (Desdemona). Maurice Browne (Iago), Max Montesole (Cassio), Ralph Richardson (Roderigo).

The Hairy Ape (May 1931)

Credits: Playwright: Eugene O'Neill; Location: London.

Cast: Paul Robeson (Yank).

Show Boat
(May–September 1932)

Credits: Director: Oscar Hammerstein II; Producer: Florenz Ziegfeld, Jr.; Book and Lyrics: Oscar Hammerstein II; Music: Jerome Kern; Based on the novel by Edna Ferber; Additional Music and Lyrics: P. G. Wodehouse, Joseph E. Howard, Charles K. Harris; Musical Directors: Oscar Bradley, Sammy Lee; Choreographer: Sammy Lee; Scenic Designer: Joseph Urban; Costume Designer: John Harkrider; Technical Director: T. Bernard McDonald; Stage Manager: Herbert Burns; Assistant Stage Manager: Murry Cohn; Venue: Casino Theater, New York.

Cast: Paul Robeson (Joe), Norma Terris (Magnolia), Dennis King (Gaylord Ravenal), Helen Morgan (Julie), Charles Winninger (Cap'n Andy), Edna May Oliver (Parthy Ann Hawks), Sammy White (Frank), Eva Puck (Ellie), Charles Ellis (Steve), James Swift (Pete), Thomas Gunn (Vallon), Tess Gardella (Queenie), A. Alan Campbell (Windy), Francis X. Mahoney (Rubber Face), Gertrude Walker (Lottie), Tana Kamp (Dolly), J. Louis Johnson (Charlie), Maurine Holmes (Hazel), Mary Hellgren (Mary), Robert Faricy (Jake), Estelle Floyd (Ethel), Evelyn Eaton (Kim as a Child), Dorothy Denese (La Belle Fatima), Annie Hart (Landlady), Mildred Schwenke (Mother Superior), Jack Daley (Backwoodsman), Laura Clarion (Old Lady on the Levee).

All God's Chillun Got Wings
(March–May 1933)

Credits: Director and Producer: André Van Gyseghem; Playwright: Eugene O'Neill; Venues: Embassy Theatre and Piccadilly Theatre, London.

Cast: Paul Robeson (Jim Harris), Flora Robson (Ella Downey).

Basilik (April 1935)

Credits: Playwright: Peter Garland (a.k.a. Norma Munro); Venue: Arts Theatre, London.

Cast: Paul Robeson (African Chief), Arts Theatre Club.

Stevedore (May 1935)

Credits: Director: André Van Gyseghem; Playwrights: Paul Peters, George Sklar; Venue: Embassy Theatre, London.
Cast: Paul Robeson.

Toussaint L'Ouverture
[a.k.a. *Black Majesty*] (March 1936)

Credits: Director: André Van Gyseghem; Playwright: C. L. R. James; Venue: Westminster Theatre, London.
Cast: Paul Robeson (Toussaint L'Ouverture), Robert Adams.

Plant in the Sun
(June–August 1938)

Credits: Director and Producer: Herbert Marshall; Playwright: Ben Bengal; Venue: Unity Theatre, London.
Cast: Paul Robeson.

The Emperor Jones (June 1939)

Credits: Playwright: Eugene O'Neill; Venue: Ridgeway Theatre, White Plains, New York.
Cast: Paul Robeson (Brutus Jones).

John Henry (January 10–15, 1940)

Credits: Directors: Anthony Brown, Charles Friedman; Producer: Sam Byrd, in association with Fred Mitchell; Playwright: Roark Bradford, based on his novel; Music: Jacques Wolfe; Musical Director: Don Vorhees; Orchestrations: Charles L. Cook, Hans Spialek; Choral Director and Musical Supervisor: Leonard De Paur; Scenic Designer: Albert R. Johnson; Costume Designer: John Hambleton; Venues: 44th Street Theater, New York, following trial runs in Philadelphia and Boston during December 1939.
Cast: Paul Robeson (John Henry), Joseph Attles (Man Named Sam/Bad Stacker Lee), Minto Cato (Old Aunt Dinah), George Dickson (Rucker), Ruby Elzy (Julie Anne), Alexander Gray (Mate/Billie Bob Russell), Robert Harvey (Hell Buster), Myra Johnson (Poor Selma), George Jones, Jr. (Julie Anne's Papa), James Lightfoot (John Henry's Papa/Deaf Man), Henrietta Lovelace (Julie Anne's Mama), Sadie McGill (Rucker's Wife), C. W. Scott (Roustabout), Maude Simmons (John Henry's Mama), J. De Witt Spencer (Mink Eye/Nud), Kenneth Spencer (Walking Boss), Josh White (Blind Lemon), Musa Williams (Ruby), Ray Yeates (Lead Heaver/A Rouster).

Show Boat (May 1940)

Credits: Book and Lyrics: Oscar Hammerstein II; Music: Jerome Kern; Based on the novel by Edna Ferber; Venue: Philharmonic Auditorium, Los Angeles.
Cast: Paul Robeson (Joe).

The Emperor Jones (August 1940)

Credits: Director: James Light; Playwright: Eugene O'Neill; Music: Colin McPhee; Venues: Country Playhouse, Westport, Connecticut; McCarter Theatre, Princeton, New Jersey.
Cast: Paul Robeson (Brutus Jones).

Othello
(October 19, 1943–July 1, 1944)

Credits: Director: Margaret Webster; Producer: The Theatre Guild (Administration: Lawrence Langner, Theresa Helburn); Associate Producer: John Haggott; Playwright: William Shakespeare; Music: Tom Bennett; Scenic and Lighting Designer: Robert Edmond Jones; Company Manager: John Yorke; Assistant Stage Managers: Rosalind Fradkin, John Ireys; Musical Conductor: Milan Hartz; Venues: Sam S. Shubert Theatre, New York, following an August 1942 trial run in Cambridge, Massachusetts, and Princeton, New Jersey; Tour: U.S. nationwide (September 1944–June 1945).
Cast: Paul Robeson (Othello), José Ferrer (Iago), Uta Hagen (Desdemona), Margaret Webster (Emilia), James Monks (Cassio), Jack Manning (Roderigo), Averell Harris (Brabantio), Robert E. Perry (Duke of Venice/Gratiano), Philip Huston (Lodovico), Henry Barnard (Messenger), Jack de Shay (First Senator), Graham Velsey (Second Senator), John Ireys (Third Senator), William Woodson (Montano), Sam Banham (First Soldier at Cyprus), Eugene Stuckmann (Second Soldier at Cyprus), Bruce Brighton (Third Soldier at Cyprus), Edith King (Bianca), Martha Falconer, Timothy Lynn Kearse, David Koser, John Gerstad, Jeff Brown, Jay Brassfield, Ronald Bishop (Senators, Soldiers, Servants and Citizens).

Othello (April–October 1959)

Credits: Director: Tony Richardson; Costume Designer: Loudon Sainthill; Venue: Shakespeare Memorial Theatre, Stratford-upon-Avon, England.
Cast: Paul Robeson (Othello), Sam Wanamaker (Iago), Mary Ure (Desdemona), Malcolm Taylor, Royal Shakespeare Company.

Chapter Notes

Preface

1. Clement Alexander Price, "A Modern Man," *Paul Robeson: Portraits of the Artist* (The Criterion Collection, 2007), pp. 8–9.
2. Ibid., pp. 3–4.
3. Paul Robeson, *Here I Stand* (Boston: Beacon Press, 1988), p. 4.
4. Paul Robeson, Jr., *The Undiscovered Paul Robeson: An Artist's Journey, 1898–1939* (New York: John Wiley and Sons, 2001), p. xiv.
5. Ibid., pp. xiii–xiv.
6. *Paul Robeson: The Tallest Tree in Our Forest* (St. Clair Vision DVD, 2007).

Chapter 1

1. Robeson, *Here I Stand*, p. 16.
2. Ibid., p. 7.
3. Ibid., p. 10.
4. Ibid., p. 11.
5. Ibid.
6. Ibid., p. 21.
7. Ibid., p. 19.
8. Ibid., p. 25.
9. Ibid., p. 71.
10. Robeson Jr., *Undiscovered Paul Robeson: An Artist's Journey*, p. 61.
11. Hilton Als, "Master of Disguise: Paul Robeson and *The Emperor Jones*," *Paul Robeson: Portraits of the Artist* (The Criterion Collection, 2007), p. 14.
12. *Opportunity: A Journal of Negro Life*, December 1924, pp. 368–370.
13. Robeson Jr., *Undiscovered Paul Robeson: An Artist's Journey*, pp. 80–81.

Chapter 2

1. Robeson, *Here I Stand*, p. 40.
2. Charles Burnett, "In the Beginning: Oscar Micheaux and *Body and Soul*," *Paul Robeson: Portraits of the Artist* (The Criterion Collection, 2007), p. 19.
3. Ibid., p. 22.
4. *Paul Robeson: The Tallest Tree in Our Forest.*
5. Robeson Jr., *Undiscovered Paul Robeson: An Artist's Journey*, p. 95.
6. Ethel Waters, with Charles Samuels, *His Eye Is on the Sparrow: An Autobiography* (Garden City, NY: Doubleday, 1951), p. 193.
7. Will Friedwald, *Jazz Singing: America's Great Voices from Bessie Smith to Bebop and Beyond* (New York: Da Capo Press, 1996), pp. 10–11.

Chapter 3

1. Paul Robeson, interview with Elsa Knight Thompson and Harold Winkler, Oakland, CA, Pacifica Radio (KPFA), January 1958.
2. Geraldyn Dismond, "The Negro Actor and the American Movies," *Close Up*, vol. V, no. 2, August 1929, p. 7.
3. Ibid., p. 9.
4. Ibid., pp. 12–13.
5. Ibid., p. 13.
6. Ian Christie, "On the Edge: Robeson, *Borderline*, and the Forgotten Avant-Gardes," *Paul Robeson: Portraits of the Artist* (The Criterion Collection, 2007), p. 30.
7. *The Bioscope*, 25 October 1930.
8. Robeson Jr., *Undiscovered Paul Robeson: An Artist's Journey*, p. 168.
9. *New York Herald Tribune*, 23 May 1930.
10. Denise Reaman, "Artist of All Seasons at 101, Salemme Believes Best Work Is Yet to Come," *The Morning Call* (Allentown, PA), 14 August 1994, p. M1.
11. Robeson Jr., *Undiscovered Paul Robeson: An Artist's Journey*, p. 179.
12. *Daily Gleaner* (Jamaica), 9 January 1932.
13. Ibid.
14. Robeson Jr., *Undiscovered Paul Robeson: An Artist's Journey*, p. 195.

Chapter 4

1. Donald Bogle, *Toms, Coons, Mulattoes, Mammies, and Bucks: An Interpretive History of Blacks in American Films* (New York: Continuum, 2002), p. 98.
2. *Punch*, 22 March 1933.
3. *Daily News-Chronicle*, 14 March 1933.
4. Als, p. 17.
5. Billie Holiday, with William Duffy, *Lady Sings the Blues* (New York: Doubleday, 1956), p. 52.
6. Robeson Jr., *Undiscovered Paul Robeson: An Artist's Journey*, pp. 207–208.
7. Als, p. 14.
8. *Robeson on Robeson* (The Criterion Collection DVD, 2007).
9. *Our Paul: Remembering Paul Robeson* (The Criterion Collection DVD, 2007).
10. Ibid.
11. *The Star* (London), 3 August 1933.

Chapter 5

1. *Paul Robeson: The Complete EMI Sessions, 1928–1939* (EMI Classics CD, 2008), p. 30.
2. Robeson Jr., *Undiscovered Paul Robeson: An Artist's Journey*, p. 209.
3. *Sunday Observer* (London), 28 April 1935.
4. *Sheffield Telegraph*, 21 February 1935.
5. George E. Turner with Orville Goldner, expanded and revised by Michael H. Price with Douglas Turner, *Spawn of Skull Island* (Baltimore: Luminary Press, 2002), p. 26.
6. Robeson Jr., *Undiscovered Paul Robeson: An Artist's Journey*, p. 212.
7. Deborah Willis, "Constructing an Image," *Paul Robeson: Portraits of the Artist* (The Criterion Collection, 2007), p. 41.
8. Harriet Akutekha Jenkins, conversation with Scott Allen Nollen, July 2009.
9. Robeson Jr., *Undiscovered Paul Robeson: An Artist's Journey*, pp. 216–217.
10. Ibid., p. 217.
11. Marie Seton, *Paul Robeson* (London: Dobson Books, 1958), p. 84.
12. Ibid., p. 95.
13. Paul Robeson, Jr., telephone conversation with Scott Allen Nollen, March 2006.
14. *The Observer*, 29 July 1934.
15. *Robeson on Robeson.*
16. *New York Times*, 27 June 1935.
17. *New York Amsterdam News*, 5 October 1935.
18. Ibid.
19. *Our Paul: Remembering Paul Robeson.*
20. Robeson, *Here I Stand*, p. 48.

Chapter 6

1. James Whale, letter to Paul Robeson, 28 April 1936, Paul and Eslanda Robeson Collections, Moorland-Spingarn Research Center, Howard University, Washington, D.C.
2. Irene Thirer, "Director James Whale Here En Route to Europe," *New York Post*, 1 June 1936.
3. *New York Amsterdam News.*
4. James Curtis, *James Whale: A New World of Gods and Monsters* (Boston: Faber and Faber, 1998), p. 269.
5. Ibid., p. 270.
6. Robeson Jr., *Undiscovered Paul Robeson: An Artist's Journey*, p. 234.
7. Curtis, p. 272.
8. Whale.
9. Curtis, p. 272.
10. *Daily Variety*, 27 April 1936.
11. Mark Gatiss, *James Whale: A Biography* (New York: Cassell, 1995), p. 126.
12. Thirer.
13. Gattis, p. 127.
14. *California Eagle*, 1 January 1936.
15. Bogle, p. 99.
16. John Landis, conversation with Robert Osborne, Turner Classic Movies, March 2009.

Chapter 7

1. Robeson, *Here I Stand*, p. 32.
2. *Sunday Worker*, 10 May 1936.
3. Robeson Jr., *Undiscovered Paul Robeson: An Artist's Journey*, p. 236.
4. C. L. R. James, "Paul Robeson: Black Star," *Black World*, November 1970.
5. Robeson, *Here I Stand*, p. 30.
6. Robeson Jr., *Undiscovered Paul Robeson: An Artist's Journey*, p. 237.
7. *The Song of Freedom* pressbook, 8-page edition (British Lion Film Corporation–Hammer Productions, 1936), p. 6.
8. Jenkins conversation.
9. Paul Robeson, "Primitives," *The New Statesman and Nation*, 8 August 1936.
10. *The Bystander*, 30 September 1936.
11. Robeson Jr., *Undiscovered Paul Robeson: An Artist's Journey*, p. 241.
12. Ibid., p. 246.
13. Robeson Jr., conversation.
14. Sergei Eisenstein, *Rabochaya Moskva*, 20 December 1936.

Chapter 8

1. Edward R. O'Neill, "Paul Robeson," in Geoffrey Nowell-Smith, ed., *The Oxford History of World Cinema* (Oxford: Oxford University Press, 1996), p. 341.
2. *The Worker*, 12 April 1937.

Chapter 9

1. Anna Lee, telephone conversation with Scott Allen Nollen, August 1989.
2. *Our Paul: Remembering Paul Robeson.*

Chapter 10

1. Robeson Jr., conversation.
2. *True Pioneer: The British Films of Paul Robeson* (The Criterion Collection DVD, 2007).
3. *Jericho* pressbook (General Film Distributors, 1937), p. 6.
4. Ibid.
5. *Philadelphia Tribune*, 20 May 1937.
6. *Jericho* pressbook, pp. 4 and 7.
7. Ibid., p. 7.
8. Ibid.
9. *True Pioneer: The British Films of Paul Robeson.*
10. *Jericho* pressbook, p. 5.
11. *Sunday Worker*, 5 October 1936.
12. Robeson Jr., conversation.
13. Robeson Jr., *Undiscovered Paul Robeson: An Artist's Journey*, p. 303.
14. Ibid., p. 309.
15. Ibid., p. 312.
16. "Paul Robeson Tells Us Why," *Cine-Technician*, no. 17, September–October 1938, pp. 74–75.

Chapter 11

1. Robeson Jr., *Undiscovered Paul Robeson: An Artist's Journey*, p. 322.
2. Ibid., p. 325.
3. Ibid.
4. Robeson, *Here I Stand*, p. 39.
5. *Manchester Dispatch*, 1 November 1938.
6. Paul Robeson, interview with Elsa Knight Thompson and Harold Winkler.
7. *True Pioneer: The British Films of Paul Robeson*.
8. Robeson Jr., *Undiscovered Paul Robeson: An Artist's Journey*, p. 331.
9. *Our Paul: Remembering Paul Robeson*.
10. Robeson Jr., *Undiscovered Paul Robeson: An Artist's Journey*, p. 332.
11. Robeson, *Here I Stand*, p. 31.
12. Price, p. 7.

Chapter 12

1. "Paul Robeson," FBI Number 100-25857, New York, 8 December 1942.
2. *The Story of "Native Land"* (The Criterion Collection DVD, 2007).
3. Ibid.

Chapter 13

1. *Our Paul: Remembering Paul Robeson*.
2. Martin Duberman, *Paul Robeson* (New York: Knopf, 1988), pp. 259–61.
3. Waters, p. 257.
4. *Our Paul: Remembering Paul Robeson*.
5. Waters, pp. 257–258.
6. Edward G. Robinson, with Leonard Spigelglass, *All My Yesterdays: An Autobiography* (New York: Hawthorn Books, 1973), p. 225.
7. *Our Paul: Remembering Paul Robeson*.
8. Paul Robeson, Jr., *The Undiscovered Paul Robeson: Quest for Freedom, 1939–1976* (Hoboken, NJ: John Wiley and Sons, 2010), p. 48.
9. "Paul Robeson," FBI Number 100-25857, New York, 8 December 1942.
10. Ibid.
11. Ibid.
12. Guy Hottel, letter to Director, FBI [J. Edgar Hoover], Washington, DC, 26 August 1943.

Chapter 14

1. Price, p. 7.
2. *Paul Robeson: Here I Stand* (Educational Broadcasting Corporation DVD, 1999).
3. *Paul Robeson: The Tallest Tree in Our Forest*.
4. *Paul Robeson: Here I Stand*.
5. *Victoria Daily Times*, 13 January 1945.
6. *Paul Robeson: The Tallest Tree in Our Forest*.
7. Paul Robeson, transcript of WHK Radio broadcast, 5 November 1944, Paul and Eslanda Robeson Collections, Moorland-Spingarn Research Center, Howard University, Washington, D.C.

8. Robeson Jr., *Undiscovered Paul Robeson: Quest for Freedom*, p. 106.
9. *People's Voice*, 12 January 1946.
10. Robeson Jr., *Undiscovered Paul Robeson: Quest for Freedom*, p. 108.
11. *Paul Robeson: Here I Stand*.
12. Robeson Jr., *Undiscovered Paul Robeson: Quest for Freedom*, p. 111.
13. Ibid., p. 117.
14. "Re: Paul Robeson," FBI Office Memorandum, St. Louis, Mo., 29 January 1947.
15. Hedda Hopper, "Looking at Hollywood," *Los Angeles Times*, 20 March 1947.
16. Ernest Morrison, conversation with Scott Allen Nollen, Saint Paul, MN, July 1988.
17. Mrs. Paul Robeson, Negro Actors Guild of America, "The Negro Contribution to Culture," 27 March 1949, Schomburg Center for Research in Black Culture, New York Public Library, NAG, box 3, 3/24.
18. Robeson Jr., *Undiscovered Paul Robeson: Quest for Freedom*, p. 146.
19. Ibid., p. 160.
20. *New York Age*, 6, 13, and 20 August 1949; 3 and 17 September 1949.
21. Paul Robeson, transcript of Golden Gate Ballroom speech, 30 August 1949, Paul and Eslanda Robeson Collections, Moorland-Spingarn Research Center, Howard University, Washington, D.C.
22. Robeson Jr., *Undiscovered Paul Robeson: Quest for Freedom*, p. 171.
23. *New York Times*, 9 October 1949.
24. Robeson Jr., *Undiscovered Paul Robeson: Quest for Freedom*, p. 181.
25. New York *Journal American*, 13 March 1950.
26. *Daily Worker*, 17 March 1950.
27. "Paul Robeson," FBI Number 100-25857, New York, 11 July 1950.
28. Robeson, *Here I Stand*, pp. 63–64.
29. Ibid., p. 68.
30. "Paul Robeson," FBI Number 100-25857, New York, 21 March 1952.
31. "Paul Robeson Security Matter," United States Government Office Memorandum, Seattle, Washington, 26 April 1952.
32. "Paul Robeson Security Matter," FBI Office Memorandum, Pittsburgh, 24 July 1952.
33. *Paul Robeson: The Tallest Tree in Our Forest*.
34. "Paul Robeson," FBI Air-Tel, New York, 8 December 1952.
35. "Paul Robeson," FBI Number LA 100-25861, New York, 15 September 1953.
36. "Miscellaneous," FBI Number 65-28939, New York, 24 September 1953.
37. Robeson Jr., conversation.
38. Robeson, *Here I Stand*, pp. 59–60.
39. Ibid., p. 62.
40. *Daily People's World*, 6 August 1954.
41. Robeson Jr., *Undiscovered Paul Robeson: Quest for Freedom*, p. 232.
42. *Daily Worker*, 16 May 1955
43. "Paul Robeson," FBI Number NY 100-25857, New York, 6 July 1955.
44. "Council on African Affairs," FBI Office Memorandum, New York, 11 July 1955.

45. *Daily Worker*, 19 August 1955.
46. Ibid.
47. Sidney Poitier, *The Measure of a Man: A Memoir* (London: Simon and Schuster, 2000), p. 88.
48. Ibid., pp. 89–90.
49. Ibid., pp. 90–91.
50. Ibid., p. 92.
51. Ibid., p. 94.
52. "Changed: Paul Le Roy Robeson," FBI Number NY 100-25857, New York, 17 April 1956.
53. Paul Robeson, *Here I Stand*, pp. 41–42.
54. Ibid., p. 48.
55. *Charlottesville-Albemarle Tribune*, 22 June 1956.
56. Robeson, *Here I Stand*, p. 29.
57. Ibid., p. 72.
58. Robeson Jr., *Undiscovered Paul Robeson: Quest for Freedom*, p. 264.
59. Robeson, *Here I Stand*, pp. 56–57.
60. *Manchester Guardian*, 4 May 1957.
61. Robeson, *Here I Stand*, p. 59.
62. Robeson interview with Thompson and Winkler.
63. "Paul Le Roy Robeson," FBI Air Tel, New York, 1 April 1958.
64. Ibid.
65. *Paul Robeson: The Tallest Tree in Our Forest*.
66. "Paul Robeson — More Music Than Politics," *San Francisco Chronicle*, 5 February 1958.
67. Robeson Jr., *Undiscovered Paul Robeson: Quest for Freedom*, p. 272.
68. "Paul Robeson Internal Security," FBI Air-Tel, Washington, DC, 26 June 1958.
69. Paul Robeson, interview with Therese Denny, London, England, August 1958.
70. "Paul Le Roy Robeson, Internal Security," FBI Number 100-25857, New York, 12 March 1959.
71. *Variety*, 3 September 1958.
72. *New York Times*, 22 September 1958.
73. Robeson Jr., *Undiscovered Paul Robeson: Quest for Freedom*, p. 289.
74. Ibid., p. 297.
75. Ibid., pp. 297–298.
76. *Baltimore Afro-American*, 26 September 1959.
77. *Neue Zeit*, 21 April 1961.
78. Robeson Jr., *Undiscovered Paul Robeson: Quest for Freedom*, p. 309.
79. Ibid., p. 317.

80. Ibid., p. 319.
81. "Paul Le Roy Robeson, Eslanda Robeson, Paul Robeson, Jr.," FBI Number 100-12304, London, 21 July 1961.
82. "Paul Le Roy Robeson, Internal Security," FBI Number 100-25857, New York, 9 November 1962.
83. Ibid.
84. Robeson Jr., conversation.
85. Robeson Jr., *Undiscovered Paul Robeson: Quest for Freedom*, p. 326.
86. "Paul Robeson, Eslanda Robeson," FBI Number 100-25857, New York, 23 January 1963.
87. "Paul Robeson Security Matter," FBI Air-Tel, New York, 19 December 1963.
88. Robeson Jr., *Undiscovered Paul Robeson: Quest for Freedom*, p. 330.
89. "Paul Robeson," CIA Cable Numbers 201-11448-309, London, 28 August 1963, and 201-11448-310, Washington, DC, 30 August 1963.
90. *Pittsburgh Courier*, 11 January 1964.
91. *Baltimore Afro-American*, 5 September 1964.
92. Robeson Jr., *Undiscovered Paul Robeson: Quest for Freedom*, p. 352.
93. "Robeson Cherishes His U.S. Heritage," *Los Angeles Times*, 16 May 1965.
94. Robeson Jr., *Undiscovered Paul Robeson: Quest for Freedom*, p. 355.
95. Ibid., pp. 358–359.
96. "Eslanda Goode Robeson Security Matter," FBI File Number 100-56680, New York, 10 January 1966.
97. Duberman, p. 542.
98. Robeson Jr., *Undiscovered Paul Robeson: Quest for Freedom*, p. 366.
99. "Ten Greats of Black History," *Ebony*, August 1972.
100. Charles Musser, "The Search for an Achievable Utopia: Robeson and Documentary," *Paul Robeson: Portraits of the Artist* (The Criterion Collection, 2007), p. 52.
101. Robeson, *Here I Stand*, pp. 31–32.
102. *Paul Robeson: Here I Stand*.
103. Willis, p. 43.
104. *Our Paul: Remembering Paul Robeson*.
105. Ibid.
106. *Robeson on Robeson*.
107. Poitier, p. 124.

Bibliography

Primary Sources

Interviews

Jenkins, Harriet Akutehka. Conversations with Scott Allen Nollen. July 2009.

Landis, John. Conversation with Robert Osborne. Turner Classic Movies, March 2009.

Lee, Anna. Telephone conversation with Scott Allen Nollen. August 1989.

Morrison, Ernest. Conversation with Scott Allen Nollen. Saint Paul, MN, July 1988.

Robeson, Paul. Interview with Elsa Knight Thompson and Harold Winkler. Oakland, CA, Pacifica Radio (KPFA), January 1958.

Robeson, Paul. Interview with Therese Denny. London, England, August 1958.

Robeson, Paul, Jr. Telephone conversations with Scott Allen Nollen. March 2006.

Original Documents

"Changed: Paul Le Roy Robeson." FBI Number NY 100-25857. New York, 17 April 1956.

"Council on African Affairs." FBI Office Memorandum. New York, 11 July 1955.

"Eslanda Goode Robeson Security Matter." FBI File Number 100-56680. New York, 10 January 1966.

Hottel, Guy. Letter to Director, FBI [J. Edgar Hoover]. Washington, DC, 26 August 1943.

Minutes, Negro Actors Guild of America, Inc. New York, 4 December 1937. Schomburg Center for Research in Black Culture, New York Public Library, NAG, box 3, 3/1.

"Miscellaneous." FBI Number 65-28939. New York, 24 September 1953.

"Paul Le Roy Robeson." FBI Air Tel. New York, 1 April 1958.

"Paul Le Roy Robeson, Eslanda Robeson, Paul Robeson, Jr." FBI Number 100-12304. London, 21 July 1961.

"Paul Le Roy Robeson, Internal Security." FBI Number 100-25857. New York, 1 April 1958.

"Paul Le Roy Robeson, Internal Security." FBI Number 100-25857. New York, 12 March 1959.

"Paul Le Roy Robeson, Internal Security." FBI Number 100-25857. New York, 9 November 1962.

"Paul Robeson." CIA Cable Number 201-11448-309. London, 28 August 1963.

"Paul Robeson." CIA Cable Number 201-11448-310. Washington, DC, 30 August 1963.

"Paul Robeson." FBI Air-Tel. New York, 8 December 1952.

"Paul Robeson." FBI Number 100-25857. New York, 8 December 1942.

"Paul Robeson." FBI Number 100-25857. New York, 11 July 1950.

"Paul Robeson." FBI Number 100-25857. New York, 21 March 1952.

"Paul Robeson." FBI Number LA 100-25861. New York, 15 September 1953.

"Paul Robeson." FBI Number NY 100-25857. New York, 6 July 1955.

"Paul Robeson." FBI Number NY 100-25857. New York, 6 January 1956.

"Paul Robeson." FBI Office Memorandum. Newark, NJ, 21 June 1949.

"Paul Robeson, Eslanda Robeson." FBI Number 100-25857. New York, 23 January 1963.

"Paul Robeson, Eslanda Robeson." FBI Numbers 100-25857 and 100-56680. New York, 30 August 1963.

"Paul Robeson Internal Security." FBI Air-Tel. Washington, DC, 26 June 1958.

"Paul Robeson Security Matter." FBI Air-Tel. New York, 19 December 1963.

"Paul Robeson Security Matter." FBI Office Memorandum. Pittsburgh, 24 June 1952.

"Paul Robeson Security Matter." FBI Office Memorandum. Pittsburgh, 24 July 1952.

"Paul Robeson Security Matter." United States Government Office Memorandum. Seattle, WA, 26 April 1952.

"Paul Robeson Security Matter." United States Government Office Memorandum. 25 June 1958.

"Photographic Surveillance (International Peace Arch Rally, featuring Paul Robeson, Held 5/18/52 at Blaine, Wash.)." FBI Office Memorandum. Seattle, Wash., 19 May 1952.

"Re: Paul Robeson." FBI Office Memorandum. St. Louis, MO, 29 January 1947.

Robeson, Mrs. Paul, Negro Actors Guild of America, Inc. "The Negro Contribution to Culture." 27 March 1949. Schomburg Center for Research in Black Culture, New York Public Library, NAG, box 3, 3/24.

Robeson, Paul. Transcript of Golden Gate Ballroom speech, 30 August 1949. Paul and Eslanda Robeson Collections, Moorland-Spingarn Research Center, Howard University, Washington, D.C.

Robeson, Paul. Transcript of WHK Radio broadcast, 5 November 1944. Paul and Eslanda Robeson Collections, Moorland-Spingarn Research Center, Howard University, Washington, D.C.

Whale, James. Letter to Paul Robeson, 28 April 1936. Paul and Eslanda Robeson Collections, Moorland-Spingarn Research Center, Howard University, Washington, D.C.

Published Memoirs

Holiday, Billie, with William Duffy. *Lady Sings the Blues*. New York: Doubleday, 1956.

Poitier, Sidney. *The Measure of a Man: A Memoir*. London: Simon and Schuster, 2000.

Robeson, Eslanda Goode. *Paul Robeson, Negro*. London: Victor Gollancz, 1930.

Robeson, Paul. *Here I Stand*. Boston: Beacon Press, 1988.

Robeson, Paul, Jr. *The Undiscovered Paul Robeson: An Artist's Journey, 1898–1939*. New York: John Wiley and Sons, 2001.

_____. *The Undiscovered Paul Robeson: Quest for Freedom, 1939–1976*. Hoboken, NJ: John Wiley and Sons, 2010.

Robinson, Edward G., with Leonard Spigelglass. *All My Yesterdays: An Autobiography*. New York: Hawthorn Books, 1973.

Waters, Ethel, with Charles Samuels. *His Eye Is on the Sparrow: An Autobiography*. Garden City, NY: Doubleday, 1951.

Periodicals

Baltimore Afro-American, 26 September 1959; 5 September 1964.

The Bioscope, 25 October 1930.

The Bystander, 30 September 1936.

California Eagle, 1 January 1936.

Charlottesville-Albemarle Tribune, 22 June 1956.

Daily Gleaner (Jamaica), 9 January 1932.

Daily News-Chronicle, 14 March 1933.

Daily People's World, 6 August 1954.

Daily Variety, 27 April 1936.

Daily Worker, 17 March 1950; 16 May 1955; 19 August 1955.

Dismond, Geraldyn. "The Negro Actor and the American Movies." *Close Up*, vol. V, no. 2, August 1929.

Eisenstein, Sergei. *Rabochaya Moskva*, 20 December 1936.

Eugene O'Neill Foundation. *Tao House Newsletter*, September 2008.

Hopper, Hedda. "Looking at Hollywood." *Los Angeles Times*, 20 March 1947.

James, C. L. R. "Paul Robeson: Black Star." *Black World*, November 1970.

Manchester Dispatch, 1 November 1938.

Manchester Guardian, 4 May 1957.

Neue Zeit, 21 April 1961.

New York Age, 6, 13, and 20 August 1949; 3 and 17 September 1949.

New York Amsterdam News, 5 October 1935.

New York Herald Tribune, 23 May 1930; 27 June 1935.

New York *Journal American*, 13 March 1950.

New York Times, 27 June 1935; 9 October 1949; 22 September 1958; 23 December 1963.

The Observer, 29 July 1934.

Opportunity: A Journal of Negro Life, December 1924.

"Paul Robeson — More Music Than Politics." *San Francisco Chronicle*, 5 February 1958.

"Paul Robeson Tells Us Why." *Cine-Technician*, no. 17, September–October 1938.

People's Voice, 12 January 1946.

Philadelphia Tribune, 20 May 1937.

Pittsburgh Courier, 11 January 1964.

Punch, 22 March 1933.

Reaman, Denise. "Artist of All Seasons at 101, Salemme Believes Best Work Is Yet to Come." *The Morning Call* (Allentown, PA), 14 August 1994.

"Robeson Cherishes His U.S. Heritage." *Los Angeles Times*, 16 May 1965.

Robeson, Paul. "Primitives." *The New Statesman and Nation*, 8 August 1936.

Sheffield Telegraph, 21 February 1935.

The Star (London), 3 August 1933.

Sunday Observer (London), 28 April 1935.

Sunday Worker, 10 May 1936; 5 October 1936.
"Ten Greats of Black History." *Ebony*, August 1972.
Thirer, Irene. "Director James Whale Here En Route to Europe." *New York Post*, 1 June 1936.
Variety, 3 September 1958.
Victoria Daily Times, 13 January 1945.
The Worker, 12 April 1937.

Pressbooks

Jericho. General Film Distributors, 1937.
The Proud Valley. Associated British Film Distributors, 1940.
Song of Freedom. 12-page edition. British Lion Film Corporation, 1936.
Song of Freedom. 8-page edition. British Lion Film Corporation–Hammer Productions, 1936.

Commercial Publicity Materials

"Paul Robeson and Elisabeth Welch in 'Song of Freedom.'" *From Screen and Stage*, no. 31. Ardath Tobacco Co., 1936.

Theater Programs

Othello: The Playbill for the Sam S. Shubert Theatre, 12 December 1943.

Recordings

Paul Robeson: Ballad for Americans and Great Songs of Faith, Love and Patriotism. Vanguard, 1989.
Paul Robeson: Freedom Train and the Welsh Transatlantic Concert. Folk Era Records, 1998.
Paul Robeson: The Complete EMI Sessions, 1928–1939. 7-CD set. EMI Classics, 2008.
Paul Robeson: The Power and the Glory. Columbia Legacy, 1991.

Documentary Films

Our Paul: Remembering Paul Robeson. The Criterion Collection, 2007.
Paul Robeson: Here I Stand. Educational Broadcasting Corporation, 1999.
Paul Robeson: Portraits of the Artist. 8-DVD set. The Criterion Collection, 2007.
Paul Robeson: The Tallest Tree in Our Forest. St. Clair Vision, 2007.
Robeson on Robeson. The Criterion Collection, 2007.

The Story of "Native Land." The Criterion Collection, 2007.
True Pioneer: The British Films of Paul Robeson. The Criterion Collection, 2007.

Secondary Sources

Biographies

Curtis, James. *James Whale: A New World of Gods and Monsters*. Boston: Faber and Faber, 1998.
Duberman, Martin. *Paul Robeson*. New York: Knopf, 1988.
Gatiss, Mark. *James Whale: A Biography*. New York: Cassell, 1995.
Nollen, Scott Allen. *Louis Armstrong: The Life, Music and Film Career*. Jefferson, NC: McFarland, 2004.
Seton, Marie. *Paul Robeson*. London: Dobson Books, 1958.
Watts, Jill. *Hattie McDaniel: Black Ambition, White Hollywood*. New York: HarperCollins, 2005.

Books on African Americans in the Cinema

Bogle, Donald. *Toms, Coons, Mulattoes, Mammies, and Bucks: An Interpretive History of Blacks in American Films*. New York: Continuum, 2002.
Jones, G. William. *Black Cinema Treasures: Lost and Found*. Denton: University of North Texas Press, 1997.

Books on Entertainment History

Friedwald, Will. *Jazz Singing: America's Great Voices from Bessie Smith to Bebop and Beyond*. New York: Da Capo Press, 1996.
Nowell-Smith, Geoffrey, ed. *The Oxford History of World Cinema*. Oxford: Oxford University Press, 1996.
Schatz, Thomas. *The Genius of the System: Hollywood Filmmaking in the Studio Era*. New York: Pantheon Books, 1988.
Turner, George E., with Orville Goldner. Expanded and revised by Michael H. Price with Douglas Turner. *Spawn of Skull Island*. Baltimore: Luminary Press, 2002.

Essays

Als, Hilton. "Master of Disguise: Paul Robeson and *The Emperor Jones*." *Paul Robeson: Portraits of the Artist*. The Criterion Collection, 2007.

Burnett, Charles. "In the Beginning: Oscar Micheaux and *Body and Soul*." *Paul Robeson: Portraits of the Artist*. The Criterion Collection, 2007.

Christie, Ian. "On the Edge: Robeson, *Borderline*, and the Forgotten Avant-Gardes." *Paul Robeson: Portraits of the Artist*. The Criterion Collection, 2007.

Musser, Charles. "The Search for an Achievable Utopia: Robeson and Documentary." *Paul Robeson: Portraits of the Artist*. The Criterion Collection, 2007.

O'Connor, Patrick. "Paul Robeson: I Came Here to Sing." *Paul Robeson: The Complete EMI Sessions, 1928–1939*. EMI Classics, 2008.

Price, Clement Alexander. "A Modern Man." *Paul Robeson: Portraits of the Artist*. The Criterion Collection, 2007.

Shaw, Ian. "Freedom Train and the Welsh Transatlantic Concert." Folk Era Records, 1998.

Willis, Deborah. "Constructing an Image." *Paul Robeson: Portraits of the Artist*. The Criterion Collection, 2007.

Index

Numbers in *bold italics* indicate pages with photographs.